D1478198

OSS

OPERATION

BLACK MAIL

OSS

OPERATION

BLACK MAIL

ONE WOMAN'S COVERT WAR AGAINST

THE IMPERIAL JAPANESE ARMY

ANN TODD

NAVAL INSTITUTE PRESS
ANNAPOLIS, MARYLAND

This book has been brought to publication with the generous assistance of Marguerite and Gerry Lenfest.

Naval Institute Press
291 Wood Road
Annapolis, MD 21402

Library of Congress Cataloging-in-Publication Data
Names: Todd, Ann, author.
Title: OSS Operation Black Mail : one woman's covert war against the Imperial Japanese Army / Ann Todd.
Description: Annapolis, Maryland : Naval Institute Press, [2017] | Includes bibliographical references and index. Identifiers: LCCN 2017013058 (print) | LCCN 2017013937 (ebook) | ISBN 9781682471517 (ePDF) | ISBN 9781682471517 (epub) | ISBN 9781682471517 (mobi) | ISBN 9781682471500 | ISBN 9781682471500 (hardcover : alk. paper) | ISBN 9781682471517 (eBook)
Subjects: LCSH: McIntosh, Elizabeth P., 1915–2015. | Women spies—United States—Biography. | United States. Office of Strategic Services—Biography. | World War, 1939–1945—Secret service—United States. | World War, 1939–1945—Campaigns—Asia. | World War, 1939–1945—Psychological aspects.
Classification: LCC D810.S8 (ebook) | LCC D810.S8 M368 2017 (print) | DDC 940.54/8673092 [B] —dc23
LC record available at https://lccn.loc.gov/2017013058

Map created by Chris Robinson.

♾ Print editions meet the requirements of ANSI/NISO z39.48-1992 (Permanence of Paper). Printed in the United States of America.

25 24 23 22 21 20 19 18 17   9 8 7 6 5 4 3 2 1
First printing

The men and women of the OSS
fought a different, often invisible war,
one for which few medals were given.
This book is an homage to them,
all of them, on every front.

CONTENTS

ILLUSTRATIONS

PREFACE

For eighty-six-year-old Elizabeth "Betty" McIntosh, the morning of September 11, 2001, was very much like one sixty years before. On December 7, 1941, the sparkling blue sky over Betty's little house on Oahu filled with waves of Japanese bombers. The roiling smoke and flames erupting from the Twin Towers on 9/11 looked identical to the smoke and flames that had emanated from the ruined white ships in Pearl Harbor. Shaking off the memory, Betty snatched up the phone, muting the volume on her television but continuing to watch the horrific scene unfolding. As an Office of Strategic Services (OSS) "living legend" and a retired case officer, she had no problem reaching the Central Intelligence Agency's Directorate of Operations and was put through to her old department, the Special Activities Division.

"Put me back to work," she said.

Before CIA there was OSS. Colorful histories of OSS abound. First and foremost on the bookshelf is scholarship on the luminous founder of OSS, William J. Donovan. There are also thrilling accounts of Jedburgh teams training and fighting with the French Resistance, frogmen pioneering underwater special warfare, and the daring exploits of Operation Norso in Norway. And then there are the biographies and autobiographies of those who went on to become CIA directors: Allen Dulles, William Colby, Richard Helms, William J. Casey. The overwhelming majority of these treatments center on World War II as it unfolded in Europe, the Mediterranean, and North Africa. *OSS Operation Black Mail* is a different, less prosaic narrative of OSS—the story of a remarkable woman who fought on a different front, in a remote and often overlooked theater of war.

Elizabeth P. McIntosh was a trailblazer in the art of psychological warfare, which she waged against the Japanese in the China-Burma-India theater of operations (CBI), a place at the time often referred to as "Confused Beyond Imagination." Her craft was black propaganda, and her mission was to demoralize the enemy through prevarication and deceit and, ultimately, to convince him to surrender. Donovan himself believed fervently in the efficacy of psychological warfare, and in 1943 he added a branch, Morale Operations (MO), to his growing organization. The people recruited for this latecomer were of a different ilk from those drawn out of the ranks of Yale, Harvard, and other esteemed faculties who populated Donovan's Research and Analysis (R&A) Branch. They were not elite soldiers poached from the regular armed forces or movie stars who flocked to OSS in search of adventure and the chance to make a difference. MO brought in a wave of artists, journalists, and people who were deeply familiar with the languages and cultures of far-flung parts of the globe. Creative types. Professionals, many too old to enlist but eager to join the war, preferably "over there." The scholars, writers, and artists destined for Asia had, through their own careers and interests, sought to understand the cultures of that part of the world as an end in itself. Now that understanding would be used to find weaknesses in a culture, to attack the unity of that culture, or, as one scholar put it, "to crack the enemy's culture up, not just crack it open."[1]

The deceptive part of black propaganda is and was point of origin. A newspaper was made to look as if it came off the presses in Berlin or Tokyo when actually it was painstakingly replicated, cut, pasted, and printed in Washington or Calcutta. A radio program purported to be broadcast from Tokyo when really it was being beamed from a tiny hand-cranked generator in Chittagong.

Betty McIntosh once said, "Never again would I feel so alive, so completely engaged in something I knew would never come around again." She served a total of eighteen life-changing months in India and China before she eventually entered service in the CIA, from which she retired in 1973. During those eighteen months, she met and worked with people as diverse as Allen Dulles, Julia Child, and Ho Chi Minh. She ordered the killing of a Japanese courier in the jungles of Burma to plant a false surrender order in his mailbag. She obtained the complete cooperation of a surly enemy prisoner of war (POW) to craft that order, copies of which were clutched in the hands of Japanese soldiers walking out of the jungle in 1945. The title of this book, *OSS Operation Black Mail*, refers to the many and various ways Betty and her crew obtained and altered personal correspondence between Japanese soldiers and their families on the home islands of Japan. By the time Betty was transferred to China, she had been made Acting Head of MO for CBI. Although more than forty-five hundred women served in OSS, to be made acting head of an operational branch over an entire theater was a stunning achievement.[2] She was extremely good at demoralizing and deceiving the Japanese simply because she admired them and had spent a great deal of time immersed in their culture. She targeted not merely the Japanese soldier but the man within: the son, the husband, the father. She knew her work could ultimately save lives but never lost sight of the fact that her propaganda was a weapon, and her intended recipients the enemy.

In the spring of 1943 a harrowing flight over the "Hump" with her good friend Julia McWilliams (later Child) landed McIntosh behind enemy lines in the city of Kunming, where she worked to provide materials to distant MO field teams. Her memories of China, like those of Delhi and Calcutta, remained vivid and give this wartime narrative an exotic dimension. Along with artist William Smith and Chinese coworkers Ma and Ting, Betty explored hilltop monasteries. She exchanged cross words with John Birch and quaffed beer with Claire Chennault's Flying Tigers. While staying on after the Japanese surrender to write an official station history for Donovan, she dodged bullets flying between Chinese Nationalists and Communists, with local warlords in the mix. Her adventures in OSS were made all the richer by the people with whom she served, a small group of brilliant artists, writers, and social scientists. This story is as much theirs as it is hers, which is what she wanted.

I met Betty McIntosh in 2010, after reading her book *Sisterhood of Spies*. I was casting about for a doctoral dissertation topic and knew of the recent declassification of OSS documents in the National Archives. After one interview, I asked Betty's permission to make her the subject of not only my dissertation but a published book.

"Why would you want to do that?" she asked.

This was not false modesty. Like many of her generation, she viewed her years of service to her country as a privilege. Five years later, after hundreds of hours of interviews and careful examination of Betty's personal papers and wartime correspondence, I had not only the product of my labors but one of the richest friendships of my life.

Immediately after the war, before such accounts were precluded by the process of classification, Betty set down her own wartime narrative in *Undercover Girl*. Copies of this manuscript have become scarce and closely held by those lucky enough to find one. *OSS Operation Black Mail* builds on Betty's narrative and is additionally underpinned by all the primary source material demanded for the successful completion of a doctoral dissertation. Betty's personal quotations and dialogue re-creations, derived from interviews, reside somewhere between history and memory and should be understood as such.

During her lengthy and rich life, Betty enjoyed "three happy marriages," which means she was Elizabeth MacDonald during the war, Elizabeth Heppner in the years after, and Elizabeth McIntosh thereafter. To avoid confusion on the part of the reader, I have elected to use the last name McIntosh throughout the narrative.

Not long before her death, Betty was brought to Langley to speak to covert influence officers. The room filled to capacity as she was helped to her seat facing the crowd. When she began to speak, she leaned toward the officers and, as one woman described it, "went totally operational." The years fell away as she described her experiences in black propaganda; some of her experiments had been effective and some had not. She had ideas for operations targeting Vladimir Putin and the Islamic State of Iraq and Syria (ISIS), among other characters and global hotspots. Although she did not even have an e-mail account, she had concocted a scheme for weaponizing Facebook. Her visit to the CIA that day was nothing short of transformative for those who heard her.

On her hundredth birthday, March 1, 2015, Elizabeth P. McIntosh was feted in the Director's Dining Room of CIA Headquarters and received scores of adoring agency employees who lined up to have their pictures taken with her next to the statue of William J. Donovan. On June 8 of the same year, she slipped away from us, and we lost a national treasure.

ACKNOWLEDGMENTS

Writing a book is a solitary and daunting undertaking. Although I have never scaled the peaks of Everest or K2, I imagine the experience is similar: exhilarating, tortuous, full of hidden pitfalls and switchbacks. Difficult and delightful terrain. Sometimes it is hard to breathe. I did not reach the summit—the completion of this project—alone. First to thank is Robert H. Abzug, teacher, mentor, and dear friend. Bob, you changed my life. Professor Betty Miller Unterberger was unrelenting in her belief in me as a scholar. H. W. Brands, Don Carleton, Roger Beaumont, and Gail Minault all gave generously of their time and guidance. Such people make me proud to call myself a historian.

Reference librarians and archivists are the great unsung heroes of history writing, and I am grateful to those manning the stacks of the National Archives at College Park, Maryland; the Library of Congress; the Smithsonian Archives; and the Schlessinger Library at the Radcliffe Institute. The CIA Museum and its team of dedicated museum professionals were generous to a fault in sharing their expertise with an outsider. James D. Hornfischer, Bill Harlow, and the editorial staff of the Naval Institute Press helped me turn a dissertation into a manageable manuscript. David Priess offered both timely advice and the gift of his friendship.

I wrote this book while serving as a camp host in a national park. My time there was an adventure, and I highly recommend it for anyone looking to shake things loose in his or her life. The numerous challenges associated with living for three years in a small RV with three not-small dogs were mitigated by the Rangers, maintenance staff, administrators, and colorful campers of Prince William Forest Park. I am particularly grateful to Tracy Ballesteros, Christopher Ballesteros, Ralph Marrantino, Stephanie Poole, Ken Valenti, Brian McIntosh, and Park Superintendent Vidal Martinez. Thanks especially to "Tall Paul" for keeping my road plowed in the winter, Doug Davidson for tending to every plumbing issue imaginable, and Chuck Ayers for always making me feel part of the National Park Service family.

I will never forget the encouragement shown me by Nick Reynolds, Rebecca Reynolds, Sam Cooper-Wall, Art Reinhardt, Sarah Dalke, Scott Dalke, Troy Sacquety, Charles Grow, Lin Ezell, Robert Sullivan, Susan Tennenbaum, Hayden Peake, Clayton Laurie, and Jim Olson. The friendship of Patrick Greenwade, Glenn Reynolds, Mark Mitchell, Brent McCauley, Sarah Crumley, Cade Crumley, Will Binford, Bailey Tipps, Cindy Anne Duncan, Jodi Jones, Cassandra Hindsley, and Mary Hindsley has continued to sustain me over many years. Will McCauley will always, always, make me laugh, which is sometimes the greatest gift of all. Toni and Dave Hiley made me the charter member of their Take in a Cold and Hungry Doctoral Student Program and are now stuck with me forever. Jan Bailey McCauley has been and will always be my sea anchor through the storms and intermittent doldrums of my life. Thank you, pal.

My last thanks go to my family. Never a day passes without their undivided attention and total adoration, so long as the treats keep coming. To Rufus, Patsy, and Bear: keep those tails wagging.

CAST OF CHARACTERS

(LISTED ALPHABETICALLY AFTER BETTY)

Betty McIntosh

Recruited into OSS for her familiarity with Japanese language and culture. Assigned to a relatively new branch of OSS, Morale Operations, she was trained in the art of black propaganda and sent to the China-Burma-India theater of operations.

Gregory Bateson

Anthropologist, husband to famous fellow anthropologist Margaret Mead. Hired for linguistic and cultural expertise in Malay. Sent to CBI in 1944.

Paul Child

Painter, photographer, mapmaker, art and French teacher, lumberjack, furniture maker, and holder of a black belt in judo. Created maps, charts, and three-dimensional layouts in the OSS branch of Field Photographic. Sent to CBI early in 1944.

Jane Foster

An internationally recognized artist who was hired by OSS for her expertise in the languages and culture of the Netherlands East Indies, later known as Indonesia. She was deployed to CBI in 1944.

Rosamunde Frame

Fluent in eleven Chinese dialects and sent to CBI in 1944 to work in OSS Secret Intelligence, she was tasked with monitoring a growing number of Chinese functionaries coming into India and being on the lookout for agents employed by the Japanese.

Richard Heppner

A junior partner in William J. Donovan's law firm called to active duty in the U.S. Army in June 1941. Brought into OSS, where he directed sabotage efforts in Operation Torch in North Africa and was then sent to CBI to initiate an OSS presence in that theater. Eventually posted as commanding officer, OSS Detachment 202, China. Heppner became Betty's second husband.

Alexander MacDonald

A fellow journalist who met Betty while he was working the police beat at the *Honolulu Star-Bulletin* and who eventually married her. As a reserve officer in the U.S. Navy, Alex was activated on December 7, 1941. He followed his wife into OSS Morale Operations in 1944, joined her in Washington, and then followed her to CBI, where he operated black radio stations and conducted operations in Burma and Thailand.

Julia McWilliams

First hired by OSS in the Emergency Rescue Equipment (ERE) Division, later promoted to senior clerk and administrative assistant. Sent to CBI in 1944. Later known as celebrity chef Julia Child.

Dillon Ripley

A dedicated ornithologist brought on board OSS for his extensive knowledge of the Netherlands East Indies and fluency in Malay. Sent to CBI in 1944, he worked both in Morale Operations and Secret Intelligence Operations in Thailand.

Marjorie Severyns

Graduated from the University of Washington, where she studied political science, international law, and history. Traveled to Japan, China, and Korea as an exchange student. Was working for the Board of Economic Warfare when she was lured into OSS, where she joined Morale Operations.

OSS

OPERATION

BLACK MAIL

INTRODUCTION

The pathways of Père Lachaise Cemetery in Paris lead one through what seems like a very old, very quiet little hamlet. Many of the crypts resemble miniature houses, with pitched roofs and columned facades, situated side by side on narrow brick "streets." Elizabeth P. McIntosh walked under trees casting heavy shade and past banks of flowering vines softening the marble edges and corners of this neighborhood of the dead. She had come to visit her old friend Jane Foster.

Among Betty's wartime friends, Jane was the second of what would become many good-byes—the curse of a long life, no matter how well lived. The first was William J. Donovan, the man responsible for making Betty part of a "pixie-like" band of friends—partners in crime, she liked to call them—including Jane Foster, Paul and Julia Child, Dillon Ripley, Gregory Bateson, Bill Magistretti, Rosamunde Frame, William Smith, and Richard Heppner.

Betty could indeed discern the pixie within people, members of a race she liked to describe as "not good enough for heaven nor bad enough for hell." Impish, eccentric, fearlessly imaginative—all were essential characteristics, but none was more important than humor. Collectively Betty's band of friends was "Donovan's dreamers." Betty early on understood that what made the Office of Strategic Services (OSS) special was the people. Among such a large cohort one could surely find lazy ne'er-do-wells dodging meaningful service. But they did not define the organization, the extraordinary ones did. And if they were not extraordinary before, many were after.

Not melodramatic herself, Betty found the trait charming in others. Not given to flights of fancy, she found such musings in others a source of useful brilliance. When she turned her gaze on people, they somehow revealed the most unique and quixotic aspects of themselves, things that made them burn brighter in memory. Her writings sparkle with those things she most treasured in her friends. She also had an irreverent, dry, and even scathingly wicked sense of humor and was not above dismissing any truly obnoxious character as a *schnook*.

At first glance it would seem Betty McIntosh's personality did little to equip her for cloak-and-dagger activities in war, but it was precisely her ability to see the good in others that made her a deadly black propagandist, a trade she could not have envisioned for herself. She did not attempt to reach the brute within the enemy soldier, but rather the homesick boy. Donovan attracted people like Betty to his great experiment and brought out in them gifts they would have otherwise never recognized in themselves. It was his genius.

William J. Donovan was as large in life as he became in death. Soft-spoken and charming, Donovan left no one who knew him untouched. The soldiers he commanded in World War I revered him as much as the men and women who served under him in OSS. His detractors were many, and their feelings toward him were not tepid. If you liked Donovan, you really liked him. If you hated him, it was a fierce hatred. There was precious little Donovan's supporters and friends would not do for "the General," and those who were threatened by him stopped at nothing to thwart his efforts. "Wild Bill," as he was known by friend and foe alike, was not wild at all but a gracious man of gentle thoughtful temperament who could wield autocratic power with the silence of a ninja. No one knows exactly when he acquired his nickname. Perhaps it was when he led his New York National Guard unit on a hunt for Pancho Villa in Texas or when, seemingly impervious to fear and danger, he led his men through heavy fire in World War I. A handsome man, he had a cleft chin and blue eyes that could twinkle, pierce, or turn soulful, draped by down-turned, heavy lids.

Long before America entered the war on December 7, 1941, Donovan had constructed a strategic vision for fighting it. He made a careful study of an Axis strategy that used propagandistic lies and deceit, diplomatic betrayal, subterfuge, and unprovoked attacks on innocent civilians. When the United States scrambled to meet this amoral threat, Donovan argued persuasively that a military and industrial buildup was not enough. Another dimension was needed, one of intellect and cultural knowledge of the enemy, along with a willingness to conduct irregular warfare. Together with Churchill, Donovan believed fervently in the power of deception. He intended to meet the enemy on his own terms, with every dirty trick the best minds in the country could contrive. To this end, he created a new branch, Morale Operations (MO), and recruited the kind of freethinkers not welcomed into the ranks of the traditional military. In retrospect, the success of his hunt for good propagandists is surprising in that the people he hired were not, per se, propagandists. For MO, Donovan sought those who were not only "outstanding in initiative, resourcefulness, and intelligence, but who also had experience in writing, graphics, printing and radio, [and/or] special knowledge of a foreign area, its people, and its language."[1] Early comers to the agency included many household names in business, media, or academic circles, but it was the later wave of recruitment for MO that began America's first official experiment with conducting subversive propaganda.

Most histories of OSS make mention of its many near-death experiences but miss the fact that black propaganda saved the agency from obliteration. The British insisted on the inclusion of psychological warfare as an essential element of Allied strategy, and when the Joint Chiefs of Staff (JCS) took a look around for psychological warriors, Donovan stood poised to take the field. In 1942 the JCS was itself an infant organization, created to present a united front to the British Combined Chiefs (BCC). It had been emerging fitfully over time in response to a lack of cooperation between the ever-expanding U.S. military branches following the Civil War.

Donovan was made chairman of the JCS Joint Psychological Warfare Committee while he was still the coordinator of information (COI). The committee did very little, but meanwhile, the COI came under the protective wing of the JCS. OSS and the Office of War Information (OWI) were both created on June 13, 1942. Donovan regretted the loss of many of his new propaganda workers to OWI, especially when the latter joined forces with his constant nemesis, G-2 (Military Intelligence) Chief Maj. Gen. George V. Strong, described by one of Donovan's associates as "a vicious man, a bully with no merit but vigor . . . does all he can do to fight us all in OSS."[2] Strong convinced President Franklin Roosevelt to draft a "death warrant" for the newly born OSS. It was slipped to the bottom of a pile by a friendly hand and lay there untended until Donovan, in a stroke of semantic brilliance, pronounced *his* propaganda to be *black*, not *white*—the purview of OWI. Donovan persuaded the president to sign a new executive order defining OWI's propagandistic functions as strictly white and overt, which left the need for black, or covert, propaganda. JCS 155/2/D officially made OSS the military's psychological warfare agency, which meant Donovan would be supplied with military manpower for his otherwise civilian agency.[3]

The process of creating black propaganda is subtle, not heroic, tricky, not courageous, and yet in the right hands its cumulative effect can be devastating. It is guerrilla warfare, a strategy for resistance. The immediate goal is not winning, but rather not losing. A huge part of creating and disseminating black propaganda is and was the guesswork, and this was especially true in targeting the Japanese. Even Westerners who had lived most of their lives on the home islands of Japan found the Japanese people "inscrutable." The Axis in Europe, however, shared a common ancestry with the Allies, in many cases not even a generation of separation. Linguistic and cultural divisions were not bottomless chasms. To Allied personnel, Germans and Italians quite simply "looked like us." Not so the Japanese.

MO officers in the Far East Division were not "old Japan hands," cohabitating the State Department with such "old China hands" as John Davies. The Japan experts rose above any dehumanizing of the enemy but nonetheless clung stubbornly to ethnocentric and condescending evaluations. Joseph Grew, an undersecretary of state who had served as ambassador to Tokyo from 1931 to 1945, was solidly in the old Japan hand camp and considered the Japanese "inert and tradition-bound." Other experts concurred, and they had the ear of the JCS throughout the war. The British were unwavering in their evaluation of the Japanese psyche as that of an "obedient herd" and a "monstrous beehive,"[4] collectively considering the Japanese immune to persuasion or trickery.

Betty McIntosh, by her own admission, had a romanticized image of the Japanese, and her approach to black propaganda work was informed by reading Lafcadio Hearn, whose writings on traditional Japan had charmed many Western readers. For Hearn, "everything Japanese is delicate, exquisite, admirable—even a pair of wooden chopsticks in a paper bag with a little drawing upon it; even a package of toothpicks of cherry-wood, bound with a paper wrapper wonderfully lettered in three different colours; even the little sky-blue towel with designs of flying sparrows upon it, which the *jinricksha* man used to wipe his face." His descriptions of the home islands were enchanting: "The whole city and the bay and the mountains begirdling it, and Fujiyama's white witchery over-hanging it in the speckless sky, all Japan, in very truth, with its magical trees and luminous atmosphere with all its cities and towns and temples, and forty millions of the most lovable people in the universe."[5]

Few Allied military analysts factored such bucolic scenes into their assessments. Following the sinking of the U.S. Navy ship *Panay* and heavy-handed incursions into China, Japanese soldiers became caricatures—small, troll-like, bucktoothed, bespectacled creatures that could be beaten by a junior varsity football team with no military training. Before Pearl Harbor the idea that Japanese could be trained as aviators was considered absurd, and even after the attack, many were convinced the pilots had to have been German.

Yet another version of the Japanese fighting man was the inhuman perpetrator of atrocities, namely against the Chinese, and there existed no small amount of evidence to back that up. Tominaga Shozo was a university student in Hiroshima conscripted and dispatched to Central China in the summer of 1941. He described participating in a typical "training exercise" for new arrivals:

> I unsheathed my sword, a gift from my brother-in-law, wet it down as the lieutenant had demonstrated, and stood behind the man. The prisoner didn't move. . . . I was tense, thinking I couldn't fail. I steadied myself, holding the sword at a point above my right shoulder, and swung down with one breath. The head flew away and the body tumbled down, spouting blood. The air reeked from all that blood. . . . Good soldiers were those who were able to kill. . . . We made them like this. . . . Good sons, good daddies, good elder brothers.[6]

In Washington, military strategists and their advisers labored to understand the Japanese, but their efforts yielded a veritable boiling pot of confusion and misconception, with small sprinkles of truth floating in the mix. OSS analysts were different. Donovan's stable of anthropologists refused to dismiss anything or anyone as inscrutable, not even a formidable enemy—the better the challenge.

This is not a typical war story. The only beaches stormed are the minds of an invisible enemy. OSS practitioners of black propaganda suffered no battle fatigue beyond frustration and impatience. Often a great deal of time and effort was expended in conception and production, after which the fruits of one's labors were sent out to be tossed from the bomb bays of an airplane or planted on a dead enemy courier. Rarely was it known if even a shred reached the hands of the intended recipient. The process was opaque on both ends: the origin of a rumor or radio broadcast obscured, the target elusive. For Betty and her friends, time on the "front lines" of psychological warfare in China-Burma-India rushed by in an eighteen-month cascade of creativity and innovation, played out on a stage where a colonial world was ending and chaos awaited. Life would never be as rich again.

ONE

VOYAGE BEFORE
THE STORM

I made it a habit never to pass up the chance for adventure.

—*Elizabeth P. McIntosh*

etty McIntosh felt herself adrift in a sea of khaki when she stepped onto the deck of the USAT *Republic*, flagship of the Army Transport Service (ATS). Four painted stripes on the stack denoted the number of months the ship had served in a war zone, dodging U-boats between New York and Europe on multiple trips and carrying up to 7,000 troops at a time. It was the *Republic*'s forty-first voyage since it had entered the service in 1931, and this was her longest cruise to date, one that would take her over 30,000 miles at sea. The ATS included 11 other passenger ships, 10 cargo ships, and 12 smaller vessels such as harbor transports, tugs, and water boats.[1]

On board the *Republic* were two thousand young members of the New Mexico National Guard, all of whom were delighted when the tawny blond reporter bounded up the gangplank. Seventeen young officer candidates already occupied the lanai suites, so Betty joined the nurses in their accommodations just around the corner from the main deck. Soldiers milled and jostled over every surface and filled all the staterooms and below-deck holds. Their cots crowded what had been a swank first-class lounge when the *Republic* served as a member of the Cabin Passenger Service fleet.

Betty was still a cub reporter at the *Honolulu Star-Bulletin* in April 1941 when she convinced her editor someone should write a story on the movement of troops to the Philippines. Together with a shipload of National Guardsmen and nurses, Betty was getting under way for a two-month out-and-back mission to reinforce MacArthur's forces and evacuate military dependents.

As the *Republic* was setting sail, U.S. relations with the Japanese were strained, but Tokyo still had not moved into Southeast Asia and President Roosevelt had yet to freeze Japanese assets in America. The Imperial Japanese Navy (IJN) was conducting bold maneuvers in western Pacific waters and the South China Sea. It was a tense, shallow, and precarious breathing space during this final modus vivendi before war. The Philippines were high on the list of likely targets for Japanese attack, and American code breakers worked feverishly, exchanging intelligence with their British counterparts in Singapore. Douglas MacArthur was six years into his ten-year plan to have 76,000 Filipinos trained, armed, and ready to defend the islands, to be accompanied by a significant buildup of airpower. Independence was scheduled to be granted on July 4, 1946.[2]

The voyage to Manila passed as a pleasure cruise. Betty made her rounds, gathering the ship's history and lore. The crew took great pride in the *Republic* and was eager to boast of her attributes. Walter W. Olsen was commander in chief of the post exchange laundry, presiding over a crew of twenty-nine helpers. He led Betty to two huge washing machines running at full capacity from 8 a.m. to 5 p.m. each day at sea. Olsen spoke of them lovingly, as though they were the ship's engines, proudly explaining the series of rinses and soakings involved in a cycle. A trip from San Francisco to Manila was projected to use up to seven hundred pounds of granulated soap to launder uniforms, jackets, and underwear. Sheets, towels, and pillowcases were sent ashore to be laundered at port. Ship's personnel paid for their clean clothes, with the highest price being fifty cents for a blue sailor's uniform and the lowest two cents for socks and handkerchiefs.[3]

Betty cornered one of the four maritime cadets on board. George Chandler Jr. dreamed of becoming skipper of a commercial liner or even going to Annapolis. He was every bit the Brooklyn boy, and eager to tell the attractive reporter all about "his" ship.

"The foist thing you do when you join the ship is to loin all the angles," he began in a serious Brooklyn accent. "After that you settle down to the woik of learning about pipelines, electric systems, the engines and navigation in general."[4]

George studied seventy-two hours a week and knew his engines intimately, backward and forward. Betty left fascinated that by the time they reached Manila, George's engineering log would show precisely how many turns the ship's huge propellers had made and how many per minute.

Discipline was relaxed among the guardsmen and young officers, with little regimentation apart from morning muster. Guitars and harmonicas appeared, and as the equatorial heat rose, more and more time was spent topside. The soldiers carried their blankets on deck and slept under the stars. They sang—their voices wafting over the deck and up from the holds—played cards, and regaled each other and the nurses with stories of recent glory days of high school football and baseball. Betty read a great deal, always nonfiction, as was her habit, and listened to what could be picked up on the portable radio. Her bunkmates were a happy group of savvy young women from all walks of life, typical of Army nurses in 1941. "Free, white, and twenty-one" was a common refrain for (white) females with a high school education who joined the U.S. Army Nurse Corps before World War II. After training and requisite years of service, nurses enjoyed a respected profession granting them the kind of independence that comes with income.[5]

Betty McIntosh was not unlike the nurses, staking a beachhead as a professional woman in a world of wives and mothers. Her independent nature was encouraged by her own mother, who had been a newspaper columnist in Washington, D.C., before she married William Peet, a sports editor, and moved with him to Hawaii, where she began teaching English at an all-Japanese high school. Betty was a popular and attractive tennis player who worked on the high school newspaper and yearbook. She was also very mischievous. Her 1931 Punahou High School yearbook claimed she was "the originator of ninetenths [sic] of the deviltry perpetrated in study hall and classroom. . . . She confronts irate teachers with an unabashed grin, stoutly maintaining her innocence."[6] Her engaging personality, however, concealed the temperament of a loner. Most days Betty walked home from school alone and stopped at the zoo to visit her "best friend," an elephant named Daisy.

After two languorous days of sailing, the *Republic* continued to slide through the sea as though cutting cream, rarely encountering a swell on the water's surface. Betty was dozing in her bunk when she was jolted awake by a grinning cadet.

"Hey, Sleepy, wake up! The ship's sinking!" he hollered from the hatchway.

"All men to lifeboats!" blared a voice, competing with a hideously loud Klaxon.

Still groggy, Betty rolled out of bed and stood unsteadily, trying to focus and listening to what sounded like total mayhem forward and directly below the deck of her cabin.

"Lucky I can swim," she mumbled, trying to remember what to do. "Life preserver, that's it."

She peered under her bunk at nothing, then moved to the closet and began tossing out shoes and a tennis racket, cursing the Klaxon. How could anyone think with that noise? Looking up, she spied what had to be the corner of the preserver, crammed in a compartment near the ceiling to make room for a box of typewriter ribbon. She dragged a metal chair and climbed on it, but the deck began pitching and rolling—maybe this was not a drill? Each time she gained precarious balance, the chair slid away as she grabbed for her target. Just as she began to see herself in a Marx brothers comedy, one last lunge pulled loose large chunks of orange cloth-covered cork and tangled straps before she was dumped onto the deck.

Trying to remember the proper procedure for donning a personal floatation device, Betty began shoving her arms into openings, hoping the snarl of straps would hold everything together. She stumbled, blinking, out onto the open deck and was abruptly halted by a cadet.

"Stewardess, you wanna break your arms off?" he yelled, explaining that the imaginative configuration of her life preserver would indeed sever her arms at the pits should she jump overboard. He made an impressively quick adjustment, just in time for the chief steward to appear.

"Report to Lifeboat No. 7!" the chief barked at her.

Betty had no recollection where that might be, so fell in with a moving river of soldiers and sailors, ending up with a hose brigade on the aft deck. No lifeboat in sight. She heard her name called faintly and headed toward the sound, clattering gracelessly down two ladders, the bulky life preserver snagging on everything possible, snapping off something, possibly an antenna, as she plowed ahead. She reached her lifeboat as it was being lowered and leaned over the rail to watch it descend. All around her, other people seemed to know exactly what they were supposed to be doing: some standing by floats lashed to the deck; others inspecting emergency provisions, hard tack, freshwater, knives, hatchets, and flares. At last a degree of calm settled over the ship as the drill wound down.

⚑

After the excitement of the abandon-ship drill, time slowed again as one care-free day turned into another. Easter morning aboard the *Republic* dawned with a spectacular ocean sunrise. Betty and the nurses were escorted to seats on the upper deck by cadets in crisp whites just as the opening bars of "God Bless America" filled the air. A piano had materialized on deck and was accompanied by a violin-playing private from Texas. Betty looked out over the scrubbed and spit-polished soldiers as they sang, the ocean behind them stretching to the horizon, everything sparkling in the brightness of the morning. Easter brunch followed, with white and dark slabs of turkey, mushroom stuffing, giblet gravy, cranberry sauce, cream puff ducks, and ice cream. It would be years before most of the young soldiers enjoyed another such a feast, by which time they were no longer young.[7]

Tuesday morning, the ship nosed into the San Bernardino Strait, the gateway to Manila. All hands were on deck to catch sight of the peaks of the Philippine Islands after fifteen days at sea. It took the entire day to maneuver through part of the 7,083 islands composing the chain, sailing past ancient craters ringed with jungle and occasional spits of white sand in the otherwise smooth Sibuyan Sea. The ship was unusually quiet, except for the hum of the *Republic*'s trusty engines and the slap of flying fish on the glassy water. The only signs of habitation ashore were curls of smoke rising out of the hills, hinting at the presence of a barrio. A telescope was passed around so that sailors could catch glimpses of stilted shacks in the cracks of the jungle. Now and then an outrigger canoe with a red, blue, or brown sail slid out of a hidden inlet.

The day passed that way until the sun became huge and red, sinking in a streaked sky behind the restless volcano, Mount Mayon, when it passed to starboard. Betty watched the ship's reflection on the water and its lacy wake. Finally, the engines came to all-stop, and the *Republic* dropped anchor for the night. The boys on the afterdeck were twirling cowboy lassoes, but otherwise the ship was silent. Betty turned in early.

Wednesday morning sauna-like mists in Manila Bay greeted Betty as she stepped through the hatch to the outer deck. Corregidor Island sat at the mouth of the bay, its barracks and bunkers carved into solid rock for concealment. Known as the Gibraltar of the United States, Corregidor was the most heavily fortified island under the American flag, designed to brunt any attack on Manila.

At the tip of the island floated a smaller man-made redoubt, Fort Drum, resembling a floating flat battleship. The city itself was hidden in a heat mirage as the *Republic* glided through the mouth of the breakwater framing the inner bay. In 1941 Manila was the largest and wealthiest city in the southwest Pacific, situated on the island of Luzon, which, in comparison to New Guinea, Borneo, Sumatra, or Java, was considered by many to be more "civilized." Manila Bay offered one of the largest landlocked harbors in the world. A deep plain lay less than one hundred miles north in an otherwise mountainous and heavily forested landscape and offered the perfect spot for an invading force to make landfall.

Onshore, days were spent exploring by jeep, that wonder of the U.S. Army seemingly created solely to be commandeered by nurses, doctors, and other officers for off-duty jaunts. If no men were along—a rare occurrence—some young GI in uniform invariably materialized to serve as a chauffeur for excursions into the mountains or picnics on the beach. Betty was usually accompanied by another reporter, Clark Lee, who later wrote *The Battling Bastards of Bataan*. When the *Republic* was scheduled to haul anchor for a run south to take on a load of hemp at Mindanao, Betty and Clark planned an excursion to locate the enigmatic "tree men" rumored to build their houses high in the branches of the jungle trees there.

They were also in search of the "Sea Gypsies," Muslim warriors of the Moros tribe who resided either in the highlands or in stilted nipa shacks suspended over the water. The Moros were famous for their weapons, and Betty and Clark had high hopes they could procure some souvenirs. The group of explorers had grown to ten by the time it disembarked at the Davao pier, and loaded with cameras and notebooks, Betty, Clark, and the others piled into three cars. A trip up into the jade-green mountains, past miles of hemp farms and the Del Monte pineapple plantation, brought the expedition to the jungle home of the elusive Moros, who appeared wearing crushed velvet hats, tight britches, large yellow earrings, and shell necklaces. The Moros, displaying smiling racks of teeth sharpened and blackened with betel juice, seemed friendly. Clark engaged in an energetic negotiation for one or more of the knives known to be specialties of the Moros, the *barong* and *kris*.

The chief, or *datu*, appraised the group skeptically, consulted a translator, and then pronounced that he required proof they were civilized folk as he was forbidden by law to transfer deadly weapons irresponsibly. A long discussion ensued, and the *datu* remained unconvinced and reticent. The ship's chaplain stepped forward and tried explaining that they had come on a big white boat that even now sat moored in the harbor. This piqued the *datu*'s interest, and he decided to convey the knives down the mountain himself in order to see this big white boat. An hour passed, during which Betty poked around and found most of the Moros' shacks stuffy and dark, furnished only with sleeping mats. The Moros seemed to be living just as they had under Spanish occupation, she decided, although the ship's doctor, who was also along, said they looked healthy enough. They refused to sell Betty any of the beads or spears lying haphazardly on the floor of their homes.

The *datu* waved good-bye to the Americans, promising to bring weapons to the village near the harbor the next morning. Upon straggling wearily back onto the dock to board the *Republic*, the travelers realized the water of the harbor had kicked up with the wind, meaning it was not possible to lower the gangplank in the heaving swells. The wild trek into Moroland quickly paled in comparison to being hauled aboard the ship by hemp rope, which is exactly what happened. Loads of hemp continued to arrive by barge until 3 a.m., and the ship sailed at dawn.

"Whether the friendly *datu* ever came down to Davao bearing weapons, we'll never know," Betty typed that night. "The strange white boat he wanted to see was threading its way back to Manila, loaded in eight hatches with half a million dollars worth of hemp."

The trip back to Luzon was peaceful after the weather calmed and a gibbous moon appeared between scudding clouds. Word went out that they were passing over the deepest spot charted in the ocean off Mindanao, 32,400 feet down to the sea floor. News also flashed from sailor to sailor that a wireless had been received informing that all transports were to be taken over by the Navy by the time the *Republic* made port in New York. There was a literal shift in the wind. Betty wrote, "War and reality seemed suddenly close again as we passed a Japanese freighter, loaded with iron ore. I was told that Japan sends an endless line of freighters to the port of Larap for this ore, loaded for 4.50 pesos a ton. In 1940 a million tons was shipped to Japan."[8]

Sunday was the ship's final day in Manila. Betty joined in the rush of last-minute sightseeing, visiting an icon of Spanish colonialism: a Byzantine-designed Roman Catholic cathedral established in 1581. Inside the huge gleaming dome, with its massive doors and vaulted ceiling, the sounds of Manila were muffled. Women with handkerchiefs covering their heads and choir boys in scarlet vestments glided across cool red flagstones. Betty sat silently. Prayer was not her habit, but seeing the Japanese freighter filled with what she knew in her heart was war matériel led her to lower herself onto the kneeling bench.

Back in the blinding sunlight, she made her way to the city aquarium and there saw her first python. He had just consumed a live chicken and coiled most of his fourteen feet of gray scales around a large branch, his eyes drooping sleepily in the sun. A zookeeper informed Betty the snake would sleep for two weeks and would be fed again about the time she reached Honolulu. Until that moment, Betty had been undecided whether to end her trip at home in Hawaii or continue the adventure on to New York with the ship. Something about the python, so sleepy there on his branch, made her decide to go home to her husband.

That night a festive send-off party was held on the edge of the bay, with tiki torches and paper lanterns casting cheerful reflections on the water. The nurses were kept on the dance floor the whole night, and Betty barely had a chance to sit down and enjoy her Tom Collins. When she did, the sight of the full moon, the colored lights, and the notes of the swing music almost made her forget that she was leaving and that staying behind—for how long, she did not know—were people she had come to know. No one knew what was going to happen. She wanted to chat with the nurses who had become her friends, but the young soldiers were determined to dance till dawn. No one wanted to say good-bye, Betty realized, and finally, she took herself off to the ship.

The *Republic* sailed. Over four hundred women and children, dependents of the men remaining in the Philippines, crowded the decks. Instead of singing soldiers down in the hold, the ship carried containers of oil and bales of hemp. The *Republic* island-hopped for several days before it set course for Hawaii, looking for and gathering up anything the Japanese might use in war production. For the most part, the women stayed on board and watched as sailors took small boats to deserted beaches on uninhabited spits of white sand and thick jungle. The calls of wild monkeys and birds carried across the water. Still officially a stewardess, Betty was assigned twenty-five mothers and children. The families had gotten used to nannies. Some mothers had never changed a diaper, and Betty knew nothing about kids. The decks swarmed with small children, tumbling like playful otters. It was a long two weeks back. Upon returning to Honolulu, Betty was the only passenger to disembark; everyone else was bound stateside. Betty's husband, Alex, was waiting for her. As always, he listened eagerly and did not complain about her absence.

ᢙ

When Betty had returned to Hawaii with a degree in journalism from the University of Washington in 1935, her father secured her a job at his newspaper, the *Honolulu Advertiser*. Ever independent, she rented herself a small bungalow above the city in the Wilhelmina Rise carnation fields, owned and presided over by Syngman Rhee, the exiled president of Korea. Each night she drove her tan Ford convertible home to her little house, which "wasn't much," as she recalled, but had a great lanai overlooking the evening lights of Honolulu where coworkers could gather for cocktails.

Her first day on the job, her father sat her at a desk next to young Alexander MacDonald, who covered the police beat. Alex was one of those "roving reporters" of the Mark Twain journeyman type who stayed a year or two on a job and then moved on to China or Japan. He fell for Betty instantly, finding her beautiful and admiring her independent adventurous spirit. They shared an intense desire to work in Japan.

Betty and Alex were wed in a traditional Hawaiian ceremony at the home of a local Congregational minister on July 3, 1937. They were driven to the waterfront, where they boarded a flying boat for the Big Island to spend their honeymoon at the Kona Inn, overlooking Kealakekua Bay. Meanwhile, Alex allowed his parents to believe they had been wed in a Roman Catholic ceremony. Knowing it would crush his parents to learn they had not been blessed by the True Church, he asked his new bride if they could retake the vows at low mass at St. Augustine's Church downtown. She knew her own Episcopalian mother would be furious but agreed. In his memoir, Alex asked rhetorically, "Who wouldn't cherish so acquiescent a bride?"[9]

The newlyweds began work on a house of their own with proceeds from recent promotions. Alex was made Sunday editor, and Betty, having moved to the *Star-Bulletin*, was working as the society editor. They found two hillside lots outside the rapidly expanding city of Honolulu on Kalanianaole Highway, the coastal road connecting Diamond Head and Koko Head. An acre each, they overlooked an idyllic lagoon ringed by coconut trees. After paying $3,000 for both lots, they hired a young architect new to the island, Philip Johnson, to work from their sketches and design a dream home.

While the house was under construction, the couple moved in with their Japanese language teacher, Professor Saburo Watanabe, and his shy wife, Keiko, for immersion instruction in Japanese language. Betty and Alex were motivated and studied hard under the professor's tutelage. They worked on grammar drills and practiced writing kanji script after dinner each night. Soon they spoke nothing but Japanese in the house, and even after their house had been completed, they continued to see the Watanabes twice a week.

A lifetime later, Betty McIntosh remembered the next few years as idyllic. "It was a wonderful relationship," she explained. "We had no children. I loved my work and so did Alex. The house was perfect, and we had a yellow tabby cat named Skeets, a rescued stray, who waited for us at the top of the steps and came bounding down when we got home from work, almost like a faithful dog."[10]

Life was good and full of promise. Not so in the rest of the world, however. Japan had already taken over northern portions of China; in 1937 it occupied Tientsin, Shanghai, and the capital at Nanking. At that time the southern entrance into Burma was an ancient trail, passable only to animals or people on foot. Within two years the trail would be remade into a vital part of the Burma Road, China's lifeline. When the MacDonalds looked over the ocean from their home, they knew the entire eastern coast of China had been occupied by the Japanese. FDR had called for a halt to the southern expansion of Japanese forces into Indochina, and the situation was getting tense in Hawaii. Alex took a commission in the Naval Reserve.

"Something's going to bust loose," he told Betty. "We're almost into it in Europe. Next we'll be fighting Japan. I'm certain of it, and I'm going to get into it now."[11]

TWO
WAR

Dinner in dark in pantry.
Outside flares from PH plainly visible from lanai.
During night machine guns on Punchbowl kept firing at planes.

—*Joseph P. Poindexter, private secretary to the governor of Hawaii*

The circle of faces was silent on December 7, 1941, lit by only a single candle set into a puddle of its own wax on the tile floor. While the scotch and sour mash had lasted, they whispered occasionally, not looking at each other, not wanting to see reflections of their own shock, pain, and fatigue. When the liquor cabinet was bare, they stopped whispering, preferring to lean back into the shadows, pulling away from fresh memories of the day and its horrendous sounds and smells. The air was stifling. Curtains were drawn over tightly shut floor-to-ceiling windows in Betty's house on a cliff overlooking Kulionuou Lagoon. Even so, muffled sounds of sirens and antiaircraft fire reached the little huddled group of coworkers from the *Honolulu Star-Bulletin* newsroom.

Twelve hours before, a wave of 183 Japanese torpedo and dive bombers, along with its escort of Zero fighters, had dropped from the clouds and flown low and unmolested across the island of Oahu toward Battleship Row in Pearl Harbor. Eighteen U.S. scout bombers and seven flying boats were conducting a dawn patrol to the west and south between Midway and the Hawaiian Islands.

This left a gap in the northern sector, and through this breach the Japanese planes slipped and streaked toward their target, the Pacific Fleet of the U.S. Navy. Along with everyone else in the Hawaiian archipelago, Betty and her husband, both recovering from festivities the previous night on Waikiki, remained blissfully unaware of what had begun to unfold.

Betty began breakfast in the kitchen of their house while Alex slept in. As she cracked eggs and leaned over the sink to watch a tiny fleet of colorful kayaks in the lagoon below, the sounds of the Mormon Tabernacle Choir stopped abruptly and a voice on the radio barked, "The islands are under attack! This is the real McCoy!" She continued to gaze at the kayaks, waiting for the music to resume. "Just more war games," she thought. The military was forever simulating an attack on the islands to train for such a possibility, there being little else to do in paradise. When the music did not return, Betty experienced a frisson of expectation. She was a reporter and felt a story coming on. A big one.

The phone jangled, and she snatched it up.

"We need to get to the newsroom!" shouted Allen "Hump" Campbell, her photographer at the *Star*. "I'm coming to pick you up." The line went dead.

Betty raced into the bedroom and shook Alex. "I think you're going to have to report for duty," she said. "I think we're being invaded!"

Alexander MacDonald, second lieutenant, U.S. Naval Reserve, murmured, "Coffee first. Then we fight." He pulled the pillow over his head. After Betty brought him a mug of coffee, she returned to the kitchen window and saw planes buzzing over the kayakers in the lagoon below. The kayakers had stopped mid-paddle to gaze upward.

"It was such an odd moment," Betty remembered years later. "I knew what was happening but refused to grasp it until Alex pointed out the red sun painted on the sides of the planes."[1]

Her husband left in his uniform, and Betty would not see him for another two weeks. Hump skidded to a halt on the gravel drive, and she dived into the passenger seat. As they raced along the highway, it all seemed to be a big mistake; the world had not changed. Apparently unaware of what had happened, people continued their Sunday strolls, walking their dogs. But as Betty and Hump neared town, traffic slowed, and Betty saw some cars already had blue paint on their headlights.

A whistle shrilled from over her right shoulder, and the roof flew off a building down the street—the two events seemingly simultaneous but not connected.

It looked to her like a pasteboard movie set had exploded. The air thickened with dust. From Punchbowl they watched the blue sky fill with white puffs of smoke.

"Antiaircraft fire," Hump said.

Hump stopped next to a street market that had clearly sustained a direct hit. Christmas decorations littered the edges of a crater where the market had been. Hump pointed to a small boy sitting in the middle of the devastation, playing happily with fistfuls of tinsel.

"Here we go," said Hump, grabbing his gear. "We need a *war* photo," he said, pointing at the boy. "*Do* something!"

"What?" asked Betty.

"Make him less happy," Hump said. "It's a *combat* photo."

"No."

"Yes."

"No!" she shouted, stopping herself just short of stamping her foot. She stood her ground momentarily, hesitated, and then marched to the little boy and pinched him lightly. It did the trick, and he started crying. Hump had his tragic snap. Betty glared at him, snatched up the toddler, and, full of remorse, carried him with her the rest of the morning, bought him anything he wanted, and forced Hump to help her find his family.

Charging into the *Star-Bulletin* newsroom, they encountered madness. Type-writers clacked deafeningly, and everyone seemed to be yelling at no one in particular. Betty immediately made ready to head to the harbor and was turned down flat.

"No women are allowed down there," her normally indulgent editor snapped.

For once she did not argue and instead had Hump drop her at Queen's Hospital, where she found nurses, fearful of more bombing, taping the windows. Hickam Field firemen were the first to be brought in. Blackened and bleeding, most unconscious, some groaning, they lined the corridor. Corpses were carried out and laid on blood-splattered steps. Those wounded who were not delirious shouted to be allowed to donate blood. Doctors shouted for instruments. Supplies remained under lock and key until late afternoon, when Army personnel arrived to open whatever cages had not been prized apart with crowbars. Meanwhile, doctors performing major surgery traded scissors back and forth from table to table, and when they ran out of operating gowns, they continued in pajamas and underwear, rags tied over their faces as masks. Doctors, nurses, and orderlies shared the work of lifting patients from blood-slicked floors and removing clothing to clean wounds.[2]

Betty spent the day helping where she could and feverishly jotting notes for stories as she heard them—people being strafed by Japanese Zeroes, picked off on golf courses and city streets. Seven days later she typed up her observations of the day:

> For the first time, I felt that numb terror that all of London has known for months. It is the terror of not being able to do anything but fall on your stomach and hope the bomb won't land on you. It's the helplessness and terror of sudden visions of a ripping sensation in your back, shrapnel coursing through your chest, total blackness, maybe death. . . . Bombs were still dropping over the city as ambulances screamed off into the heart of the destruction. The drivers were sodden when they returned, with stories of streets ripped up, houses burned, twisted shrapnel in charred bodies of children. In the morgue the bodies were laid on slabs in the grotesque position in which they died. Fear contorted their faces. Their clothes were blue-black from incendiary bombs. One little girl in a red sweater, barefoot, still clutched a piece of jump rope in her hand. . . . Who would have known blood could be so bright red. I went to a bombed store on King St., where I often, times past, stopped for a coke at the cool drug counter. Nearly seven little stores, including my drugstore, had been completely burned down. Charred, ripply walls, as high as the first story, alone remained to give any hint of where the store had been. At the smashed soda fountain was a half-eaten chocolate sundae. Charred bon-bons were scattered on the sidewalk. There were odd pieces lying in the wreckage . . . half burned Christmas cards, on one, the words "Hark the Herald" . . . still visible, the rest charred. . . . There were twisted bed springs, half burned mattresses, cans of food, a child's blackened bicycle, a lunch box, a green raveled sweater, a Bang-up comic book. . . . I ran out of note paper and reached down and picked up a charred batch of writing paper. . . . There was the irony of Christmas tinsel, cellophane decorations. A burnt doll with staring eyes, singed curls and straw bonnet, like a miniature corpse, lay in the wreckage.[3]

When darkness finally fell, nervous soldiers began firing at any light they saw until they were ordered to stop shooting out the headlights of police cars. A terse suggestion was made that the police turn off their lights like everyone else. Friendly fire crackled invisibly in the night amid a storm of chaos, anxiety, and rumor: there would be additional attacks with Japanese pouring down out of the mountains; Japanese parachutists had been dropped wearing green uniforms with an orange sun on their left breast.

"Thank God the men did not carry out all the orders [to shoot]," commented Carl Eiffler, at that time serving as an Army captain. "We would have lost a hell of a lot of delivery men, garbage men, and some boy scouts." Late in the night, a B-17 made the dubious decision to drop a group of American paratroopers. Miraculously, none were hit, but as tracer bullets continued to lash the night sky, frazzled antiaircraft gunners finally downed four of six U.S. planes attempting to land on Ford Island from the carrier *Enterprise*.[4]

No one at the *Star* wanted to go home to Honolulu. Betty's house, a favorite destination for after-work cocktails, was remote and seemingly safe, so ten of her coworkers followed her home along the darkened highway, their caravan resembling a nocturnal funeral procession. Inside, Betty went straight to the sideboard, poured two fingers of Glenlivit scotch whiskey in Alex's favorite crystal tumbler, tossed it down, caught her breath, then poured another. She passed the bottle off to a reporter from the sports desk who then grasped it by the neck and raised it to his lips for a deep draw. Betty headed off to get out of her bloody clothes and into the shower. Normally, the group would have crowded onto the sun terrace running the length of the lagoon side of the house, but this night they pulled cushions from the couches and sat on the floor, together and yet alone, each hiding from what might come next. The Hawaiian archipelago had gone dark, and residents huddled and sheltered as the British had done for two years.

Fear-stoked emotion settled over Oahu as thickly as the oily blanket of black smoke in the harbor. In the newsroom Betty typed, "In the nightmare of Monday and Tuesday there was the struggle to keep normal when planes zoomed overhead and guns cracked out at unseen enemy. There was blackout and suspicion riding the back of wild rumors . . . parachutists in the hills, poison in your food. Starvation and death were all that was left in a tourist bureau paradise."[5]

Japanese Americans quickly found themselves objects of attention. Daniel Inouye, Betty's former Punahou High School classmate, rushed through Honolulu to report to his Reserve Officer Training Corps (ROTC) headquarters as the first wave of bombs fell.

"You dirty Japs!" he screamed into the sky, choking on tears. At his station he found his fellow Japanese American cadets standing unhappily to one side while other students received rifles.[6]

In the days following December 7, 1941, Betty visited the Red Cross centers, canteens, evacuee districts, and even the motor corps headquarters. A nurse from Hickam recalled dropping to the floor when bullets stitched a row across the wall over her head. A nurse from Schofield begged Betty to get word to her sweetheart "somewhere in Honolulu" that she was still alive. A nurse at Pearl Harbor was gathering scraps of paper and pencil stubs for boys in the hospital desperate to send last messages home before they died. A small girl named Freeda, clutching a big doll named Nancy, whispered to Betty that "daddy has been killed at Hickam." In one of the upland plantation hospitals during those first nights, nurses stumbled down darkened corridors, slipping through doors to prevent the escape of any sliver of light. They worked in the glow of blue-covered flashlight lenses casting ghoulish shadows on frightened patients. The only real sound was of crying babies in the nursery who somehow felt entitled to food regardless of the bombings.

⚜

Eight hours after the Pearl Harbor attack, the Philippines were hit. On the outskirts of Manila, the singing soldiers of the New Mexico National Guard rushed frantically to their antiaircraft guns as Japanese bombs rocked Clark Field. Pilots had earlier scrambled into the air when reports of the Pearl Harbor attack came through, but encountering no Japanese and not comprehending the extent of the unfolding calamity, they were directed to return to base for lunch. Their planes sat neatly, wing tip to wing tip, when the pounding began. Sergeants and their men were caught servicing the aircraft and dived for cover with no officers in sight. Darkness fell, searchlights pierced the night, and not until dawn was it revealed that all forts and airfields around Manila had suffered direct hits. The nurses Betty had so recently befriended ran through strafing fire to the hospitals, the ground erupting around them.[7]

In the city of Manila, the sound of shots became almost constant, with no indication as to whether the noise was from snipers, antiaircraft guns, or cars backfiring. Hospitals overflowed, taxis and gasoline were commandeered, drugstores were emptied of bandages and iodine, and mob violence broke out in hardware stores over the few remaining flashlights left on the shelves. Windows everywhere were painted dark green. A news story describing the heroics of the

New Mexico National Guard sergeants at Clark Field eventually made it to *Life* magazine, but Army censors blocked anything suggesting the true extent of the destruction. Instead, stories came in from Douglas MacArthur's head-quarters about American success in the air, suggesting the Japanese were being repulsed. America remained unaware that any such offensive was impossible in the Philippines.[8]

When Japanese troops landed on the plain north of Manila, U.S.-Filipino troops retreated to Bataan, the thirty-mile peninsula along the bay where Betty and her friends had celebrated their send-off party under a full moon. The Americans who stayed behind when the *Republic* sailed now watched as Army personnel dynamited oil storage tanks, filling the sky with more smoke and flames. Japanese troops poured down the streets and boulevards on bicycles and tiny motorcycles. Freelance journalist Annalee Whitmore wrote about the nurses in Manila: "There could be no Dunkirk here . . . where would the boats sail to? It was a war without a rear to send to for supplies. It was a war with Japanese on all sides, long-range guns in all directions, planes overhead everywhere. No relief. No escape."[9]

The nurses had no medication for gangrene, no quinine for malaria. Shrapnel wounds were legion, especially after the Japanese bombed the hospitals, leav-ing medical personnel with shrapnel wounds themselves. The friends Betty had left dancing that last night in Manila were among the seventy-seven Army and Navy nurses captured by the Japanese as they swept south and took the island of Corregidor. It would be years before Betty learned their ultimate fate.

The Japanese juggernaut swept across the East Indies in February and March, seizing vast supplies of raw materials, especially oil, from Dutch control. The native population was astonished at the ease with which its overlords were interned or set on the run. General Count Hisaichi Terauchi, commander of the Southern Expeditionary Imperial Army Group, first attacked Borneo, then Miri, the major oil-production center in northern Sarawak. His force consisted of a battleship, an aircraft carrier, three cruisers, and four destroyers. They moved in a three-pronged attack from Davao.

Japanese movement south into Malaya was a "bicycle blitzkrieg" as shock troops pedaled their collapsible bicycles down the peninsula. The earliest rep-resentatives of the Greater East Asia Co-Prosperity Sphere were Japanese pros-titutes, brought along by the *kempei tai* (military police) to win hearts and minds.[10] The Japanese had done their homework and immediately cultivated interests the British had neglected, opening new mines in backwater east coast states to produce manganese and bauxite. Members of the native population were put to work and paid.[11]

Rangoon was yet farther on the western side of the dateline from Pearl Harbor. Claire Chennault and his American Volunteer Group (AVG), known to all as the Flying Tigers, learned of the attack on Hawaii and the raids on the Philippines and Wake Island at noon, when a radioman ran out to the control tower at Toungoo and thrust a message into Chennault's hand. Chennault had only eighteen combat-ready P-40s, so ground crews set to work feverishly trying to assemble more planes. The Japanese could come bursting over the nearest mountain at any moment, with only one British civil servant posted on the Thai border with field glasses and a radio to serve as an early warning net. Suddenly, every Buddhist monk in saffron robes aroused suspicion, and many did in fact later prove to be active enemy agents. Chennault's tiny force was immediately tasked with defending the Burma Road, which began at the Lashio railhead and terminated on a high plateau in China in the city of Kunming. New P-40s began lifting into the sky the minute the last bolt was tightened and spread themselves out across the thousand miles between Rangoon and Kunming.[12]

Bombers flew over the rice paddies and jungles of Thailand toward Rangoon. Waterfront docks and railroad yards erupted under the barrage, and demolished oil refineries belched roiling oily smoke. Homes of the rich and poor alike were pulverized. In a series of Christmas raids, squadrons of Japanese fighters strafed the city, flying low along main avenues and killing hundreds of civilians. The land invasion began January 20, when 18,000 Imperial Japanese Army (IJA) troops moved over the Thailand frontier, and General Tomoyuku Yamashita's 25th Army began its advance toward India. In its path stood 25,000 troops of the British 1st Burma Division and 12,000 troops of the 17th Indian Division—about 4,000 British and 8,000 natives. The Japanese outnumbered them two to one and had momentum on their side.[13]

Britain could spare nothing from its own current situation in Europe to aid its colony, and delusional official thinking concurred that the historic invasion routes up through Thailand—mere goat paths, really—could be effectively defended. The British leadership was wrong. When the Japanese punched north, British forces became hampered by reliance on motor transport and paved roads. Yamashita captured tin mines intact and cut the port of Rangoon off from the rest of the country. Japanese warships swept into the Bay of Bengal, easily dispatching a British naval detachment and eliminating Allied coastal shipping. In the city of Rangoon, looting erupted when police deserted their post and doors to prisons and lunatic asylums were thrown open. The British abandoned their trappings of empire and fled in desperation as an army of refugees squeezing onto the narrow jungle paths headed north.

The trek was horrific. Monsoon rains turned the trails into mud rivers. Men, women, and children, British, Burmese, rich, poor—all were struck with dysentery; already weakened from loss of blood after giant leeches dropped from the trees and attached themselves. There were great acts of individual heroism. Wally Richardson, a British forestry official, closed up his house, gathered a motley group of 108 refugees, and led them through the Naga Hills to safety. Oliver Milton, a British major, brought more than 100 refugees out by following trails he had learned over his years of extracting teak and searching for mineral deposits. Norman Richardson was fourteen years old. His mother died on the retreat, and he continued on, leading out three of his brothers and sisters, one being an eleven-month-old baby who died in his arms before the family reached safety.[14]

The Japanese people did not receive news of the attack on Pearl Harbor with any great excitement. The reaction was more one of baffled consternation, followed by a realization that their long war—it would stretch to fifteen years—now included Britain and America. As the news blared from radios, the people in Tokyo responded as expected after decades of patriotic education. Rallies were organized for marches to the Imperial Palace. By that evening banner "extra" headlines in newspapers proclaimed Japan's "great victory" at Honolulu.[15] Within days posters appeared along the streets, in streetcars, and in restaurants saying, "Slaughter them! The English and Americans are our enemies! Advance like a hundred balls of fire!"[16]

Newsreels appeared in Tokyo, and the public enjoyed seeing "parachutes blooming in the sky over tropical areas, military flags whipping in the wind over the Aleutian archipelago . . . an image of their national flag [outlawed by the Dutch] being handed to Indonesian school children in explanation for occupation."[17]

🦢

Someone at Scripps-Howard Newspapers took an interest in Betty's articles reprinted in the *San Francisco Chronicle* and took her on as a stringer. When the Japanese attacked, Betty was designated a war correspondent, covering what would become the Pacific theater of war, under the command of Adm. Chester Nimitz. Even with a newly issued uniform and press credentials, she could not get to Pearl Harbor, where the scene remained horrific, for days. Dead mynah birds, doves, and sparrows, concussed by bombs, lined the streets. Betty rode with Hump as he steered the jeep past flattened buildings and the mangled, smoking ships in the harbor. Oil and diesel fumes suffused the air, never going away but merely shifting with the sea breeze. When she saw bubbles rising up from the stricken and submerged *Arizona*, she never dreamed they would still be surfacing decades later.

War correspondent or not, Betty was told by her editor at the *Star-Bulletin* that all attempts to report news from the islands were being heavily censored. It would in fact take two years for the full extent of Pearl Harbor's devastation to be made public and seventy before Betty's first piece, written the first week after the Japanese bombing, saw the light of day in the *Washington Post*. Within two hours

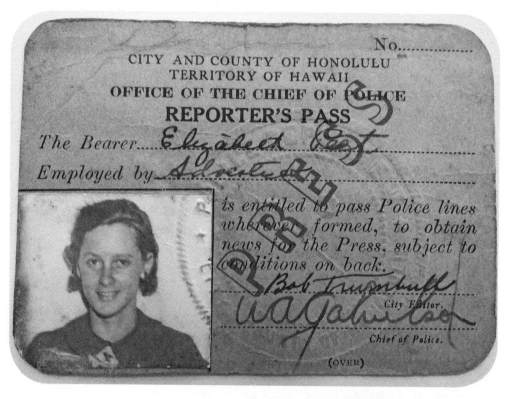

Betty's press pass issued by the Honolulu Police Department
National Archives and Records Administration II, College Park, Maryland

of the attack, Army and Navy censors instructed radio announcers, "All eye-witness stories are out. . . . All detail of places are out. . . . Don't mention or speculate on size of attack." Unsmiling Army censors were stationed in newspaper offices and ordered to read any and all copy coming off the presses. Ever the rebel, Betty tried everything to get her stories out, including sending them through the mail to college friends and newspaper colleagues on the mainland. The recipients later showed her pages filled with black holes, whole paragraphs devoured by some evil monster, leaving only the lifeless conjunction scattered here and there. The screening of all postal mail was placed under the control of a single Army reserve officer who had undergone a flash course in censorship training. His assembled staff was pulled from a grab bag of retired teachers, housewives, society girls, five concert pianists, three artists, five interior decorators, and a variety show cast of ex-concert singers, orchid-raising authorities, and others.[18]

Betty loathed them all, individually and as a group. To make matters much, much worse, Alex, working for naval intelligence, finally and fearfully confessed to being one of them.[19]

"I'm *checking*, not *censoring*," he declared, somewhat lamely. They sat at the outdoor table on the lanai, attempting to enjoy a rare dinner together. Alex tossed crumbs to their pet duck, hoping to distract his wife. It was not working.

"Oh please, Alex!" she responded, stabbing her steak for emphasis. "How could you agree to do this? You are a traitor to our profession!" It was one of their rare fights, one he was losing. Appealing to Betty's patriotism was getting him nowhere. When he left the next morning, their parting was strained and sad.[20]

Not the most patient of people in the best of times, Betty, when thwarted, became as grimly determined as any soldier charging a rampart, and this indiscriminate smothering cloak of censorship had become the enemy. Meanwhile, on the mainland, many Americans, being familiar with only Honolulu and Waikiki Beach, did not even know where Pearl Harbor was. Newspaper stories initially described it as a home port to a large part of the nation's fleet of destroyers, battleships, and cruisers and as "a naval base somewhere in the Pacific." Newspaper correspondents were at a loss, phoning each other to ask, "Where the hell is Pearl Harbor?"

"I hadn't the faintest idea where Pearl Harbor was," a reporter for *Time* later remembered.[21]

Like a trapped fish, Betty sought any escape through, around, or under the censorship net cast over the islands. She found herself writing a story on the female skipper of a fishing junk who had been ferrying supplies to outlying islands. She called the woman for further information and learned the next trip was slated to take donated medicine to the island of Molokai, the location of Father Damien's famous leper colony.

"I'd like to go with you and write about this," Betty announced to the skipper, a slight but salty woman who quickly made it clear she suffered no fools.

"There's Japanese subs out there," she replied flatly. "It's not safe."

"Right!" Betty beamed. "When do we get under way?"

The two women cast off early the next morning from Oahu for the all-day voyage. Betty had never been on a junk but always loved watching them on the water. Their sails raised and lowered like a venetian blind and were usually red, like this one. The skipper gave her a quick tour, proudly pointing out a shiny Cummins diesel engine in the center hold. There was no wheel, only a six-inch handle, the tiller, that controlled a large rudder.

"All the power of the engine is directed at the rudder, which is really big, and not every junk has an engine like mine," explained the captain proudly. "We'll make good time."

Once the junk reached open water, Betty's bravado dissipated somewhat, and she found herself watching for a periscope to pop from every passing swell. The specter of packs of Japanese submarines haunted everyone in the islands, even before Pearl Harbor was hit. Japanese subs had the previous summer been manufactured, fitted, and slipped into the water to train for the coming attack. Cruiser and destroyer captains in the U.S. fleet regularly communicated "Something is down there," and some spent days chasing what most thought were phantoms.[22]

Betty knew that on the morning of December 8, IJN lieutenant Kazuo Sakamaki had beached his midget sub on a reef not far from the lagoon below her house. The young sailor was thrown onto the sand by the surf practically into the arms of Lt. Paul G. Plybon, who was patrolling the shoreline. Later that morning a submarine base repair officer was sent out to have a look at the midget as it lay jammed in the reef, waves crashing over it. The officer could not fit inside—a detail that led to endless racist comments about the Japanese and their tiny submarines—so one of Betty's Japanese American friends swam out and easily climbed in. He later described to her the empty rice, vegetable, and fruit cans he found littering the interior. Subsequent interrogation of Sakamaki revealed that he and his shipmate, who did not survive, had peered through the periscope of their I-24 midget submarine at the red and green landing lights of Hickam Field the night of December 6. Music from tiki bars carried clearly across the moonlit water. Behind and around them, no less than thirty larger submarines waited silently.[23]

With images of sharklike submarines in her head, Betty was relieved when the palm trees of Molokai heaved into view. The dock was crowded with people eager for the much-needed supplies. Betty manned the lines and when the boat was secure stepped onto the transom and made to hop to the pier. She was stopped cold by an officious man in what had probably once been a white lab coat and told no one was allowed on the island. He summoned two boys who off-loaded the cargo before unceremoniously tossing the lines back to the boat and hauling their bounty toward distant huts, presumably housing the lepers. Betty sat glumly astern and watched as the crates disappeared into the jungle, along with her story.

The women decided to anchor off a deserted beach on the Big Island for a midafternoon swim. The warmth of the sun and the satisfaction of completing a mission in the service of others combined to diminish Betty's disappointment and returned to her a brief sense of normalcy. Having no bathing suits, they threw caution to the wind for some indulgent skinny-dipping—not such an unusual thing in the islands. After cooling off, they hauled themselves back aboard just as a chorus of wolf whistles reached them from the shore. What appeared to be an entire National Guard unit crowded onto the erstwhile deserted beach, clapping appreciatively. There remained nothing to do but wave, get dressed, and fire up the engines.

Christmas was not only somber that year but strangely never-ending. Although festive lights had been pulled down and fir trees had never arrived from the mainland, yuletide packages, delayed in the mail, continued to arrive as late as Easter. Amid gas masks, barbed wire, and bomb shelters (swimming pools were considered the best), some islanders improvised with scant decorations placed on bushes and shrubs, where they hung forgotten for months. For the MacDonalds, Christmas simply did not happen. Their beautiful little house on the cliff was heavily shrouded with the blackout curtains Betty had sewn, blocking the cool cross-ventilating breezes for which Philip Johnson had artfully positioned the windows. The wall of glass facing out over the cliff could provide a beacon visible for miles out to sea, guiding Japanese patrols right to their lagoon—a perfect landing spot. Spending time inside the house with the smallest light, even a burner on the stove, was stifling. Alex and Betty's pet duck, whose routine never varied from spending his days in a swimming pool down the hill and his nights in the house, became impossibly confused and lost when the swimming pool was turned into a bomb shelter, and he could not find the window always left open for him at night. Betty finally retrieved the duck and brought him home, showing him how to find the darkened, half-opened window.

In the early hours of April 26, Mauna Loa, the ever-restless volcano on the Big Island of Hawaii, decided to add her energy to the mounting global confrontation. A spectacular eruption brightened the sky over the city of Hilo, eleven miles away, with a red glow that made it possible to read a newspaper by its light before that coming dawn. The eruption brought multiple causes for alarm. Not only was a slow but huge wall of lava moving itself steadily toward the city, threatening not least the water supply, but the goddess Pele had also flagrantly broken all the blackout restrictions. Now the river of molten lava provided a brilliant beacon, easily spotted by Japanese reconnaissance aircraft prowling hundreds of miles away over the Pacific. Army Air Corps bombers scrambled to drop tons of explosives to divert the flow, a tactic known to have worked beautifully in 1935. How well it was working this time was still unknown; it would take close inspection to assess the situation.

At the *Star* six days later, Betty's editor saw her heading his way through the newsroom as he was pouring his first cup of morning coffee and tried to duck into his office. Like a cat, she was in the door before he could kick it shut with his foot. He retreated behind his desk and glowered at her over the top of his mug, only then realizing she was dressed, not in her press uniform, but in jeans, some sort of flannel shirt, and laced hiking boots.

"Heading to the Aleutians?" he asked.

"Mauna Loa. It's been spitting fire for a week. Don't you think someone should have a look at it?"

"No."

"I've got a friend, Bonnie Clausen, a tall, rangy chap from Colorado, used to climbing rocky mountain trails. He's going up and I want to go too. It will make a great story, and the censors can't possibly hide an erupting volcano."

"Sure they can," he said.

But he could find no good reason to deny her the story, and so Betty met Bonnie at the airport for the short hop to the Big Island. They set out at first light, climbing steadily from 6,700 to 10,000 feet, aiming for a rest house halfway up the mountain. The trail snaked through forests of scrub and finally opened onto a black lava field stretching for miles of lunar emptiness. Betty's breath was coming harder in the altitude, but Bonnie was not even winded. She began to mildly resent him. The trail devolved into slippery loose pebbles. Betty barely had the energy to admire semiprecious olivine stones, remnants of former eruptions, and "Pele's hair," crystallized lava threads covering the ground like spun silver.

It took seven miles and half a day to reach the rest house, where the whole panorama of Mauna Loa stretched above and below them, disgorging unearthly undulating black taffy-like masses of pahoehoe lava. The volcano was pocked by stubbled cinder cones from previous eruptions, strewn with a fudge-like crystallization. The candy metaphors were inescapable, Betty realized. Five more miles would bring them to where lava fountains spewed five hundred feet into the air. Following a white plume of smoke, they began the climb, eyeing distant flames tossing black lava into the air with ominous rumbling, extra pairs of boots hanging around their necks. With an unmanly shriek, Bonnie fell through a brittle, hollow lava tube up to his waist, cutting his arms and hands as he scrambled out before Betty could reach him to help. Her first pair of boots gave out less than halfway up the mountain, the soles ripped and melted. As she changed them, Bonnie tested what looked to be a solid pahoehoe flow with a stick and watched the lava collapse into a bottomless abyss. From then on they stuck to the crunchy aa flows piled over the pahoehoe like frosting on a cake, offering sharp but solid footing. They traversed this way four miles, climbing cinder cones so massive they hid the fountains from view. The red cones contrasted with black lava and moving over them was like climbing a treadmill. Concentrating on this exercise kept them from noticing the last cone had been cleared until hot roaring waves of sulfurous air slammed into them. Betty felt her breath pulled from her as her face was peppered with softly floating tufts of "Pele's hair." Larger, bright bits of lava had begun to fall and cling to their clothes. Betty found it oddly light, like feathers.

Then there it was: the crest of the giant gaping cone, an impossibly loud roaring cauldron of fire, the opening to hell. The fountain shot in bursts from the mouth of the cone, which had built to two hundred feet over three days. A crack had opened on the side and from it leaked a quicksilver of red molten lava, flecked with chunks of black rock. Despite feeling as if she were standing in a furnace, Betty found herself transfixed. She wanted to get closer and began to move. She had barely heard Bonnie's shouted admonition before, with no warning, a portion of the cone collapsed, releasing a torrent of lava in their direction. Bonnie grabbed her hand and they ran for their very lives, the hiss of hot lava stinging their backs as it flew at them. Reaching safety, they watched as the spot where they had stood became a molten lake. Betty bent over to gulp air, her hands on her knees. She watched the lava, the air above it alive with what looked like giant orange glowing fireflies. For the second time in six months, it felt as if her world had turned inside out, and somehow she still lived. Betty smiled.

As the sun was setting, Betty and Bonnie crossed the last mile of what she later described as "jagged, knife-like lava that was so brittle that it sang when the wind swept over it." They had both gone through two sets of tennis shoes and boots—all now ribboned—by the time they reached the mountainside rest house. There they found a festive party of Hawaiian cowboys and their wives who were planning to trek the mountain the next morning. They cheerfully offered tin cups of some sort of white lightning, probably distilled from poi. Betty took hers in three swallows and held out her cup for more. Bonnie took one sip before succumbing to delayed shock and altitude sickness, whereupon he proceeded to gasp for air, vomit, and faint.

"It's blackout hour," announced one of the cowboys, dutifully extinguishing the lantern.[24]

Betty typed up the story, but it was once again snagged by the censors and never published. Hawaii continued to be gripped by fear of another attack, but the extreme measures to protect citizens were beginning to chafe. A special source of resentment was the registration and fingerprinting of the entire population of the islands over the age of six. First suggested by the Mortuary Committee before December 7 as a valuable means of identification in the event of a disaster, the fingerprinting project was so well planned that the printing presses for thousands of identification cards were up and running by 1:30 p.m. the day the Japanese hit. This was the first mass enumeration and fingerprinting project of civilians in the nation's history. The whole business was wildly unpopular among islanders, who resisted the mandate to carry the fingerprint cards with them at all times.[25]

Betty herself detested the requirement. It came to her editor's attention that the police suspected, for no earthly reason, that the downtown whorehouse was actually a secret forgery shop, altering and printing out false identification cards. She was assigned to accompany the police on a raid of the establishment and "get the story." She agreed, largely out of curiosity, having never been to a whorehouse. She found the small rooms in a big house reminiscent of a beehive. The women of the night were not happy to talk to her and were not forthcoming, nor were the numerous embarrassed men on the premises. No trace of an illicit forgery operation was ever found.[26]

THREE
RECRUITMENT

OSS was a weird and wonderful organization.
—*Jane Foster,* An Unamerican Lady

The morning of May 25, 1942, Betty woke up in an old jail and decided to pen a letter to the folks. Writing on newspaper letterhead, she explained the jail was in Hot Springs, Virginia, and had been built in 1860. It still had heavy carved wooden doors and other hints at its former use but was now an affordable inn, charging $4.50 a day for food and lodging. Not bad for an expense account. Betty was in Hot Springs covering a food conference for the Newspaper Enterprise Association (NEA). The conference resembled an international fair, with delegates from forty-four countries, all in native dress. Russians in army greatcoats wandered among Chinese, bearded Rajas, and monocle-wearing British. The air hummed with discussions of the future of world food markets and distribution.[1]

The few pieces of war zone reportage Betty managed to get past the brick wall of censorship had impressed Scripps-Howard, and in early May she had been proffered a job in Washington, covering stories of interest to women. Her bags were packed in record time, and within a week she stood on the doorstep of her Aunt Virginia's Georgetown brownstone, where she would rent a third-floor room at fifteen dollars a month. The room was a godsend, as wartime Washington was bursting at the seams and housing was virtually impossible to find.

The food conference was one of Betty's first assignments, and she relished the change of scene. In her letter to her parents, she described walking along "those wonderful Virginia roads that lead through cow pastures, into tiny woods, past streams that ripple over white pebbles, among grazing sheep, wild blackberries, violets, quince trees and ancient stone wells." She attended Sunday services in one of the red-steepled Episcopal churches, where the sermon was "swell," and ate a dinner that evening of southern fried chicken, spoon bread, fresh peas, and strawberry shortcake. A party was thrown for the press at a palatial homestead housing most of the delegates. She felt certain the party "must have consumed all the liquor in the rationed state of Virginia. There were 89 of us, and about one case of Scotch—you can imagine how far it went."[2]

Betty's column was called Homefront Forecast. Its mission was to provide American households with an ongoing order of battle from the rationing front. Betty attacked the assignment with gusto. It was a new day for female reporters, especially in the nation's capital, where the most important press conferences took place. Promising young male reporters had been sent abroad, opening the domestic field up for women, some of whom parlayed the new opportunities into assignments to Europe. By the end of the war, 127 female reporters and photographers would be given military credentials to cover war stories overseas. As of 1942 Betty was not one of them and remained desperate to stake a beachhead as a true war correspondent, preferably in Asia. As the center of decision making, Washington seemed a step in that direction.

Women were not, however, welcome in the smoky back rooms of the National Press Club, where the real stories were harvested. Female reporters had started their own press club in 1919, but it never provided the access to inner Washington that came with the boys' club. Eleanor Roosevelt, who missed nothing, went on the offensive in 1930 and began holding weekly female-only press conferences to pressure news organizations into hiring at least one female reporter.[3] For Scripps-Howard, Betty was the girl.

Betty found the Roosevelt White House to be bustling but pleasant, and her ebullient eagerness quickly endeared her to the staff, from the First Lady's Secret Service to the secretaries and even the butler. Mrs. Roosevelt was warm and welcoming, grasping Betty's hand as she entered a formal parlor, saving the cub reporter from an impulse to curtsy. The interviews were brief, businesslike, and "no tea party," according to Betty.[4]

Within a month she was restless. The work was not as challenging as working in Nimitz's theater had been, censorship notwithstanding, and the capital was not the exciting place she had hoped it would be. She crafted Homefront Forecast as a sort of chalk talk for consumers, describing the vital importance of contributing household items for the war effort and communicating statistics about how everyday frugality contributed to the release of thousands of tons of critical metals. Reducing the metal used in sunglasses had, for example, saved the government 166,000 pounds of nickel silver. Banning the manufacture of slide fasteners, hooks, and eyes reportedly saved 8,000 tons of copper for war production. New slide fasteners were becoming available in plastic, thank goodness. The War Production Board (WPB) was urging the use of pin cushions in "saving our limited supply of needles." Steel crochet hooks were out, together with steel knitting needles. A newly designed "war mop" would have shorter handles, less yarn, and possibly a plastic frame. On yet another front, the Department of Agriculture's scientists announced the development of "extra special eggs" being laid by the twelve-pound midget white turkey, and for those readers with a "victory flock," soybean meal was pushed as feed for poultry.[5]

In Japan, rationing had been a fact of life since 1938. "Voluntary austerity" saw the disappearance of fashion items and cosmetics; women's permanents were limited to three curls per customer, and with the attack on Pearl Harbor, metal drives collected teapots, hibachi, and any other metal object. Sugar, milk, rice, cooking oil, meat, and fish had been rationed for almost a year. Adults were allotted 11 ounces of rice, 1.8 ounces of fish, and the same amount of meat daily and 3.2 ounces of cooking oil per month. Sunflower seeds were distributed to be pressed for oil.[6] The shops in Tokyo had begun to close—fishmongers, tempura shops, paper goods and shoji shops, fan shops, bakers. Bakers had to give their machinery to the government because iron was already growing scarce. Everything was the "national defense" color: khaki. No gold thread could be used in kimonos, and kimono sleeves had to be short to save on fabric.[7]

"You can blame your shiny nose on the war, lady," Betty typed one particularly hot afternoon, pounding the keys of her Olivetti in a pique of bored frustration, "because a lot of our better powder puffs are now in the *service*." Warming to a scolding, lecturing tone, she continued, "And if you've been putting off building that outside summer grill, you can't use a cement shortage as an excuse!" Did she care that cement had recently been reallocated to Group 3 in the WPB supply list and was thus available, now that most of the wartime jobs using cement—185 million pounds of it—had been completed? No, she did not. She found herself taking perverse pleasure in learning that clothing manufacturers were cooperative but not happy. Rayon was scarce, which meant no lining for purses, bed jackets, negligees, bathrobes, and even shoes. The hosiery industry was taking a big bite out of available rayon (nylon stockings were few and far between), second only to the 500,000 pounds the Army used in a year for tire construction. Shoe choices were dwindling, with fall shoe styles reduced by 60 percent, and gone were any unnecessary leather overlaps and lacings; colors were limited to black, white, russet, and brown. The WPB was apparently working overtime to design a model "war shoe."[8]

After Betty had typed this last bit, she conjured in her mind a black pump with tank treads replacing sensible low heels, a vision that threatened to send her into a fit of giggles. The fact that America's industrial engines were running full tilt, devouring raw materials and scrap, was extremely important; she knew that. Pushing away from the typewriter, she decided she needed to walk the Capitol grounds to renew her patriotism. Instead, a stroll around the National Mall reminded her that it resembled a shanty town, covered with temporary buildings. Because of the housing shortage, a houseboat city filled the Potomac. Betty sighed. "Maybe I should get a Dachshund," she thought, apropos of nothing.

"I'm wearing the uniform of a war correspondent, but the war is elsewhere," she complained to Ernie Pyle on one of his infrequent trips home from the front. He was cavalierly unsympathetic.

"Why do you want to go overseas and get shot?" he said, and then to rub it in, "Women don't belong in foxholes." Before she could flare back at him, he added, "Just read all about the war in my columns. . . . That'll give you the whole picture."[9]

The war marched on, and there she was, still safe on the home front. Never one to maintain a consistent prayer life, she nonetheless began praying for a break that would take her closer to the action. Apparently, that's all it took.

Betty McIntosh's OSS recruitment was unexpected and somewhat kismet, quite in keeping with William J. Donovan's operation. She was wandering through the exhibits of a Department of Agriculture convention when approached by a "friendly, elfin-faced major" who a moment before had been engrossed in a display of chicken-feather-lined sleeping bags. "He seemed to have stepped out of the fifth dimension," she later wrote, "with his one kewpie-like curl swirling below his overseas cap."[10] She found herself telling the major that she had been a reporter for six years; she had been at Pearl Harbor; no, she did not think the island Japanese were disloyal; and in fact she had studied and spoke passable Japanese.

"Have you ever considered working for the government?" he interrupted.

"Not exactly," she responded hesitantly, not knowing where this was going.

"You would have a chance to make a real contribution to the war effort," he continued, "with the possibility of an overseas posting."

He now had her full attention and explained further that he could not—so sorry—explain the nature of the work, as it was secret. But he was certain she would qualify. From his briefcase appeared three government application forms that he instructed her to fill out and mail to the OSS. "Time is of the essence," he whispered before vanishing into the mist.[11] The mysterious and seemingly chance encounter was anything but. The major was the father of a fellow Punahou High School graduate and knew of both her language proficiency and her desire to travel to the Far East. He had been looking for her.[12]

Betty would never have envisioned herself becoming part of a quirky, super-secret spy agency created in the shadow of war. Although patriotic, she did not consider herself the least bit heroic, and although crafty when circumstances required, she could not sustain a straight face for long if accused of an outright lie. She just did not have it in her to be deceitful or deceptive. Dodgy maybe, but not deceptive. Or at least that was what she thought. Later she would come to realize that part of the magic of OSS was that it "harnessed the pixie in us."[13]

Within days of mailing her application, Betty received a cryptic letter directing her to report to an address on E Street. She arrived in a cab, the driver pulling up to a roller rink and pointing to the National Institutes of Health complex on Navy Hill. Most new recruits who tried to find the super-secret spy agency on foot found themselves walking the length of Constitution Avenue to Foggy Bottom, looking in vain for a sign. Cab drivers, on the other hand, all seemed to have been let in on the secret. Betty started up the hill, noting the distinct odor of beer in the air. Donovan's OSS Headquarters at Twenty-fifth and E were housed in a series of limestone and brick buildings, surrounded by a wall and perched over the Heinrich Brewery, the Riverside Roller Skating Rink, and the Potomac River. Betty presented her papers to a gate guard and was directed to a building to be processed.

In the secret OSS fingerprinting room, Betty found herself standing next to a fellow recruit, a woman who looked to be her same age, with blond hair and a ready but impish smile. They shared a grimy, ink-blackened towel and began speaking to each other out of the corners of their mouths, having just been instructed to speak to no one.

"Look," Jane Foster whispered, "just what kind of organization is this?"

Betty told her what she knew, which amounted to little more than her encounter with the elfin major.

Jane Foster was an artist who, although not a household name, was internationally recognized for her caricatures. Having studied under Expressionist Lyonel Feininger, Jane produced work that bore echoes of Pablo Picasso, Wassily Kandinsky, and Amedeo Modigliani, both in the fluidity of her contour drawing and sketching and the cubist elements of her collages. But she was flagged and then poached from her position at the Board of Economic Warfare for her knowledge of the language and culture of Malaya and the Netherlands East Indies. OSS often conducted such raids on other government agencies, a practice that did nothing to endear Donovan to his fellow patriots in Washington. Jane's background made her irresistible to OSS recruiters, as she had traveled and worked in Bali, Java, Sumatra, Borneo, Malaya, Thailand, Indochina, the Philippines, Japan, and China and was proficient in Malay, French, Dutch, and Italian.[14] Her reputation as an artist was not unimportant. Regarding the OSS recruitment process, Edmond Taylor observed that Donovan had a high regard for artists who were also intellectuals, as "what he wanted from his artists" was not necessarily art but "ideas."[15] As it turned out, artists and journalists made up a sizable portion of his organization.

Betty and Jane had been brought into a newly formed branch of OSS, Morale Operations (MO), where they would learn the art of black propaganda. Their job was to bend all their creative energies to destroying the morale of the Japanese soldier, as well as his family back home, infecting both with defeatism and a burning desire to end the war. The goal was to deceive and trick the enemy into surrendering, thereby saving many lives on both sides.

Their first step on the road to becoming MO specialists was a stern lecture from a gruff second lieutenant whom Betty would forever remember as having "a dead cigar in his mouth [and] who looked as if he had just been recruited from a detective agency." The cigar never left his mouth as he rushed through

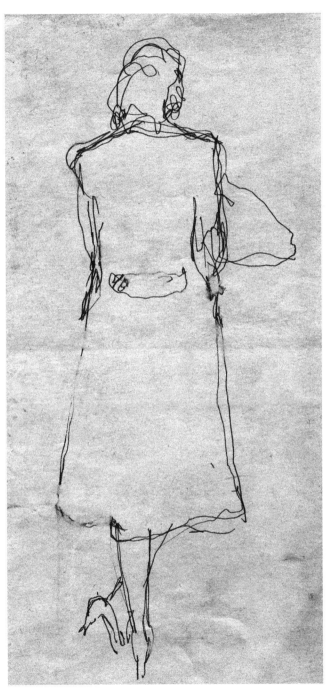

Sketch of Betty McIntosh by Jane Foster
Reproduced with permission of
Elizabeth P. McIntosh

the words of their swearing in, which struck Betty as "something like a sorority oath that we would never—repeat never—reveal what went on behind the OSS velvet curtain."

"OSS is an undercover organization authorized by the Joint Chiefs of Staff," he began. "We are anonymous. If people ask you what you do here, tell 'em you're file clerks."

Behind his head hung a large poster with a pink ear and the words "The Enemy Is Listening." Their next encounter was with a uniformed gatekeeper, to whom they identified themselves. Betty was starting to have nervous thoughts, imagining whatever she said, "no matter how trivial, was immediately to be picked up by radar and transmitted to the security officer."[16]

Duly chastised and warned, the two headed off on a long quest to locate their new offices in Building Que and their commanding officer, Maj. Herbert Little. Drifting past open doorways, glimpsing map-covered walls, the two women finally found an empty suite of offices where an irate repairman was ripping telephone extension wires out of the wall, cursing whoever had moved and not taken the damned phones with them. No, he did not know where MO had relocated, and he did not care.

For the next hour, they searched the buildings and grounds covering the side of a steep hill with the brewery on one side and the naval hospital on the other. A malty aroma from the brewery seeped into the buildings of the new spy agency, competing with the smell of incinerated animals from the National Institutes of Health on the top floor. Climbing uphill, they entered a tunnel connecting the Central and North Buildings, arriving at last at the new location on the top floor of North. The new recruits knew they were home when they found their major, standing on a chair, tacking a large map of Asia to the wall. Piles of office furniture surrounded him as though they had washed up with the tide.[17]

"Welcome, girls!" he beamed at them. "We're informal around here. Good to see you two. Hand me a tack until I get Manchuria anchored, and we'll talk business."[18]

From a locked safe, he retrieved *MO Manual, Revised,* a dog-eared mimeographed bible for MO. The document had been prepared by the European branch of MO, in close cooperation with the British "cousins," and based largely on the black propaganda activities of the Special Operations Executive (SOE). Black propagandists in SOE endeavored to make their faked leaflets and newsletters look as though they had been printed under difficult conditions within

Germany or, more often, occupied countries. White propaganda was broadcast by the BBC, and disseminated in leaflet form, urging the deposing of Hitler, and often accompanied by the statement: "This could have been a bomb."[19]

The rest of the Far East MO contingent filtered in. Desks were allocated and arranged, and introductions were made. Dr. John Holladay, a medical missionary to Thailand, was at first something of a reluctant recruit with a troubled conscience. In days to come, he would maintain a wall of stacked newspapers on his desk so that he could sit almost hidden behind it. He was quiet even when not behind his wall. By the end of the war, however, Dr. Holladay would overcome his scruples as a man of God and parachute into Chiang Mai, his former parish, with, as Betty later proudly noted, "some of the blackest MO ever perpetrated against the ancestry of the Japanese emperor." He set up and ran a medical clinic there as his cover.

Occupying a desk adjacent to Dr. Holladay was another missionary, the elderly Miss Lucy Starling. The major was particularly proud of her, exclaiming, "She's learned everything our schools can teach about guerrilla warfare. You should see that lady strip a machine gun! She's taking up judo now—look at her! She only weighs 105 pounds! And she's sixty-five if she's a day!"

Miss Starling handed the major an outline for the establishment of an underground network near Chiang Mai, insisting that she be allowed to "jump in" and instruct the natives in the use of demolitions.[20] Paul Frillman was a missionary in Hankow, China, when he was pulled into service as Claire Chennault's chaplain for the Flying Tigers. Once in the field, much later, he learned he had actually been "recruited" into OSS when it took over intelligence gathering for the 14th Air Force.[21] Rosamunde "Rosie" Frame was born in Shanghai to highly educated missionary parents. Her mother, Alice Browne Caldwell, was president of Yenching University. Rosie graduated from Mount Holyoke College in 1937, was a concert pianist, and was fluent in eleven Chinese dialects. Betty liked her immediately and would always remember her as a small, energetic, and adventurous woman, irresistible to friends and enemies alike.[22]

Dr. Dillon Ripley, a relatively new PhD from Harvard, was a dedicated ornithologist brought on board for his extensive knowledge of the Dutch East Indies and, like Jane, a fluency in Malay. His dedication to the study of birds was indefatigable, and he could at any moment abruptly walk away from a conversation, drawn by the song of a tufted titmouse. His devotion to the peoples of Sumatra and Borneo was likewise passionate. When naval intelligence rejected him on medical grounds—he was underweight from a bout of malaria—Donovan's man Joseph R. Hayden gave him a home in OSS. Hayden had planned to send Dillon back into the South Pacific, but the plan was foiled by the implacable wall of Douglas MacArthur. So Dillon was shunted to MO.[23]

Charles Fenn was a second lieutenant in the U.S. Marine Corps, a job that was actually merely his cover; he had gone straight from basic to OSS training school. Charles, who preferred to be called Fenn, had left home at seventeen to seek adventure on the high seas. He eventually became a news photographer for the picture magazine *Friday*, a left-wing version of *Life*. By 1940 he was photographing the effects of the Japanese occupation in China, and in mid-1941 he began covering the war in North Africa, Asia, and Burma (with Gen. Joseph "Vinegar Joe" Stilwell) for the Associated Press (AP). His talent as a photographer and journalist, combined with his experience in China and ability to speak Mandarin, led him to an appointment as an OSS specialist. At that point, OSS was still recruiting almost exclusively from among the wealthy, elite, and university-educated, and as an immigrant from a working-class family, Fenn felt himself somewhat a fish out of water. His recruitment marked a shift in the agency as it reached beyond the "Oh So Social" to expand the talent pool.[24] Assigned to MO, Fenn was put in charge of Burma because he was the only one to have actually been there, and Betty became his new assistant.[25]

Betty found Fenn huddled in deep discussion with two other men in uniform. Since Major Little had referred to him as "our man who walked out of Burma with Stilwell," Betty assumed they were hashing over the "real" situation there and sidled close to listen before she introduced herself. Instead they were arguing about the relative merits of Army, Navy, and Marine Corps post exchanges, specifically with regard to candy bars. The two Navy lieutenants touted the almond bars at the naval commissary, whereas Lieutenant Fenn insisted on the superiority of chocolate marshmallow creams.

The recruitment net being cast for such "unmilitary" branches as MO, Research and Analysis (R&A), and Field Photographic pulled in Paul Child, a "painter, photographer, mapmaker, art and French teacher, lumberjack, furniture maker, and holder of a black belt in judo." Paul was a floater, coming and going to offer advice and assistance to MO before he moved on to R&A and Field Photographic.[26]

Gregory Bateson—along with his famous wife, Margaret Mead (who ended up in OWI)—was a natural candidate for OSS. Born in England, Bateson had traveled widely through Europe, but it was the considerable time he spent in the field studying Balinese and New Guinea cultures that brought him to the Far East corner of MO.[27] His specialty was schismogenesis—the tendency in relationships for parties to become differentiated. He had been eager to apply his expertise to black propaganda in Europe, envisioning all sorts of schemes to increase divisions within German society, promote tensions, and create cleavages where none existed. He attempted to explain his technique as a "sort of emotional ju jitsu." Rebuffed by British hostility both to any sort of approach based on psychology and to government manipulation of, or meddling in, morale, he sailed to America in disgust. OSS welcomed him with open arms.[28] Like Dillon Ripley, Gregory's brilliant obsession led him to frequently drift off into his own thoughts. He was often seen wandering the halls in his tropical khaki field shorts and ever-drooping knee socks. He had the uncanny ability to get lost but never seemed to care.

Betty and Jane stumbled down the drive of Navy Hill that evening in a mild state of shock. They had clearly been drawn into a contingent of colorful characters pulled from a carnival grab bag. Before they left, they had learned that the OSS Personnel Office declared itself to be issuing paychecks to every nationality and occupation; also represented were members of the Canine Corps, carrier pigeons, and an elephant. Eventually their MO team would grow to include a private detective, the producer of the Lucky Strike Hit Parade, an Olympic broad jumper, a traveling patent medicine salesman, and a dog fancier.[29]

FOUR
LEARNING
TO LIE

Oh, what a tangled web we weave,
when first we practice to deceive.
—*Sir Walter Scott*, Marmion, *Canto vi, Stanza 17*

The first day of MO training covered the objective: "We hitherto law-abiding Americans were authorized to contact and manipulate underground groups and *agents provocateurs*" through lying, rumormongering, exploitation of superstitions and fears, and forgery, among other things. Betty learned, "In MO work, we must not restrain our imaginations. Out of twenty wild schemes there might be one that would really work—and save lives."[1] The primary goal was not necessarily to get the Japanese soldier to do anything in particular but rather to plant seeds of hopelessness and resentment over his conditions: *The Imperial Army officers are getting better rations. The government is lying through its teeth about the strength and position of the enemy. The puppet troops are planning to revolt and kill Japanese troops in their sleep.*

Black propaganda was a strategic weapon designed to do one big thing—weaken the enemy's will—not affect the outcome of a particular battle. The goal was to target the man within the soldier—the son, husband, father—and likewise to connect with Japanese mothers, wives, and children, planting a virus of doubt and desolation that could then reverse infect the soldiers, creating a circle of despair. In planting false information, it was not necessary to make the target believe the falsehoods but simply to disrupt his focus.

Before the war Betty had wanted, passionately wanted, to travel and work in Asia, and when that dream was overrun by events, she nonetheless remained fixed on the same destination. But finding herself in a room full of anthropologists and missionaries who had not only worked in Asia but become experts on that part of the world was intimidating to the point of panic. Even Jane, who came off a bit self-deprecating, scared Betty. Over beer the previous evening, Betty had listened enraptured as Jane hit the highlights of her failed marriage to a Dutch plantation owner in Batavia, months spent painting in Bali, and somewhere in there, the completion of a master's thesis on stone sculpture of the Batu Islands, for God's sake! Suddenly Betty's attempts at learning about Japanese culture and language through living a brief time with the Watanabes seemed a mere dalliance. Betty also convinced herself she knew nothing about China and even less about Burma, and thinking of India merely brought to mind the Taj Mahal and elephants. Somehow she had hoodwinked someone into thinking she belonged in the company of scholars and adventurers.

Jane pulled Betty out of this funk, confessing that although she knew more that the average American about Indonesia, her knowledge of China was limited to a brief spell of babysitting an infant panda bear en route to Batavia.[2] In the days to come, the two of them became inseparable, and although they took their OSS training seriously, it was hard not to find the whole of it slightly comedic, especially the paramilitary courses. Jane took delight in suggesting the PhDs might have trouble learning which way to point their rifles.

Betty came to refer to OSS training schools as "never-never land." They were in fact a series of safe houses, national parks constructed by the Civilian Conservation Corps (CCC), and the Congressional Country Club, all scattered over the states of Virginia and Maryland. The schools intended to familiarize OSS operatives with the finer points of guerrilla warfare and espionage tradecraft. As with all things OSS, the training for American intelligence officers was invented virtually overnight. Donovan's first training director was neither a combat veteran nor a spy but an R&A psychologist who, like most Americans, had no experience as an undercover agent, let alone the knowledge to train one. He rose to the task, however, attending the British SOE training school in Canada (Camp X) along with his designated training staff. Booklets were copied, advisers recruited, and the British taught them all they could, from how to pick a lock and blow a safe to how to use radios, listening devises, codes, and ciphers.[3] Donovan quickly decided liberating safecrackers from prison and casting a net for amateur ham radio operators would significantly speed things up. The safecrackers had proven experience with stealth, and the hams could be taught.

The new Far East contingent of MO was not shipped to one of the secret training facilities but instead climbed aboard a troop transport bound for Area E, located on two country estates and in a former private school north of Baltimore. A two-week basic secret intelligence (SI) course there covered such topics as learning to maintain a cover identity, surveilling, and avoiding being surveilled. Approximately midway through the course, a troop transport deposited the group at Area F for a three-day crash course in survival and weapons training required of every OSS agent, male or female. This was the Congressional Country Club in Washington, a facility deemed acceptable for female personnel to acquire some basic familiarity with weapons.

OSS was a boon to the debt-stricken Congressional, if not its salvation. When Donovan surveyed the fairways, streams, lake, and thick-wooded underbrush, he saw an ideal setting for a school of irregular warfare. He offered to lease all four hundred acres for $4,000 a month with a promise to repair any and all damages. Almost overnight a tent city covered the tennis courts, the ballroom was converted into classrooms, and the pool was covered for administrative space.[4] The manicured grounds of Congressional were turned into obstacle courses and submachine gun and pistol ranges, and a mock fuselage of a C-47 sat on the putting green to be used for parachute training. Although live ammunition was fired over the heads of the trainees as they crawled across the turf, there was but one fatality when a recruit jumped up and took a round trying to avoid a snake.[5]

The interior of the club retained much of its civilian decor, and the dining room, bar, and even the bedrooms were furnished. Military recruits who had been living in tents before volunteering for this secret duty were shocked to find themselves billeted in plush bedrooms with private baths. As the war progressed, more military-style furnishings were brought in, but meals continued to be served in a resplendent dining room. Even at the national parks, some meals were chef-catered affairs. Aside from those being trained to live off the land, such as Special Operations (SO), Donovan wanted his people to become highly skilled quickly, not subjected to boot-camp conditions.

Betty rather enjoyed the burrowing into sand traps and learning to throw grenades on the fairways. She had spent only a few hours on the firing range with a handgun before she was led out onto one of the greens, presented with a machine gun, shown its basic operation, and then told to "give it a try." She gave the trigger a confident pull and held it. The gun took on a life of its own, bucking and jumping, as though trying to free itself from her. In that moment she remembered a summer spent on the Idaho ranch of her college roommate and a horse who must have been this machine's cousin. As she had on the horse, Betty maintained a death grip on the trigger and stayed in the saddle while she was spun in a circle. Chunks of turf and dirt erupted around her orbit, and she vaguely registered men scattering and diving like startled birds.[6]

Meanwhile, Jane found herself in a room full of men around a long table arrayed with a variety of weapons: pistols, machine guns, hand grenades, and limpet mines. The young lieutenant in charge proceeded to take each weapon apart, explaining its operation and passing the parts around to be examined. Jane accepted each piece, examined it appreciatively, and murmured polite exclamations such as "Very interesting indeed!" Afterward, she was taken to a golf green near where her friend was terrorizing other men. The lieutenant tossed her what she assumed was a live grenade, and she tossed it back to him. The exercise was over when Jane stomped over to MO chief Herb Little.

"I did not join OSS to handle lethal weapons I will never use," she announced. "I am resigning." Herb explained soothingly that it was a simple exercise for recruits—standard operating procedure.[7]

Back in the clubhouse, Betty found herself gazing at black footprints on the ceiling. Military bunks had been brought in and stacked as high as they would go, and men on the top bunk had to brace their feet on the ceiling to steady themselves as they pulled their boots on.

The Far Eastern Orientation Course gave them two weeks of classroom lectures and map work, along with truly enjoyable presentations by such luminaries as Ruth Benedict and Margaret Mead, titled "Factors the MO Operator Must Take into Account in Implementing the Black Directive," "Japanese Intelligence Work and Secret Societies," and "Culture, Social Structure and People of Thailand, Burma, Malaya, and Indo-China." Sessions concluded with films on the various regions and the helpful "Chocolate and the Soldier."[8] Betty enjoyed the required texts: *Modern Japan* by Chamberlain and Stewart, *Changing China* by

Taylor and Stewart, and the *OSS Pamphlet on Japanese Government*. She studied for the map tests and became proficient at locating cities, boundaries of provinces, and traces of the Burma and Ledo Roads.[9]

Betty heard Jane snickering quietly one afternoon and looked to see what lesson had tickled her. Jane read aloud, "'Check those below that are customs of the Chinese people.

They sit on the floor instead of chairs

They eat with chopsticks

Their village government has always been democratic

All their women have bound feet

They honor older people and have a strong family loyalty.'[10]

I'm checking all of them, just to be safe," she said. Betty did not respond and began diligently flipping ahead to locate the correct answers.

As for Burma, the best possible introduction came one day when the little MO group was summoned to meet their first man from the field, Col. Carl Eiffler. He was reputed to be a "fabulous, powerful man of action whose super-human energy was responsible for the establishment of the OSS base in northern Burma—Detachment 101."[11] The members of Detachment 101 had received none of the training being provided for MO Far East Division. Eiffler's men, tasked with containing the Japanese in North Burma and reopening supply routes to China, had set out with no blueprint, either for training natives in guerrilla tactics or setting up a base camp. They had received little to no instruction in methods of irregular warfare before they were sent to the one place such skills were most in demand. Some had received abbreviated instruction in sabotage. Most knew precious little about Burma and so read and studied during the long sea voyage to India.[12]

The colonel was bringing film footage of agent training—agents being Kachin Mountain warriors—and air drops in the jungle. Everyone eagerly awaited his arrival, but nine o'clock came and went with no sign of Eiffler. The major's phone rang. He waved Betty over and commanded, "Go down and escort Colonel Eiffler to this meeting. The guard won't let him in because he doesn't have an OSS badge!"

Betty found the colonel pacing up and down in front of the guard, and upon spotting her, he "turned savagely" and for the guard's benefit loudly explained that when he left for the Burmese jungles "OSS didn't have any badges!"

Ignoring Eiffler, the guard asked Betty to identify him. Then, to make matters worse, the guard asked the colonel about the contents of his film canister. The colonel sarcastically replied that it contained "enough plastic to blow you to hell and I have a good mind to set it off." When the man from the field was finally liberated, his audience listened raptly for three hours as the colonel described how he convinced the fierce mountain people of northern Burma to join forces with the Allies. Betty took careful notes and later wrote,

> Armed with his .45 and a magician's kit, he set out to recruit Kachins. . . . While Jap patrols were seeking out the mad American colonel, sometimes only a few miles away, Eiffler set up his show in the village square. He made coins disappear. Flowers grew out of pots before the eyes of the astonished audience. He drew cigarettes from the ear of the headman. Upon the symbolic climax, the colonel claimed most of his recruits. He fired his .45 into the air, and from the sky dropped a headless miniature Japanese soldier. Through the interpreter he explained that this was a sign that the Kachins should join forces with the great white father in fighting the Japs![13]

Burma was a single entity only to the British, not to the indigenous people who lived there. Before the Japanese invasion, the typical British household in Rangoon was ringed with gardens and stables of horses and boasted a well-stocked wine cellar and library, along with plush Oriental carpets and a concert grand piano. Innumerable Burmese servants were ever-present, hovering to offer a silver tray with gin or scotch and sodas. Up the Irawaddy River, the hill country folk lived in an entirely different world. The Kachins were small people with high cheekbones strongly resembling Himalayan Sherpas or Apache Indians in North America. They made their home within the curve of mountains extending down from the Hukawng Valley along the Tibetan plateau to the Shan States bordering Siam (Thailand). Respecting no borders, they could be found in the Indian province of Assam to the west and Yunnan China to the east. The Kachins were fierce fighters. Each man carried an ornamented swordlike knife capable of cutting an enemy in half when it was swung in a flashing arc. The Kachins specialized in sweeping down from their villages on inaccessible mountain ridges, wreaking havoc, then vanishing into the wilderness.

Naga headhunters lived in the jumble of mountains, some up to 10,000 feet in height, that ran from the Dikko River, near Nazira, across Burma to the

Hukawng Valley, where the Kachins lived. Those Naga living close to India were relatively peaceful, but just twenty miles into the hills began the territory of the headhunters. The heads of white men were not particularly prized but would not be summarily rejected if one was endeavoring to present a romantic offering to a girlfriend or to improve the fertility of either the rice crop or the women of the village. Nagas traveled in bands, tirelessly springing and leaping on sinewy, muscular legs up and down trails so steep they crossed climate zones from tropical to alpine.

As the MO Far East Division in the spring of 1944 studied the theater to which it was to be sent, the Japanese 15th Army, with three divisions, was turned back from capturing British rail and supply stations in the twin battles of Imphal and Kohima. Commander Kokotu Sato signaled, "Our swords are broken and our arrows gone,"[14] and contrary to his orders, he began a retreat from the Imphal Plain back through Burma, an unprecedented act of disobedience. The three divisions leaving Imphal were forced to embark on a devastating trek over and through the mountain and jungle homes of Kachin warriors and Naga headhunters, a reverse of the nightmarish British flight. Back when the Japanese began their main invasion and were making for India in January 1942, the officers conducted the same training regimen that had made such an impression on the Chinese: hanging prisoners upside down for the rank and file to use as bayonet practice and strafing columns of refugees as target shooting. Most of the country had immediately been put under tyrannical martial law by the *kempei tai*. Japanese commanders showed open contempt for Burmese sensibilities, desecrating Buddhist temples and insulting village elders. Natives were pressed into forced labor along with Allied POWs in a futile attempt to repair the country's infrastructure, which had been destroyed by the retreating British.

The Japanese had charged toward India as experienced guerrilla jungle fighters, cleverly camouflaged and packing their collapsible bicycles and inflatable rubber rafts, along with enough rice ball rations for many days. Reeling from losing Singapore and fleeing Rangoon, the British quickly about-faced from seeing the average IJA trooper as a little yellow monkey to seeing him as a jungle-fighting super-soldier. The simple fact was the Japanese had trained in jungle warfare and the British had not. But by 1944 the retreating IJA units were reaping what they had sown. The villagers were no longer welcoming, and the Naga had sharpened their knives. With their supply lines disrupted and their ranks decimated by disease and predators, the Japanese were no longer so formidable and by every measure increasingly ripe for demoralization and intimidation.

Classroom instruction, weapons training, and introduction to tradecraft finally behind them, the MO staffers got down to work. Each week they gathered around large tables and scrutinized strategic intelligence reports, then came up with themes for subversive printed material and other black directives. They communicated and collaborated with smaller outfits in New York and San Francisco, code-named Marigold and Green's. The New York unit employed Japanese American personnel who had special security clearances to produce subversive materials from captured letters, magazines, and newspapers; they also monitored Japanese news broadcasts.[15] The MO team learned all about publication of fake newspapers—the entire process of feature writing, layout, typesetting, and printing. While other commodities in Japan grew scarce, newspaper circulation had exploded as the war progressed, and although each newspaper competed with the others, all were managed by the government. Every paper produced a local publication in occupied territories, dividing them into spheres. The *Asaki* published the *Java News* in Malay; *Yomuiri* published *Burma News* in Burmese.[16] With the right equipment, all of them could be faked.

𝍖

The cafeteria line in Que was gossip central for Betty and Jane. There they learned OSS news and the most recent developments concerning the issei (Japanese Americans born in Japan) and nisei (first generation Japanese Americans) working in the New York office. The Japanese Americans had reportedly been subjected to increasingly threatening glares from New Yorkers and forced to begin climbing the back stairs in stealth. Jane speculated this was exactly the sort of sneaky behavior that would increase their chances of being shot.[17] The large Chinese population out in San Francisco allowed Green's issei and nisei to move about more freely than they could in other cities. Thirteen Japanese Americans had transferred to Marigold and Green's from Catalina Island, along with one POW captured at Attu in the Aleutians.[18]

Betty began a deliberate campaign to convince Herb Little to bring her husband, Alex, into OSS. Major Little had long since joined the ranks of those who referred to Betty as "indefatigable." Her persistence and Alex's own proficiency in Japanese paid off when Alex found himself assigned to a secondary MO unit using Japanese Americans at the Collingwood estate near Washington. He moved into Betty's little third-floor room in Georgetown, and they resumed the semblance of a normal life, albeit a secret one, convincing Aunt Virginia they were leaving each morning for jobs with Scripps-Howard.

Collingwood housed issei personnel and the MO shop, serving mainly as a training facility for black propaganda radio. Recruits included Takashi Ohta, who was folk singer Pete Seger's father-in-law, and Joe Koida, former newspaperman and Communist Party activist. Their work focused almost exclusively on the Agana Plan, which was one of Donovan's schemes to wedge into the Pacific theater by locating a fifty-kilowatt transmitter on Guam. OSS analysts believed in the existence of an underground opposition movement in Japan, and the scripts generated for Agana were intended to snag enemy listeners by "hitch-hiking" on a frequency used by the Osaka central radio station each night when it signed off. When the Secret Service learned of the Collingwood operation in October, it immediately shut it down, not wanting "Japanese" near Washington, for security reasons.[19]

When Collingwood was shuttered, Alex, along with his issei and nisei, was sent to an MO facility on Catalina Island, off the coast of southern California. The island was owned by Mr. Wrigley, the chewing gum king, and had been commandeered for OSS sea and survival training, taught by famous mountain climbers and big game hunters with experience acquired in most of the jungles and remote terrains on the planet.[20] Special dispensation had to be granted for the MO personnel to move to the island, as persons of Japanese ancestry had been barred from the West Coast by executive order, an exclusion not lifted until January 2, 1945. Whereas Alex could take a boat to the mainland on weekends, the issei and nisei found themselves virtually marooned on Catalina Island; their only contact with the outside world had been reduced to radio and mail. When they were not training to perpetrate black propaganda, they spent their days fishing and their nights watching the lights of Newport Beach shimmering invitingly across twenty-seven miles of channel.[21]

Spring of 1944 continued on. Betty cultivated a long-distance working relationship with Capt. Max Kleinman at Marigold, sharing material and intelligence. When she came into possession of a Japanese magazine or cartoons of Sumo wrestlers, she sent them to Kleinman for his artists to use as models for uniforms, armament, and equipment. She ordered prints of duplicated popular cartoons with altered messages. She conceived her own cartoons, asked Kleinman to have his artist draw them, and then had each reproduced with writing and made to look as if the page had been torn from a magazine, page numbers and dates faked in. She imagined the text for a watercolor with a dead Japanese soldier, covered with a dirty, bloody battle flag, the overall picture one of destruction and despair. Her text read, "Hundreds of millions sing the Bugle Call to Charge. But only the soldiers dying on the battlefields know the meaning of the song, written by Private Toshio Yamamoto, a young college student, just before he died in a Burmese jungle. This pamphlet is produced by the Nihon Heiwa Domei, a peace organization of Japanese who are fighting for the welfare of a greater Japan."[22]

The process involved in producing one piece of material that might or might not be approved to send abroad was lengthy and painstaking. And even if a piece was sent abroad it would not necessarily make its way into the field for dissemination. Detailed work filled the MO file cabinets, but getting it where it needed to go seemed almost impossible.

Down the hall from Betty, Jane worked to come up with her own ideas for Malaya and Indonesia, but whereas Betty's material was bottlenecked, hers could not even get that far. The Netherlands East Indies posed a problem for OSS. Japanese occupation had been total and was secured by the collaboration of President Sukarno. Queen Wilhelmina's speech from Holland on December 6, 1942, made vague pronouncements about possible changes in colonial policies postwar; maybe the East Indies could be made a commonwealth or federation following the British model. This was classically too little too late. Japanese occupation had turned the situation upside down in Indonesia. Nationalists shed no tears for Dutch humiliation and initially welcomed the invaders as liberators. Self-described "educated young Indonesians" responded positively to promises of coprosperity, inasmuch as it offered liberation from Dutch subjugation, and were initially willing collaborators in Japan's new world order. Suddenly it had become permissible to display the Indonesian flag and play the Indonesian national anthem. Educated "natives" were quickly elevated into administrative positions vacated by interned Dutch, drastically raising their living standards. Early on, the Greater East Asia Co-Prosperity Sphere seemed to be working as billed and did not offer fertile ground for the introduction of Allied propaganda, black or white.[23]

Jane had lived in the warp and woof of Dutch colonialism while married to Leo Kampfer, a plantation owner and secretly an officer in Dutch counterintelligence. Her liberal temperament chafed to see the overt colonial paternalism and exploitation of the native Malay, and her outrage led to painful marital discord and eventually divorce. She could easily understand how the Japanese were able to insert themselves into a volatile situation and exploit it as surely as had the Dutch. In addition to her troubled thoughts and memories, she now had the added frustration of lack of access to her MO target. Although Douglas Mac-Arthur had "allowed" Donovan to operate in Indonesia and Donovan had definite plans for subversion and espionage in the archipelago, he had neither a staging area nor contacts within the country. The Dutch left no network of agents in place, and although some scattered Allied forces were on the ground, they possessed no radio transmitter with which to make systematic reports. The use of black propaganda as a weapon depended entirely on means of dissemination.[24]

🎋

Just as the humidity and predictability of Washington were dancing on Betty's last nerve, she reached home one evening to find her aunt, visibly upset, waiting on the front steps.

"I had to find out from a total stranger that you are leaving!" Aunt Virginia cried.

"What?" asked Betty.

"A strange man who said he was from the *OSS*," her aunt continued accusingly, "said you were leaving, shipping off for *India*, and could he rent the room?"

"So much for secure and secret communications," Betty thought, recognizing the familiar signature of OSS paradox. She excitedly called the transportation office and was officiously reminded that such confidential information could never be "revealed over the wires." The man on the phone then proceeded to tell her not to get in any rush as she would first be going to Assessment School, commonly referred to as "S."[25]

Hurrying to the cafeteria line the next morning, Betty rendezvoused with Jane. They cornered their friend Jan, a survivor of "S." He began by describing it as "a sort of mental clinic."

"What they try to do out there," Jan told them over coffee, "is to explore your personality: What will you do under pressure? How do you make friends? What situations frighten you? What goes on up here?" he explained, tapping his forehead with his coffee spoon.[26]

"S" was a new level of vetting for OSS, whereby a group of eminent psychologists would screen all candidates as to whether they could withstand the emotional strain of overseas duty. It had been established when Donovan, after being cornered by his desperate staff about the rapidly ballooning agency, was forced to admit that recruitment was spinning out of control. A psychological-psychiatric assessment unit, modeled on the British vetting procedures being carried out in London, was needed. Once Donovan had been persuaded there was a problem, he wanted whatever the British had.

"I want it done in a month," he ordered. "You will get the best people from the army and from civilian life. You'll get an estate in the country and I want it done in a month."[27]

The staff of "S" included Dr. Richard S. Lyman, a neuropsychiatrist from Duke, along with a number of medical doctors. They struggled to screen candidates for positions for which they had no concrete job description. How does one identify the temperament of a sleuth? Months passed before enough men and women went through the program for the doctors to process feedback and begin understanding how OSS job descriptions should be structured. When Betty, Jane, and Dillon Ripley, the ornithologist, arrived at "S," precious little of this information had been compiled and processed, so the experience was still an ongoing experiment for candidates and assessors.[28]

The first morning they were picked up in a weapons carrier and driven through the countryside with twenty young men in fatigues. Upon reaching their destination—a 118-acre estate in Fairfax belonging to the Willard Hotel family—they were shown to their "quarters," actually plush bedrooms in a colonial mansion. Then they were put into testing groups of four students each and provided a "student information sheet" describing the jobs they were being considered for, in this case MO. For the staff, MO topped the list of specialties for which the candidates had no prior work history and therefore no "evidence of aptitude or ability." How could they assess whether these psywar aspirants were up to the task, and in the case of MO, what exactly would that task entail? Years later the doctors of the OSS Assessment staff marveled that out of thousands of candidates, virtually all of them were "able to tolerate the indignities and ordeals that we invented for them."[29]

MO had its own unique requirements, first and foremost a willingness to toil at something for which there would be no rewards, not even intangible ones. The battle to demoralize the enemy never concluded with clear victory or defeat, and rarely was there any indication an operation had achieved a desired result. Not only were patience and imagination required, but so was an oversized tolerance for deferred gratification. Additionally, the practice of deception was viewed askance by everyone else involved in the war effort. MO was unsavory in the eyes of the military, government, and Allies, but none of this mattered because it was valued by one person: William J. Donovan.

Ground rules were laid. The candidates were instructed to assume a "split personality" and choose cover identities. They were to maintain cover at all times among themselves, but role-playing was suspended during one-on-one testing with the psychologist. Betty, always the nervous one, was relieved. Since everyone in her small group was playing the same game, how hard could it be? So she commenced to imagine that "the flippant, brash soul of a stenographer named Myrtle had transmigrated into my body." The situation quickly became problematic when Jane impishly chose "Betty," intrepid newspaper reporter, as her cover. Encountering this mental hazard, Betty constantly and inadvertently broke cover by responding to Jane's assumed student name.

"I could never remember to respond to Myrtle, the first test of an alert agent," she later remembered ruefully. "Neither could I continue to live in the same body with Myrtle, whom I was beginning to loathe at the end of the three-day course. She even broke me of the habit of chewing gum!"[30]

Dillon, now "Butch," apparently tried to assume the identity of one of the safecrackers OSS recruited for sabotage. This did not hold up well when without thinking he began identifying the birdcalls surrounding them during outdoor exercises—the "piercing note of the ruby-throated grippe, the warble of the double-breasted fit and the indigo nuthatch, the excellent trill of the triple sec and dove-tailed cote."[31]

At the end of three days, the Assessment staff recorded that "the candidates had been asked questions to which they did not know the answers; knew answers to questions they were not asked; played with blocks and built bridges over waterless rivers; put mannequins together and pulled Gestalt figures apart."[32]

Upon graduation Betty ceased to be a civilian but was not firmly in the military. Males recruited into the OSS, after being assessed as physically fit and of draft age, were usually designated as "specialists" and inducted into the U.S. Army, Navy, or Marines. Then they completed training and were somewhat arbitrarily awarded a rank and pay grade commensurate with previous professional qualifications and life experience. The situation for women was slightly more complicated. OSS command determined that its women would be inducted into the Women's Army Corps (WAC). For people like Betty, with professional civil service ratings, this was entirely acceptable. They were given officer status with the attendant relatively high pay. Those women who were secretaries, however, were destined to become enlisted personnel, with a starting salary of sixty dollars a month, much lower than they would have received in civilian life. The inequity was eventually resolved with a compromise: an "assimilation" into the military ranks whereby one became subject to the Articles of War with all its restrictions, the most inconvenient being that one could not quit without being court-martialed. Betty was awarded the assimilated rank of captain, corresponding with her civil service rating.[33]

Following graduation from "S," Jane was working quietly in her office one afternoon when the door banged open and a man in a sergeant's uniform dumped an Abercrombie & Fitch (A&F) duffle bag onto the floor. "Foster, here's your overseas equipment," he announced and left. Jane examined the gear: bedroll, tropical pith helmet draped in green mosquito net, two oral thermometers, compass, canteen, canvass leggings, Hamilton military wristwatch, dog tags.[34] OSS personnel received an inordinate amount of quality gear, much of it purchased with unvouchered funds by Donovan, who, like other generals, outfitted himself with special togs. A&F famously supplied such adventurers as Theodore Roosevelt, Amelia Earhart, and Ernest Hemingway, so it was natural Donovan would want his people decked out in something a cut above standard government issue. Most OSS personnel were therefore a stylish lot, in a roguish sort of way. Assimilated or seconded officers typically received more bounty than enlisted personnel, one of the few distinctions in rank that were occasionally noticeable in OSS. Often it was the case, however, that officers shared the finery, offering their goose-down A&F sleeping bags to enlisted personnel destined to parachute behind enemy lines.

This Is No Picnic
From the collection of
H. Keith Melton at the
International Spy Museum

Betty received more issue than Jane, to the point that she was, as she wrote in a letter home, "loaded to the gills."[35] Closing her own A&F flight bag proved difficult. She also had a footlocker with, in addition to the tropical gear, some "operational equipment"—boxes of squash and tennis balls, which would "be of value when trading with the British." There were also included trinkets such as lipstick and cigarette lighters, which were the equivalent of beads and pelts for trading with the "natives," such as potential Burmese agents. Betty would soon learn the natives already had their own lipstick and lighters. Part of the arsenal for dealing with the British "cousins" were several lovely ball gowns. To top all this off was helpful reading material to prepare her for the mission ahead: a book titled *This Is No Picnic!*[36]

FIVE

IN THEATER

China Burma India was the stuff of legends;
Americans used to say that you needed a crystal ball and
a copy of *Alice in Wonderland* to understand it. . . .
It had everything—maharajas, dancing girls, war lords,
head-hunters, jungles, deserts, racketeers, secret agents.
  —*Theodore White and Annalee Jacoby,* Thunder out of China

Miami was the port of embarkation for Air Transport Command (ATC) flights to Asia, and in the summer of 1944, it was a deserted resort town catering almost entirely to service personnel. Betty, Jane, and Marj Severyns, a dour analyst who found herself attached to the MO team, were billeted in the Floridian Hotel, where most of the opulent decor had been replaced by government-issue furniture, file cabinets, and khaki. The surroundings should have made the war seem closer, but it did not. Balmy breezes, palm fronds, swimming pool—all belied global events transpiring in European forests or bloody coral Pacific atolls.

In fact, Florida reminded Betty of Hawaii, only hotter. She was sipping a coke by the pool, writing a letter to her parents on ATC stationery, when Marj silently joined her and began flipping through two publications: *A Guidebook to Calcutta, Agra, Delhi, Karachi and Bombay*, published by the American Red

Cross of the China-Burma-India Command, and *YANK's Magic Carpet*, printed and distributed by the Staff of the China-Burma-India Edition of *YANK*, the Army weekly at Calcutta, India.

"Listen to this little description of what will be memorable to us in India," Marj said. "'You'll remember some beautiful Indian women—the tall Sikh girls in their loose white pajama pants, the doe-like Hindus in their warm-colored wrap-around sarees which reminded you of Western negligees; Moslem beauties decked out in gilt, silver and silk for a religious festival; and perhaps the round gentle face of a Burmese refugee working as secretary in a headquarters office.'"[1] She threw the booklet down in disgust. "Who writes this stuff?" she huffed.

Betty retrieved the booklet. "*Yank*. It's written for GIs. See?" she said, pointing to the cover, which depicted a cartoon U.S. soldier sitting cross-legged on a flying carpet as it sailed over what had to be the Himalayas.

"And are we not GIs?" Marj demanded.

"Government issue?" asked Betty. "Not really. More like Abercrombie and Fitch."

Marj gave Betty what had come to be known as the "Severyns stare" and stalked off.

Severyns, which she made clear she preferred over her Christian name, was aloof almost to the point of coldness. She appeared on the surface to have no imagination, but when it came to going after facts and useful intel, she was like a ferret. Jane had once unkindly suggested an actual facial resemblance to the creature. Severyns had orders for Delhi, where she would help Betty set up an MO shop.

After three uneventful days, the women were summoned to present themselves and their bags for departure. That afternoon Betty and Jane waited for Jane's name to be called for boarding, only to learn she had been bumped and would follow on a flight the next day. The two friends would not see each other again for months. Betty later learned Jane had gone missing at one point, disappearing into the jungle on the Gold Coast of Africa for days, making sketches and studying indigenous art. When she reemerged, unrepentant, she was simply put on another plane to Karachi.[2]

On July 17 Betty was eight thousand feet over the Amazon, composing another letter to her mother and father as the jungle, a vast green carpet with the huge river moving sluggishly through it, stretched endlessly below. The pilot made a point to dip the wings when the plane crossed over the equator, signaling the passengers could start a "short snorter," a dollar bill signed by everyone on the plane to commemorate the crossing.[3]

What might have been an exotic adventure was tempered by the drab sameness encountered at every refueling stop. There were the same Army heavy dishes in the mess halls, the same candy bars in the Army post exchanges, and seemingly the same young American boys in khakis and fatigues, no matter if it was Accra, Maiduguri, Khartoum, Aden, or Masirah. When the C-47 lifted off from the island of Ascension, in the middle of the Atlantic Ocean, it passed through a notch in the hills strewn with the wrecks of planes that had not made it.

Betty did see baboons, toucans, and cockatoos and later described "tawny camels, with skin that looked like the drawn top over an apple pie. . . . A giraffe at El Fashar coquettishly kicked up his heels when Lieutenant Lee blew a smoke ring at him; ridiculous small gray donkeys at Khartoum gravely carried their long-legged passengers." There were "long marches of prairies, covered with tall-topped thatched huts, negroes in shorts, and giant ant hills." On the final approach to the airfield on Masirah, the plane suddenly heaved over on its side and plummeted toward the earth. As a loud roar filled the air, Betty saw the man in front of her raise his hand as if to ward off a blow. Miraculously, the pilot pulled out of the dive abruptly, snapping everyone's head back. Only the lightning fast reflexes of the pilot had saved a collision with another transport converging on the same course.[4]

The trip was exhausting, but by the time they reached Karachi, Betty and Severyns had managed to forge the semblance of a friendship in anticipation of working together. The weary travelers were finally deposited in New Delhi by an indifferent driver at a nondescript building referred to as the "Taj." Severyns called upon some Urdu out of her GI handbook on India (not the flying carpet version) to wake a sleeping sahib and ask for their quarters. It was close to dawn when Betty flung herself down on a damp cot, not bothering with mosquito netting—malaria be damned.[5]

The next morning, bleary-eyed Betty and Severyns were lectured by a young sergeant on proper Indian protocol vis-à-vis themselves, the natives, and the British "cousins"—rules to be observed so as to not upset already tenuous relations with the latter. The women were expected to employ a gaggle of westernized Oriental gentlemen (WOGs), including but not limited to men who shined brass and shoes. One must have, in addition to the ever-present bearer, a sweeper, a dhobi for laundry, and if she owned pets, a dog wallah. One of the residents reportedly kept a pet mongoose named Fifi, and the mongoose wallah quickly assumed a lower status than the dog wallahs. The army of bearers, who served as personal servants, butlers, valets, grooms, messengers, and even midwives in a pinch, was a semipermanent fixture in the various villas and palaces, remaining through generations of maharajahs and British officers. Getting used to a bearer took some adjustment for Americans. For the British, the bearer was, of course, taken for granted, as was stopping the war promptly at 10 a.m. and 5 p.m. daily to take tea.[6]

OSS Headquarters Delhi had located itself in a large Edwardian house, the previous residence of wealthy British businessmen and typical of the luxurious living that was the heritage of colonial conquest and occupation of India. The advance team of OSS men had endured life in a tent outside the city before they were able to move into the new billet, which was palatial in comparison and similar to many villas found throughout India built by wealthy maharajas and commandeered during wartime.[7] When they first arrived, many Americans were put off by such ostentation in the midst of war, but as Charles Fenn later observed, most "got over their ambivalence enough to take advantage of the gracious living . . . steaks, chicken curries, and cheap (although limited) booze, plus having a host of Indian servants ready to salaam, and dancing every evening."[8]

Betty and Severyns took a Tonga, a pony-driven taxi, to the OSS wing of China-Burma-India (CBI) headquarters and reported to their commanding officer (CO), the young and handsome Col. Harry Berno.

"Just what is this—MO?" he asked suspiciously. "I know—propaganda stuff, like OWI."

Colonel Berno was a fan of the OWI camp. OWI had bought up entire pages in the *Delhi Statesman* and run a series of historically instructive articles on how America won her independence. The Indians, especially the "Quit India" Indians, loved it. The British did not, and ergo, OWI was doing everything right so far as Colonel Berno was concerned. Betty assured him that their target was the morale of the Japanese soldier; they were to collect material and use it to produce black propaganda. Their new CO appeared unimpressed and somewhat disappointed to learn the newcomers had no plans to needle the British. He pointed out there was no equipment to spare for their operations, and it was against regulations to go to outside channels—as in, to the British—to get any. Having made himself clear, he asked if they would join him for dinner with a couple of generals that evening, say, around seven.[9]

Betty and Severyns agreed to the dinner and were dismissed. They boarded another Tonga for a trip through the rain to 32 Feroz Shah Road, a former dentist's office and now the command post for MO Delhi. They ducked out of the deluge and announced their presence to a first lieutenant, a bespectacled young man bent over a Japanese newspaper. A sign was taped to a filing cabinet near his desk: "Beware of the Kraits."

"I'm just one of the help—Bill Magistretti," he said modestly. Magistretti was actually R&A but was making himself available to help get the new MO shop up and running. Bill had gone to Heain Middle School in Kyoto, Japan, and actually prepared for the Buddhist priesthood. Supporting himself through Berkeley as a busboy, waiter, and cloakroom attendant, he studied Oriental languages, including medieval Japanese, to go along with a fluency in French. When OSS discovered him, he was translating Japanese technical manuals on petroleum antiknock fluids. He had, more significantly, conducted an analysis of Japanese propaganda in the vernacular press.[10]

Betty liked him immediately. He poured tea for the three of them and began a rundown on the situation in CBI. Because of increased American presence in the Pacific, Japanese troops had been secretly shifting troops there from Burma; the Allies had gleaned this information from captured documents. The British Ministry of Information (BMOI) had picked up Japanese propaganda being sent into conquered areas informing the citizens that the Japanese were withdrawing and granting de facto independence to these countries. This, as Bill observed, would set things up to be "a nice mess after the war."[11] OSS Detachment 404 had recently moved from Delhi to Kandy, in the mountains of Ceylon, and was charged with coordinating intelligence and operations conducted by OSS and the British SOE in the Far East. This included recruiting natives from enemy-occupied territories in order to reinsert them, by airdrop or submarine, into their home countries so that they could gather intelligence on Japanese order of battle and many other things. Most important, these agents were also used to disseminate black propaganda.

"Coordination" was not the watchword of CBI, where areas of authority overlapped. The first OSS presence in the theater was Detachment 101, which hit the ground running and immediately became a thorn in the side of the British, largely because the Americans could not be controlled. That never changed, but throughout the war the British made repeated and futile attempts to rein in Detachment 101's activities, which involved training indigenous people in the

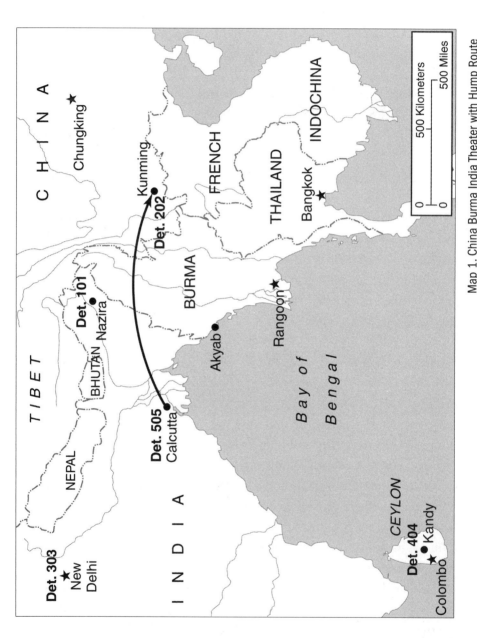

Map 1. China Burma India Theater with Hump Route

art of waging guerrilla warfare with Western weapons. The British had great misgivings about American clandestine activities with people who were subjects of the Raj. Fear of independence movements underlay most of the British hostility, and it was not helped by a strong belief in OSS that the Allies should live up to the principle of the Atlantic Charter, which asserted the rights of every people to choose its own form of government. When OSS-British relations reached an all-time nadir the summer of 1943, delegates to the Quebec Conference created an overall integrated command and superimposed it on the theater. Lord Louis Mountbatten took charge of the new Southeast Asia Command (SEAC) with umbrella authority. Donovan parried by creating yet another OSS Detachment, 404, now giving him two detachments in the theater, one to continue running free and one to come under British oversight. In an effort to make everyone coordinate activities, a "P" Division was created as a joint Anglo-American panel intended to vet operations.

Betty quickly grasped her most immediate problem in getting the MO shop up and running: equipment. Technical concerns presented themselves at every turn, starting with the kind of printing press required to begin actual production of black propaganda. Sometimes an offset press, which made no indentation on the paper, was needed for printing leaflets, documents, magazines, or posters. Letter press left a physical indentation, and if that was not present on a page of newsprint, any reasonably observant, let alone suspicious, Japanese reader would notice. The cold reality was that OSS MO Delhi had neither offset nor letter. OWI was in town, but a brief outreach to them revealed the same wall of disdain and hostility that had separated the former siblings in Washington, and besides, they too were underequipped. The British owned both presses, but they were using them for white propaganda, just like OWI, and besides, they did not like the Americans and found black propaganda distasteful and a waste of time and matériel. In addition to presses, Betty needed the correct paper, as Japanese newsprint was of a cheaper, courser grade than American. The cousins had that too.

The good news was that Bill Magistretti not only was a fellow "Jap lover" who bore no animus toward that other "enemy," the British, but also played tennis. Betty was a high school tennis star. Bill had carefully charted the somewhat predictable breaks in the afternoon rains, which allowed a quick set or two.

"We play until the rains resume," he told her. "Then we have gin tonics."

On the Tonga ride back to the Taj that evening, Betty found herself bolstered by Bill's good-humored equanimity. She formulated a plan for developing a professional working relationship with the British in order to fulfill her orders as she understood them. It involved a great deal of creative bartering, schmoozing, and outright begging. Upon arriving "home," she met the owner of Fifi the mongoose, her new roommate. Joy Homer was the granddaughter of Winslow Homer and daughter of famous singer Madame Louise Homer.

"Fifi guards us against kraits," Joy said and went on to explain that the krait was a deadly indigenous reptile. The banded variety was known as the "two step," as that was how far one could walk after a bite. Kraits could hide anywhere, in the dust, in shoes, inside a radio.

Another housemate joined them for cocktails—concoctions that reminded Betty of the one and only taste of moonshine she once sampled in Arkansas. Rosamunde Frame had made the Pacific crossing with Julia McWilliams and Gregory Bateson. Julia thought she was going to India but landed in Bombay to learn she was being shifted to the SEAC headquarters of Lord Mountbatten, where she would join Jane Foster. Frame had been destined for China, but women were as yet not welcome in that theater, so she was shuffled to Delhi, where she waited. Betty was a bit in awe of Rosie's reputation as a "real spy." Frame's new orders, which she freely shared in a very un-spy-like manner, were to monitor the growing number of Chinese technical ordnance people coming into India and to be on the lookout for Japanese puppets.[12]

Rosie Frame had a definite air of mystery. No one knew exactly how old she was—twenty-four? twenty-five? thirty?—and she was not telling. She seemed to possess multiple personalities and was different things to different people, a talent Betty assumed made one a good spy. Whereas Betty saw Rosie as tough and self-sufficient, Paul Child found her fragile and overly dramatic after she had complained of a muscle strain on their first date. He later altered his opinion, describing her in a letter to his brother as a person who had "real brains, is sensual, direct, and spirited." Paul tended to psychoanalyze his coworkers and speculated that Rosie was conflicted and troubled owing to the loss of her dynamic and spiritual mother who had been dean of women at a Protestant college in Peking. Mostly he liked listening to her speak Mandarin.[13]

In the days that followed, life settled into a tropical routine revolving around work at 32 Feroz Shah Road: tennis, evening engagements, and the day-to-day technicalities of living through an Indian monsoon. Betty was wandering through an outside market, clutching an umbrella, when she spotted a white bull terrier puppy. She later wrote, "I fancied the animal smiled at me. He turned out to be a mentally retarded sort of happy hormone, a pink-nosed, pink-eyed, under-vitamined dog called Angel Puss, who every one said should be thrown back in the developer!" Angel Puss immediately nosed under the mosquito netting and settled on Betty's cot. Fifi the mongoose peered at the newcomer from her drawer.[14]

Her excursions into Delhi brought home to Betty that she really was in India, with its explosion of colors ranging from brick red to curry and golden yellows to faded shades of purple and green. The working women were extraordinarily beautiful and stately, with perfect postures acquired by balancing stacks of bricks on their heads. Multiple bangles chinked around their slim ankles as they swept streets and dug ditches, their singing floating above all the other street sounds. Less pleasing were the vast number of flies covering everything the least bit organic. Sick beggars were thick with them. A helpful Englishman explained it was a sure sign of impending death because "flies always know." Especially upsetting were the flies crawling over the faces of babies sleeping in the sun.

Whereas Betty, Joy Homer, Severyns, and Rosie adjusted to their rather cramped quarters at the Taj, their friends Joan Bondurant and Maureen Patterson, classmates from the University of Michigan, had rented themselves a bungalow on Tughlak Road, a spacious house with that greatest of Asian luxuries: separate rooms. Living and dining areas and bedrooms were complimented by a large garden and servants' quarters. Betty and fellow Taj inmates teased the duo relentlessly about their opulent digs, given they were presumably receiving the same standard $2,900 per annum salary as all other P-3 analysts.

Joan and Maureen were in fact the real spies. They were conducting one of the most sensitive operations in the theater: penetrating and understanding the goals of the Indian Nationalist Movement. Maureen Patterson got her OSS start in San Francisco sorting printed Japanese-language materials confiscated from temples and homes when Japanese Americans were removed and interned. She followed her former professor to India and was assigned translation of captured materials for R&A. During the day Joan and Maureen performed the duties for which they had initially been recruited: analyzing materials such as photographs, postcards, and travel brochures—anything that might be of help to Detachment 101, General Stilwell, or MO. At night they changed into slinky gowns and spied on the British, or more specifically, British attitudes and activities vis-à-vis the Indian Nationalist Movement. Small social gatherings at the bungalow garnered reciprocal invitations to formal dances at the Imperial Hotel and dinners in private homes. As important were the invitations to the Chelmsford Club, established by the Indian elite after they were excluded from the British Gymkhana Club. All the while the duo was gathering spot-on intelligence about the pending formation of the state of Pakistan, the maneuverings of the Muslim League, and British attempts to keep the colony intact. The women operated a short-wave radio to monitor broadcasts from Japanese-occupied Singapore from one of the "spacious" bedrooms.[15]

These activities were of course strictly forbidden. OSS was not supposed to do any back-channel investigations or reporting under the terms of the Roosevelt-Churchill agreement that had made it possible for the U.S. Army to operate in India. The British were convinced OSS was fomenting revolution among the Nationalists, which Maureen later wrote "in a small way was what our OSS unit was up to!" Joan Bondurant made her specialty the analysis of Gandhian thought and action and later authored the book *Conquest of Violence*. The two women surreptitiously met with individual Indian National Congress leaders as they were released from jail: Pandit Nehru, Maulana Azad, Sarojini Naidu, Muhammad Ali Jinna, and B. C. Roy, Gandhi's personal physician.[16]

The British government had essentially promised the Indians their independence in the India Act of 1935, but the Indian Nationalists did not wholly believe the British. When Gandhi launched his Quit India Now movement instead of supporting the British war effort, he was jailed for two years, ensuring continuous public unrest for the duration of the war.[17]

Meanwhile, Jane Foster was settling into a rather idyllic setting in the mountains of Ceylon. Having arrived in Colombo after her jagged jaunt from Miami, she passed quickly through the OSS encampment on the coast and then boarded the Toonerville Trolley, a British-operated train serving the military and making daily runs up through the mountains to Kandy. It was known as a delightful four hours of bacon, eggs, and tea on the morning trip and gin tonics on the evening return, all served by native waiters. At least two hours were spent climbing ever higher, with two engines straining through tunnels, through forests, and around cliff-hugging curves. The air, strangely, did not cool with the ascent but continued to feel like the tropics below, where rice paddies nestled in the steep mountain valleys and elephants bathed in rivers. On the many stops, native people crowded the tracks, waving with exaggerated motions and flashing the V-for-victory sign.[18]

Lord Louis Mountbatten, commonly known as "Supremo," had made the surprising decision to pack up his entire outfit in Delhi and move sixteen hundred miles south, five hundred miles farther from the fighting in Burma. The new Kandy headquarters became, as one historian wrote, "a byword for luxury and elegance," with opulent accommodations and a "sleek fleet of limousines."[19] Lord Mountbatten and his staff reportedly had a thirty-member band and a golf course. Jane was met by an Army jeep and taken to her billet, the Queen's Hotel. The establishment was a planter's oasis before the war but appeared to her like much else in the theater, neglected and shabby. It was filled with the cousins—women of the Women's Royal Naval Service (WRENS) and Royal Air Force (RAF) pilots—along with ten OSS women, Gregory Bateson, Paul Child, and Dillon Ripley.

Dillon was chief of SI for Detachment 404 and bent his energies to the gathering of intelligence, making frequent hazardous trips into Burma. He also found himself in the thick of the "tangled skein" that was Thailand. Nowhere else in Asia was conflict between OSS and the British more intense than in Thailand. Mutual antipathy reached such a pitch that OSS, with State Department backing, made preventing the British colonization of Thailand a primary plank of wartime strategy.[20]

Japanese strategy called for using Thailand, a country that had never been colonized, as a staging area for invasions of Burma and Malaya. Right-wing Thai field marshal Phibun Songkhram agreed to join with the Japanese in exchange for territorial gains in the Shan States and northern Malaya. Phibun's rival, Pridi Phanomyong, worked with SOE and OSS to support a vigorous anti-Japanese underground. Free Thai, mainly students studying in America and England, were recruited for infiltration. Far from being cooperative, Thailand was a cauldron of opposing aims and conflicting postwar Allied plans, resulting in a race to insert teams and establish radio contact with Bangkok.

Dillon spent every minute of his spare time traveling in Ceylon in a jeep with a hired driver and a man on loan from the Colombo Museum of Natural History who served as his assistant in bird collection. Dillon was renowned among the small circle of wartime birders, and once on a mission in the jungles of Burma, he encountered a British lieutenant general who had heard of him— "the OSS ornithologist"—and asked for help on a manuscript he was preparing on the birds of Burma.[21]

Jane's accommodations in Kandy were pretty much on a par with Betty's—nothing really to complain about for a Westerner in Asia during a war. Her room was a mere cubby hole with hot running water, but she was alone, which suited her temperament. The day after her arrival, she was jeeped to Detachment 404, which amounted to a cluster of shacks on an otherwise exquisitely beautiful tea plantation. A group of OSS men, most of whom had PhDs, lived on site. The shacks, called *cadjans*, had palm-thatched roofs over a frame of two-by-fours based on a traditional unit, which was one room measuring ten by eighteen feet and divided to accommodate several desks. There was a four-by-four-foot window opening with unpainted shutters, warped and rippling with termite runs. Since the compound was encircled by a high barbed-wire security fence, the shutters served mainly to shut out especially heavy rainfall. Each room had exactly one twenty-five-watt lightbulb strung from the ceiling, compliments of the British supply officer from Mountbatten's headquarters.[22]

Jane expected to be greeted by her friends from Washington, but she found only Paul Child in the *cadjan*, sitting in a comfortable easy chair in a central cubicle. A large acetate map of the entire theater was tacked to one wall and covered with grease-pencil messages, news clippings, and radio monitorings. Paul's own paintings were mounted on the other walls.

"My office is the wonder and glory of Detachment 404," Paul, with his customary modesty, pronounced.[23] It was also gossip central for the compound, and Jane quickly became a frequent visitor, flopping down on a worn loveseat to tell funny stories, brainstorm ideas, and bemoan her inability to get her black propaganda into Malaya. Gregory and Dillon usually wandered in. When not plotting to insert teams into Thailand behind the backs of the British and under the noses of the Japanese, Dillon worked to help Jane make contacts in Malaya. The British had blocked OSS Operation Jukebox, aimed at putting agents on the eastern shore of the Malayan peninsula. In fact, the British and the Dutch were thwarting all of Dillon's efforts to make contact with natives in Malaya and Sumatra. "It would be as if," the Dutch representative told him, "Great Britain should send agents into the United States to stir up the negroes, or sent a representative to Puerto Rico to express British sympathy for Puerto Rican aspirations for independence."[24]

Paul had arrived in Kandy the previous March and endured endless frustrations with building plans, recalcitrant workers, a lack of materials, and no hope of being adequately supplied. A social creature, he was dogged by loneliness. His ennui evaporated like sweat in the high desert with the arrival of Jane Foster, whom he would describe in a letter to his twin brother Charlie as "a new and interesting gal . . . an artist, intelligent, talkative and a comfort to me." Even her deficits—"wild hair and a messy room"—intrigued him.[25]

Immediately upon her arrival, Jane learned her coworkers were all in the hospital, a former Franciscan monastery, with dengue fever and took a jeep to visit them. She believed her own earlier bout of dengue, which she had contracted in Bali, would keep her draped in a cloak of immunity, but she instead found herself a guest of the ward within days. The clogged drains at the Queen's Hotel were apparently a nursery for mosquitoes.[26] Paul himself was stricken with a frightening rash from feet to knees but was controlling it with a mysterious ointment that he determined never to part with until war's end. The dampness was unrelenting; envelopes fell apart, pins rusted, towels smelled sour, and shoes molded. The bands of their Hamilton watches disintegrated. Giant blue bees droned in the air and termites seemed to appear at every turn. A newcomer to Detachment 404 arrived on a Monday with his entire wardrobe locked in a steel trunk. When he got around to opening it on Thursday, all the termites had left him were a few buttons, buckles, a copper penny, and the hobnails on his boots.[27]

Jane recovered from her bout with dengue fever and settled into her own MO routine. Each morning she and Paul, having staked out a private table, had breakfast. Invariably Julia, having embarked on a silent campaign to win Paul's heart, hovered nearby. Jane's arrival brought a discouraging retrenchment, but not a full-scale retreat. After breakfast, Jane, Paul, Julia, Cora DuBois, Gregory Bateson, and Liz Paul, a secretary, were picked up by a weapons carrier and transported to the plantation for work.

For Jane the day was spent scrutinizing what little there were of intelligence reports from occupied territories, gleaning names of Japanese military personnel, civilians, and their collaborators, specifically Malay or Indonesian. She passed the reports on to Julia, who routed them elsewhere. Jane would then sit back and think, staring into space, sometimes for hours, dreaming up schemes to convince Japanese soldiers that people were sleeping with their wives. In a field station report, she outlined her technique: "so simple that it can be read at a glance . . . so small it can be transported without entailing too much risk . . . posted quickly and secretly in public places, such as the walls of a privy."[28]

Jane had two helpers, Abdul and Hadji, who rendered her brochures into Arabic and Malay. She began writing radio scripts for black "freedom stations," which operated on the hopeful assumption that shortwave broadcasts would undermine Japanese reluctance to surrender by inducing a "public discussion" about the issue of surrender of their troops. Per guidelines from Washington, reference to the existence of Japanese POWs, without mentioning any numbers, was one possible tactic. In such a reference, it was important to never question bravery, to never use the word "surrender" (*kosan, kofuku*), and to avoid any suggestion that the prospective captive might be repatriated home after the war, the official thinking being that to return would be a disgrace. Finally, Washington had decreed that the release of names and photographs of prisoners was forbidden (a rule that changed later in the war).[29] This did not mean there could not be a release of *fictional* names and photographs.

OSS Detachment 404 was not plagued by the same lack of equipment as the Delhi office was. Jane's problem was getting her printed material to target. The only real option was dropping leaflets by Spitfires, flown by the British. She quickly began arranging for this to happen, which involved a great deal of creative bartering, schmoozing, and outright begging.

SIX

OPERATION
BLACK MAIL

The Japanese are a slow-thinking and
naturally cautious people.
—*British military attaché to Tokyo, 1940*

Betty's initial optimism upon arriving in Delhi was quickly beginning to fray. All of her carefully conjured schemes were dependent on access to equipment, which she did not have, and as of yet she had not met a cousin who could be cajoled. A large part of the problem was the British attitude toward the Japanese soldier, which had thus far in the war been shared by most of the U.S. Army and the JCS. The British thought that trying to manipulate the Japanese was a losing proposition and a waste of time and resources because the Japanese were either too indoctrinated with fanaticism or too dull witted to be hustled. This was the inherited gospel of Peter Fleming, the man in charge of British deceptive tactics for CBI. Fleming had tried allowing the Japanese to "capture" forged letters and documents exaggerating India's defensive position during the 1942 Burma campaign and thereafter concluded that "subtle items" like forged letters were far above the heads of the Japanese, who could rarely be relied on to reach obvious reasonable conclusions, no matter how strong the hints.[1]

Late 1944 brought a slight shift in thinking, not only in Washington but among the British Chiefs of Staff. "Despite his indoctrination," one report noted charitably, "the regimented fighting man of Japan is fundamentally human." Anthropologists and other social scientists weighed in with their analyses, and the Japanese soldier began to emerge from the mist as an individual, with varying "normal" degrees of disenchantment with the course of the war, combined with basic homesickness.[2]

Bill knew a British major over in the Southeast Asian Translation and Interrogation Center (SEATIC) compound who was "gruffly pro-American." Major William Clark held the keys to the MO kingdom in the form of captured Japanese printed material: letters, postcards from home, diaries, field manuals, magazines. Major Clark—"Willie" to his friends—was serving with distinction as an undercover agent in Malaya when the country was first overrun and spoke flawless Japanese. As they slogged through the rain in Bill's jeep, Betty wondered if her Japanese counterpart—there had to be one somewhere—was encountering similar difficulties, if he had been reduced to begging.

Willie peered at them over horn-rimmed glasses and began a spluttering tirade: "Now what? I see you are coming to rob me of important documents. And bringing female reinforcements! This time I shall be adamant. Nothing leaves this building!"[3]

Bill ignored the major and proceeded to a back room. Willie did not protest, and Betty realized this was a familiar dance for the two of them. The major offered her a cigarette, and she demurred—did she not have plans for her cigarette ration? In an instant Willie's attitude shifted, and a deal was struck. He would allow her to dip her hand into some damp sacks recently captured in the jungles of Burma in exchange for her allotment of Lucky Strikes. While Bill hauled the bags from the back room, Willie explained he was working on a problem.

"Have you ever been to the Philippines?" he asked her, and when she said yes, he produced a photo album with the insignia of a Japanese infantry unit. "This was compiled by a Japanese combat artist," he said. "It chronicles the travels of the unit from when it left Yokohama until it was wiped out at Myitchina. We've identified Mandalay, Rangoon, the Kokoda Trail, but I need to know where this is." He pointed to a photo of a group of Japanese soldiers in a motor boat, the *Mabuhay II*, moored to a dock. "I know it has to be the Philippines," he asserted.

Betty instantly recognized the Standard Oil shed and nipa shacks near the docks of Davao, on Mindanao. Clark beamed and made notations. His new friend Betty was welcome to call him "Willie."

The bags held "pitiful momentos"—family photos, good luck charms, letters, and wrapped stacks of clean, dry postcards. Betty had no trouble reading the simply scrawled messages, many in pencil. All were stamped with an Imperial Army post office star and censor's chop. The men of the Mori unit Higashi tai had written a total of five hundred postcards on the eve of battle at Myitkina. "What a shame the families will never receive these last messages from their loved ones," Betty mused aloud.

Bill observed that since the cards had already cleared the censor, they could hypothetically be placed back in the mail stream to the home islands. Betty stared at him and suddenly saw the possibility of her first feasible operation since she had arrived in CBI. They could erase the penciled colloquial kanji script and substitute different messages. If they could get the cards in the mail and past the censors, this would be the first black MO to make its way into the heartland of Japan.

"It's a cinch," Bill said. "Our 101 agents can slip this mail pouch into the Jap postal system that's still working south of Mogaung—there's a damned good chance nobody'll check cards that have already been censored!"[4]

The practice of tampering with personal mail had been perfected by the British, who regularly captured mail, altered it, and reposted it into Germany, during World War I. The Soviets had likewise been at the practice for many years and were quite good at it. OSS officer Edmond Taylor, one of Donovan's black propaganda pioneers, recounted specific "fiendish" cases and promoted the technique as one that was extremely indirect, often containing no obvious political propaganda. A soldier at the front would receive letters "telling him his children, evacuated to a country village, were dangerously ill owing to the inadequate care and food" being provided by the German government. The object, Taylor asserted, "was merely to shake the soldier's nerves, make him hate the war."[5]

Bill and Betty agreed on several common themes for the altered messages for the folks at home in Japan: the IJA in Burma was underequipped and being defeated; U.S. bombers passed overhead daily to mass for bombings of Japan, and soldiers were unsettled by rumors of strikes on the home islands. Underlying message: The war is lost.[6]

Willie agreed that this was indeed a fiendishly good idea. The mail was intended for Honshu Province. No doubt the local papers there had been insisting the war was going swimmingly, so it would be unsettling to get a glimpse of the real conditions in Burma. Willie snatched one of the cards, erased the words,

and deftly wrote in kanji: "Obasan, where are supplies from home? We are starving in the jungle. How can we fight without bullets?"[7] Willie was so pleased
with himself he offered to round up a posse of nisei and come to the Taj that
evening to help with the project. When the group showed up, the Indian gate
guard held the British invaders at bay until Bill ran down to rescue them.

They began work and, for the first hour or so, debated how to make the
altered messages believable. With the exception of Willie, everyone involved was
a "Jap lover." Missionaries and their children, like Bill Magistretti, knew what
the experts in Washington and London were reluctant to acknowledge: that each
Japanese individual was human and did not necessarily succumb to the hive
mentality. American missionaries in Japan before the war had supported and
encouraged a Peace Party, comprising mainly Japanese college students, before
they fled to avoid prison. The missionaries knew that a sizable portion of the
population viewed war with the United States as suicidal, and many who held
this belief were university students. A 1934 petition denouncing the militarists
had been signed by a million Japanese, but now those signees were silent.[8] Where
were they? How many Imperial Japanese troops now in Burma had been a part
of that movement?

Most Western military experts thought the Japanese soldier clung to a fierce,
single-minded adoration of the emperor. But a tradition of deep dedication to
family had existed in Japan before written history, predating and rivaling devotion to an emperor. When Betty and Alex shared tea with Professor and Mrs.
Watanabe, a joss stick always burned on the family shrine, offering prayers of
devotion to departed family members. While the MO recruits were learning the
art of black propaganda back in Washington, someone had brought in items
captured in the Pacific, including a *senninbari* belt, worn by Japanese soldiers
under their uniforms. The belt was covered with tiny stitches, painstakingly
knotted by the soldier's loved ones, each stitch a prayer for his safe return. Betty
remembered running her fingers over the stitches, imagining the women who
cherished that soldier and would never see him again.[9]

Operation Black Mail overflowed from the MO office to the dining room at
32 Feroz Shah Road. At one point Betty and Severyns served tea and sandwiches
from the pantry. The mood was upbeat, with everyone elated to be doing something constructive. Bill had already solved the problem of getting the cards back
into the Imperial Army mail flow: Detachment 101 would do it.

When Col. Ray Peers, the commander of Detachment 101 came through later that week, Severyns had a proper military memo prepared to hand over with Betty's mailbag. Betty explained in her most persuasive voice that if the colonel's agents could get the postcards reinserted into the Japanese mail stream, it could very well be the "first black penetration of Japan proper." Three days later Colonel Peers sent a personal courier confirming one of his Kachins had done the deed. "Mission accomplished," he wrote. "Every reason to believe material will reach objective."[10]

Soon another treasure trove arrived: a captured sack of letters en route to Japanese soldiers from the home islands. Operation Black Mail was still in business. Betty and her colleagues worked from the originals to write new letters:

> I hope that you are in good health. It has been seven months since we have had word from you but we know you are safe as the army has not notified us differently. How I wish the mail was faster! I have not been able to write often because of long hours at the factory.
>
> Michiko and Tetsuo are in the nursery at the factory and I have little time to spend with them. I will be glad when the war is won and we can settle down to normal family life once more.
>
> This is just gossip, but if I repeat it to you do not say anything as it may get back here and it would be embarrassing. However, do you remember Ikeda's wife? She was from Kyoto? He has been away in China and Burma for five years now, and she has only had letters from him four times in that period, although he said he wrote her weekly postcards. Well, the truth is that she is going to have a baby. She went on working at the factory until it became noticeable then she was asked by the foreman to leave as the effect was bad on the others. She went back to her parents place.
>
> Such things are happening all over the city, I am told. It is probably because so many men are away and the women get lonesome.
>
> Do not worry about me, as I am too busy with the children, the work at the factory, and defense duties after work . . . I am beginning to look like a coolie. However, you must admit that five years is a long time to be away from your wife and children, is it not? They tell us it will be after India is conquered. I pray that will be soon. The children send their best wishes. I will try to enclose notes from them in my next letter.[11]

"Do you think 'coolie' is the right word?" Betty asked Severyns. "I'm looking to express to poor Yoshi that because of home front deprivations in the face of a war gone bad, his young wife is looking more like an old sack . . . a bag . . . something derogatory."

"Yes, I understood that," Severyns said flatly and then continued her work silently, offering nothing. Betty stared at her for a second and then carefully folded the letter. "Coolie" it was.[12]

Betty's next forgery took a stab at the lies being fed the home islands with regard to Japan's forward momentum in Burma. While a poor soldier huddles in the jungle rain, wracked with dysentery, hiding from the relentless raids of the U.S. 10th Air Force, picking the meat from a dead snake, he will at long last receive what he hopes will be an uplifting letter from home:

Are you in good health?

I have been reading the papers about the glorious victories our troops have been winning in Burma. How wonderful that you are among the brave soldiers marching ahead into India. Every day after school the children and I study the map of Burma we have cut out of the Fujin Kurabu. We mark your progress across the mountains and jungles with a flag. Taro is proud and tells his friends that his father is beating the Americans and the British single-handed. Out of door life must have browned you like a native! The papers tell how sturdy and strong our troops have become in Burma after living in the sun. It must be thrilling to advance under the powerful air arm of our Eagles and see the weak enemy fall before you like straw before a sickle [or some apt expression].

On the home front we are pulling our belts tighter. Sacrifices are worth it, though, when we know they are being made so that you and your comrades will be getting all the food and ammunition you need.

We hear by the grapevine that as soon as the brave troops of Japan have conquered India and freed the Indians from the yoke of the hateful British, that our men will be coming home for permanent station. This is indeed gratifying and I am praying daily that you will soon be on your way home. It has been so many years since we have seen you. You will not know the children. In spite of the rations I have been able to scrimp and save enough so Taro is healthy and strong. Take care of yourself. Mother and father send best wishes.

Chieko[13]

Black Postcards

DESCRIPTION: In October, 1944, a batch of 78 Japanese postcards were captured outside Myitkina, in a field P.O. box. The cards had been written by men of the MORI 10120 Unit Higashi tai on the eve of battle, were censored and censor stamped. The censor "nan" or stamp was that of the coy commander. The cards were addressed to persons in Central Honshu.

The MO Delhi unit, assisted by Nisei, erased messages on the cards written in pencil. Black messages were inserted. The cards, together with an equal number of untouched ones written in ink, were re-mailed farther down the line in Burma. If delivered, they are the first known OSS black propaganda to reach Japan proper.

PURPOSE: Black messages inserted in the cards purported to (1) tell the homefolks that the Japanese army in Burma was not well equipped and that they were being defeated; (2) U.S. bombers passed overhead daily to mass for bombings of Japan; (3) that troops were disturbed by rumors of strikes on the homefront and government upsets; (4) that the war was lost.

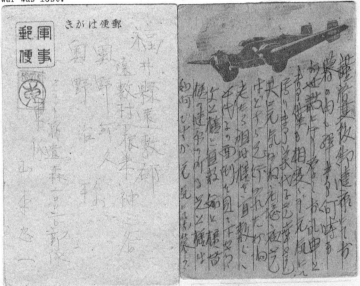

TRANSLATION OF CAPTURED POSTCARD
(Words in parenthesis were erased--underlined words are black inserts)

Salutation: I presume that you are well. I thank you very much for all that you are doing. I am fine. Are Miyoko-san and Miyuki-san in good health? Where did Ito-san go? Please take care of aging mother. Please look after Chiyoko. My regards to father and Ken. (I'm praying for your health. How is brother? Please live happily.) <u>At the front here we are disturbed about the government crisis</u>. Please keep safe.

Example of black postcard with altered message. "At the front here we are disturbed by the government crisis [in Tokyo]" was inserted at the end of a soldier's message to loved ones back home.
National Archives and Records Administration II, College Park, Maryland

꒭

In Kandy Jane was hard at work creating a fake newspaper, the *Burma Shimbun* (Burma news). Her fake articles stressed the impending "siege of Japan"; reported Chinese receipt of vast amounts of matériel captured from Germany and Italy, which strengthened Chiang Kai-shek's already huge army; and casually mentioned the rotation schedule of U.S. soldiers in Burma. Many Japanese troops had not seen home in seven years.

> American Soldiers—Spoiled Boys
>
> It is reported that wealthy America is spending several millions of dollars in their so-called rotation policy to console the spoiled American soldiers who are located in the Far East. Transports for those who have completed two years of combat duty are leaving India for America every month, and after two months leave they will be given one year's duty in America. American soldiers who are continuing their war of resistance in the jungles of Burma have plenty of supplies, rations, and medical care and live a luxurious life incompatible to the jungle. But their only pleasure is to leave as soon as possible and an easy job. And in spite of this they are angry at having their hours lengthened. Let us compare the feelings of our heroes.[14]

The scorpion and tarantula populations of Ceylon underwent something of a baby boom as the summer monsoon progressed. Only recently had a scream gone up from one of the girls' rooms in the hotel when a live tarantula turned up on a dressing table. The room boy was summoned, and though he was as frightened as everyone else, he nonetheless, in true Buddhist fashion, scooped the creature up in a large towel and shook it out the window over the main street.

A chronic lack of supplies had ground projects to a halt, bringing listless ennui to Detachment 404. To relieve the boredom, someone positioned a three-foot-long dead iguana under a secretary's chair and said, "Don't look now Virginia, but I think *there's something under your chair!*" The results were predictable. A young British naval commander dived out his window one day after a very much alive six-foot cobra appeared in his office. A baby cobra had been trapped by someone and was living in a large bottle in another office and being fed frogs every day.[15]

Paul's infatuation with Jane continued. He took to dropping in on her in the evenings, finding her surrounded by sketches, half-written letters, negligees, and pajamas, with a chipmunk on her shoulder and a bottle of beer in hand. She had "collected" men of all kinds—Malaysian, Australian, and those of undetermined nationality or ethnicity—and they drifted in and out as she regaled them with stories in various fictional accents. Paul described a typical Jane episode to his brother, Charlie:

> Yesterday her chipmunk fell out of the hotel window onto the slanting roof over the servant's quarters, one story below. This roof is about forty feet above the ground, but she was out of the window like a flash and down the drain pipe to the roof, her mind wholly on her pet. Picture to yourself the horror of several stodgy British military characters who, hearing an unwonton scrabbling and clucking on the roof, looked out, and there saw Janie on all fours, a banana in each fist (for bait), alternately cursing and cooing in English and Malay.[16]

Betty was surprised to learn from Jane that her husband, Alex, had turned up in Kandy. The MacDonalds had communicated little since Betty had deployed to India, and it bothered her how little it bothered her. Alex was becoming almost ephemeral, floating on the edges of her life and thoughts. She was not sure how he had managed to be sent to the same theater as she—no doubt some foul-up back at Que—but a couriered message from him revealed that his ultimate destination was Thailand. By that time the theater had undergone a split into India-Burma-Thailand (IBT) and China, but apparently, Alex's orders had been cut before Thailand was made part of Betty's sphere of operations. Few people bothered to follow the shifting kaleidoscope that was CBI, now IBT. Meanwhile, Alex played sets of tennis with the residents of Detachment 404 until he was sent to set up an MO shop down south in Colombo. Edmond Taylor wanted Alex to quickly develop a "freedom station" that would operate out of Chittagong and beam black propaganda into Thailand.[17]

Alex appealed to both Betty and Jane for help writing radio scripts. He inevitably altered Betty's, to her great annoyance. When the scripts began circulating to OSS detachments and outposts for use by various black transmitting stations in the theater, suddenly everyone became a critic, and MO chief James Withrow began receiving scathing memos. From B. M. Turner: "It almost sounds as if it were being delivered by a Church Sewing Circle." From Frank McGramm: "It is the type that a high school debating society might prepare; lacks fire, suspense, drama." Great doubts were expressed as to the literacy of the Thai people, and the overall consensus was that Thais would not respond to a "fireside chat." The chorus of critics insisted broadcasts should cater to the average Thai's "sense of dramatics."[18]

"Who *are* these people?" Alex complained to Betty.[19]

Years later Betty recalled Operation Black Mail as a personal turning point. Although she felt slightly conflicted when she pictured the recipients of those postcards—young wives, mothers, sisters—and the fear and sadness they would have undoubtedly experienced, as well as the poor Japanese soldier reading his own substituted letters, she nonetheless found within herself a sense of accomplishment unlike any she had experienced as a journalist. At first she thought it was the long-awaited chance to be a part of the war effort, but as time went on, she came to recognize it was the act of deception itself which apparently came easily and intuitively to her. On some level she knew she could never return to the person she had been.

SEVEN
RUMORS
AND THREATS

Tell the story casually, and don't give yourself away
by being overanxious to launch your rumor.
—Morale Operations Handbook

Almost every propaganda scheme built on rumor, and Betty's rumor of choice was "War with Russia," as in a second Russo-Japanese war. She gleaned from some of Willie's captured diaries the IJA soldiers' inordinate fear of the specter of hordes of Russian cossacks pouring down through Manchuria, eager to exact revenge for the humiliations of 1905. The Russians had thought the 1905 conflict was going to be, for them, a "Small Victorious War,"[1] but they had lost miserably, and decades later, scared Japanese soldiers in the jungle, hearing of their predecessors' victories but not seeing them, found the idea of vengeful Russians coming from the north to be unsettling at the very least. Japanese POWs had confirmed for their Allied interrogators the very real fear that if Germany fell, Russia would invade. Betty conjured up an "Open Letter to Japanese Soldiers," authored by the fictitious Shugi Watanabe.

1. The Soviets are massing troops on the border, extending railroads, lengthening bomber bases in the Maritime Provinces.
2. Their leader, Marshal Blucher, is anti-Japanese and eager for another No Mon Hon Incident.

3. Japanese troops on border are becoming corrupt and out of "fighting practice."

4. Russia will declare war as soon as Germany falls.

5. We Japanese Communists—some 300,000 strong—are trying to reach soldiers to the south to warn of the coming threat to Japan.

 You must know that the homeland faces destruction, like the cities of Germany, with militant Russia massing on the northern borders, ready to avenge the Russo-Japanese War, England and America fleets poised with air arms to strike at Japan from the Philippines and South East Asia. What, then, is to be done?[2]

As a matter of course, the Japanese were known to dismiss "Red" propaganda as quickly as Allied, but Betty had faith in her scenario in this case. The Japanese Communist Party had been the only political party in Japan to openly oppose involvement in the war, although it did so as an entity that had been outlawed since 1922.

The best lies are built around a grain of truth—a lesson from MO School—and the truth was it was getting harder and harder for the Imperial Japanese government to mislead the civilian population. The Marianas Islands had been retaken, primarily to provide a base of operations for the new B-29 Superfortress heavy bombers, poised within striking distance of the heart of Japan. India- and China-based B-29s of the 20th Bomber Command were now hitting industrial targets in Japan, constrained only by how much fuel could be gotten over the stretch of the Himalayas known as the Hump. American forces were preparing to renew the offensive in northern Burma before the end of the year.[3] If the Japanese government was still denying the obvious presence of Allied bombers, perhaps it was time to believe someone else.

The government-controlled press in Japan could not deny the bombing but always identified the targets as hospitals and schools. Rumors were taking the place of information. It was common belief that if the Americans were victorious, they would prevent the birth of Japanese babies by castrating all Japanese men or sending them to exile on distant islands. The former U.S. ambassador to Japan was widely and falsely quoted as saying, "The only good way to deal with the Japanese was to kill them."[4]

Hideki Tojo lost his hold on power after the loss of Saipan. At its peak his control over the Japanese people rivaled Hitler's over Germans; not only had he become prime minister in October 1941, he also held the posts of minister of war, home minister, and foreign minister simultaneously. In February 1944 he added commander in chief of the General Staff to his responsibilities. His July resignation gave the MO team an opportunity to take advantage of what they hoped was a wave of uncertainty rolling across the Japanese home islands and through the ranks of the IJA and IJN.

In addition to "War with Russia" rumormongering, Betty was further convinced of one sure bet: superstition. Bill Magistretti was in complete agreement. The Japanese took prognostication seriously, and OSS intelligence knew the value of a well-placed astrological prediction or explanation of events. As the war progressed, more and more diaries were captured in the Pacific, and these logs painted a vibrant relationship between the Japanese soldier and the spirit world.[5] Many believed those who died in "special attacks," such as kamikaze or suicidal efforts, continued to live invisibly all around them in a spiritual form. Lafcadio Hearn had written eloquently, "The dead never die utterly. They sleep in the darkest cells of tired hearts and busy brains—to be startled at the rarest moments only by the echo of some voice that recalls their past."[6]

Betty created a Hindu sage, the illustrious Pundit Inbramunyum Rao of Yokohama, who based his observations on the Panchagrahakuta (combination of five planets). The planets had aligned July 20 and were due to do the same August 18. Swami Rao explained the "conjunction of five planets was a rare and unusual event," and doubly ominous was the occurrence of two such conjunctions in a single year. Appalling disaster was predicted for August 18, when Mars, the planet of aggression, and Rahu, the planet of violence, were in the "evil aspect known as papakarhariyoga which presages military and diplomatic catastrophes for the Axis powers." The malevolent rays were to fall especially hard on military leaders, particularly naval commanders, Leo being in the house of the sun, the ruler of Japan. Evil aspects were drawn to this sign magnetically and threatened Japan with disaster. "He who is forewarned is forearmed. Therefore let Japan's leaders take warning from the heavens and prepare against the impending disasters and catastrophes."[7]

Back in Washington, Ruth Benedict lectured that Japanese POWs strongly believed that even if Japan were bombed, the country would not be weakened "because they were forewarned." If the leadership warns the people that they will be invaded, then this knowledge cannot but work in their favor, and the invasion will be seen as the result of "actively [pulling] the enemy toward us."[8]

Conversely, if the military does not forewarn the people about a catastrophic event, then the event is not only a disaster but a betrayal. This message underlay the prognostications of Mr. Inbramunyum Rao of Yokohama. His news should have been well-known and official, not available only through the Hindu Protective Society of Japan, which published the horoscope as a warning to Japanese. Mr. Rao warned that "care must be taken to protect the people in the homeland from disasters such as earthquakes and tidal waves."[9]

Mr. Inbramunyum Rao was such a hit around the office Betty and her colleagues decided to conjure up a genuinely Japanese Nostradamus: Tsunekichi Watanabe. Watanabe was not only a clairvoyant but a thorn in the side of the *kempei tai*. His career began with a faked article in a faked Hong Kong newspaper. "Watanabe, Traitorous Japanese, Catspaw of Enemy" details his apprehension by authorities who uncovered an "insidious plot, [the 'truth'] in which a Japanese traitor was a catspaw for vile communistic and British-American propaganda." The public was warned to be eternally vigilant against such British-American "thought stratagems" as those promulgated by scoundrels like Watanabe and to recognize certain predictions as being "so obviously ridiculous that any Japanese would only laugh at" them. For example,

> Because the enemy has superior material and wealth, I predict that they will retake Guam by next October, and will send our fleet to home waters by a route that will never be reported to the Japanese press.
>
> Formosa will be bombed next fall from land and sea and, according to my calculations, the Americans will be able to build a fleet twenty times as large as the Imperial navy by next November. They will attack Japan with fleets of planes day and night by the end of this year.[10]

The article continued, "A series of leaflets, crudely printed, but well-written" were discovered hidden under a board in Watanabe's room, along with a makeshift printing press. His young accomplice, Sabu Ito, managed to elude police (and was thus free to wage MO warfare when it was least expected). The Hong Kong paper was backdated to January 1944, allowing plenty of time for Watanabe's "predictions" to play out.

Mr. Inbramunyum Rao and Tsunekichi Watanabe, along with his sidekick the young Sabu Ito, all remained mute, their voices shut away in a file cabinet in the MO office at 32 Feroz Shah Road because MO Delhi continued to work with no printing press. The thrilling start of Operation Black Mail gave way to a tedious plateau of procurement issues and evaluation of confusing intelligence from multiple sources, including eight operatives in the field. Betty was receiving her own intelligence and keeping Major Willie Clark on retainer by funneling her cigarette ration to him. For every delivery of Lucky Strikes without a quid pro quo from Willie, he owed her more and more. She was gracious—he was a friend after all—but kept a balance sheet in her head, hedging against the day she would need to call in some chits from that particular cousin. Her source from the field was Charles Fenn, the free-ranging OSS Marine who prowled through Burma and into China, gathering intelligence for Claire Chennault as well as Betty and black propaganda teams throughout the theater. When a packet from Fenn arrived, the little MO group in Delhi huddled over it as though a gift had dropped from heaven.

Fenn was sending back information and implementing MO schemes from the field in support of Detachment 101 military operations. As an OSS operative, he carried orders from the Navy giving him clearance to travel wherever his duties required, allowing him to roam and take jaunts outside any local chain of command. In June 1944 he was sent to China, where he met up with General Chennault, whom he had known when he was a journalist covering China for the Associated Press. Chennault was keen to have MO agents provide his pilots with psychological briefings concerning the people they would be bombing. After the Japanese drive across southeastern China from Hankow to Canton, it became temporarily impossible for Fenn to use Chinese agents, and so he was left to work alone, spreading rumors to counteract deceptions planted by the Japanese in advance of their campaign. In addition to this dangerous work of fighting lies with lies, Chennault urged Fenn to conduct SI and provide target information, details on Japanese troop movements and order of battle, and most important, weather conditions. Eventually Fenn was able to establish an extensive Chinese agent network to conduct his MO rumor campaigns and gather the necessary intel for Chennault.[11] Fenn was a one-man OSS super-agent.

Allied propaganda relied heavily on leaflets, and MO in CBI eventually generated many, many leaflets. But radio was considered the very best way to promulgate rumor and misinformation, and so Betty and Jane continued writing scripts for Alex. Jane had spent a great deal of time mulling over all possibilities, sanctioned and unsanctioned (by Washington), before she crafted her scripts. She sat at her desk trying not to be distracted by surrounding conversations, clattering typewriters, and the ever-present construction coolies whose habit was to stand at the window and stare at her until she chased them away.

Some days Jane found herself incapable of producing anything at all and resorted to cheering herself up by consorting with the British. They adored her wit and welcomed her as the only American allowed into their Shakespeare theatrical group.[12] She also enjoyed the pleasant diversion of wrangling dinner invitations from Mountbatten's staff. Coexisting with the British was dicey, but Lord Mountbatten charmed everyone, spreading oil on the waters with his cheery elegance and extravagance. At the Queen's Hotel, Jane and the others came to accept a lack of running water, the ever-present roaches, tarantulas, and occasional cobras.

Jane was grateful to be awakened each morning by a Singhalese boy with tea and hot water for her wash basin.[13] The constant difficulty Jane encountered in getting her material to target was more troubling to her than tarantulas or cobras. She had been recruited to OSS MO as a specialist in Malaya, Indonesia, and Indochina, only to learn no OSS agent networks existed in those places and precious few operated in China. Neither the British nor Chiang were keen on OSS networks, as they were well aware of American sympathies for most anyone looking for independence or, in the case of China's Communists, governmental control. She could possibly seek the help of the four hundred or so coast watchers, mostly Australian military officers, New Zealand servicemen, Pacific islanders, or former plantation owners and ex-colonial officials who had stayed behind in the hills after Japanese occupation. They were now equipped with air-dropped radios and reported on Japanese movements and air operations. But the coast watchers reported to MacArthur in Australia, and MacArthur did not share his intel with Donovan's people.[14] The British and Chinese had only intermittent contact with sketchy sources in Thailand and Malaya.[15] Gregory tried to locate an old friend in Malaya to gather intel for Jane. He had no luck but did learn about a couple of Chinese organizations: a Malayan leftist organization and a group belonging to Chiang's spymaster, Tai Li. Both were anti-Japanese but were at present more engaged in fighting each other.[16]

At this point Gregory, who continued to wander around a bit dazed and lost in his own thoughts, his tropical knee-high socks perpetually drooped in a puddle around his ankles, was the subject of a flurry of paperwork between OSS and the U.S. Draft Deferment Committee. When Gregory received his orders to India, Donovan expended a great deal of effort extracting a passport from the State Department for him and a permit from the local board of the Selective

Service Committee for Gregory to leave the country. Now it was necessary to extend the anthropologist's permit. Gregory ran afoul of a formidable woman whom he had never met—Mrs. Ruth Shipley, the Cerberus of Passport Control. Historian Richard Harris Smith later wrote of Mrs. Shipley: "She ran State's passport division as her own personal empire [and] insisted that Donovan's agents travel abroad with their passports clearly marked *OSS*. It took considerable discussion at high levels to convince State that clandestine operations were simply incompatible with Mrs. Shipley's whims."[17]

When Gregory first shipped out, Donovan's office patiently explained to the local draft board, which in turn had been stonewalled by Mrs. Shipley, "We desire to send Mr. Bateson abroad to perform important confidential duties for this agency. The confidential nature of this work makes it impossible for us to disclose his destination at this time." At some point the required permit was issued, but getting it extended after it expired on June 27, 1944, set off a Kafkaesque bureaucratic firestorm, one that was oft-repeated throughout the life of Donovan's secret agency. The draft board informed OSS, "Inasmuch as this agency has no means of knowing when and if an employee returns to this country before the expiration date of his Permit, the responsibility for requesting an extension must necessarily rest with the Branch."[18] The back-and-forth continued for some time, as OSS fought to keep clandestine agents like Gregory legally deployed.

Meanwhile, there were file cabinets of rumors waiting to be circulated:

- Ba Maw's visit to Tokyo has convinced the Japanese that Burma is well able to stand on her own two feet; therefore, the Japanese Army is retiring from Burma to protect the homeland from invasion.
- The Burmese National Women's Corps is being used as an organization of prostitutes for the convenience of Japanese military personnel, and a number of unmarried women of this organization are already pregnant.
- Members of the Burmese Independence Army have protested against the Japanese use of temple compounds for their own ends. The Japanese feared a revolt and with desertions increasing have disarmed most of the army and broken it into small units.
- A former laundry building on the east side of L'Kemmedine Road across from Ahlone Station is the storage place of Japanese explosives that will be used to raze the city.

- Several village headmen have gained rewards and good treatment for their villages by turning over to the Allies Japanese deserters who were passing as Burmans and living in the hills with Burmese women.
- The American-British forces are being very lenient for the acts of a few Burmans, and they are not blaming Burmans who were compelled to work for the Japanese. Even some of the early traitors who switched to the Allied cause are receiving fair treatment.[19]

Much of the material waiting to be sent to the field had been developed by Dr. Ina Telberg, one of the experts who had given MO training lectures in Washington. She occupied the position of desk chief in Calcutta and was considered the brains of many an operation. Her analysis of intelligence was incisive, and she was especially adept at providing specific targets for poison-pen letters, false orders, and rumors. She also divided her time between Calcutta and Kandy and was constructing a brilliantly deadly project to besmirch the reputation of Prince Fumimaro Konoye.

Konoye was highly respected by the people of Japan, had been prime minister, was a confidant of the emperor, and had been instrumental in Tojo's resignation. He held to paternalistic samurai values and was considered a "pillar of strength, wisdom, patriotism, and irreproachability." Damaging his reputation could, Telberg believed, inflict a grievous blow to the morale of all Japanese. She planned to use black newspapers and rumor to cast him in the role of someone attempting to "wriggle out of responsibility" for Japan's stalled progress in the war. She wanted materials disseminated to associations and societies in Thailand and Malaya that she believed held vast numbers of civilian and military Japanese. Intelligence identified these groups as chosen for fifth-columnist "stay-behinds" once the Allies reoccupied both nations.[20]

MO relied on military intelligence and R&A assessments for the rumor campaigns but often tried to work off what OWI was putting out as factual news. Extracting useful news stories from OWI, however, could be more difficult than dealing with the British. Enmity between the two organizations ebbed and flowed with the OSS-OWI feuds in Washington and the degree to which field stations were in contact with their respective D.C. headquarters. Left to their own devices in the field, OWI writers, MO black propagandists, and British of every ilk could be friends, so long as the relationships remained clandestine.

EIGHT

LAYING DOWN
THE SWORD

A Japanese soldier should not surrender. Even if he were
taken prisoner when he was wounded and unconscious,
he could not hold up his head in Japan again;
he was disgraced; he was "dead" to his former life.

—*Ruth Benedict,* The Chrysanthemum and the Sword

It was August 1944, and the snake charmers of Delhi were out in force, sharing crowded street corners with beggars and burning braziers. Betty carried the taste of Delhi in the dust between her teeth and was struggling to accustom herself to the smells. Bouncing over the Jumna River in the back of a bicycle rickshaw, she gazed down at hundreds of dhobis, the clothes washers, standing in shallow water, the sound of garments slapping against flat rocks like scattered applause. Horses, bullocks, and water buffalo shared the river with splashing children, all seeking relief from the heat. Her trip to the market for Christmas gifts had been a success, and she was hopeful the leather goods and trinkets might reach her parents by December. It was nice to be alone in her room that evening. Writing home was a respite from endless, albeit pleasurable, rounds of tennis, dancing, and cocktails with the British.[1]

Her letter was filled with the best of India—hibiscus, gaily dressed natives, kites, and the sound of tonga bells—but did not mention the storm clouds of

famine gathering over the country and the undercurrents of fear and desperation. Two nights earlier, an OSS Operations Group (OG) man had insisted on
walking her home from the Gymkhana Club, and the next day he stopped by
her office with a loaded .38-caliber pistol. "Take this with you when you go out
at night," he said. She hefted the gun and looked at him. OG guys were not to
be trifled with. Serious and mysterious, they were always in some version of a
uniform, always poised to disappear for weeks at a time, which they often did.
Being around an OG was humbling. While she schemed at her desk to strike
fear into the heart of a Japanese soldier, the OG guys were moving through the
woods with Naga headhunters, bringing real fear, the kind no forged missive or
well-phrased pamphlet could begin to match. While she swatted tennis balls after
work, the OGs were planting explosives and eating bugs. At least that is how
she imagined it. So now she did not try to explain that her evening clutch could
not possibly hold such a thing as a .38, and he did not ask. Instead, he took her
down to the river for some practice. It took a while, but he was at last convinced
she could hit the side of a building, with enough focus. He walked her home,
and she never saw him again, which was probably good, because getting ready
for evening engagements always presented the same dilemma: the gun fit in her
beaded evening bag only if she jettisoned the compact and lipstick. So the gun
remained in her lingerie drawer. Every time.

One steamy morning Severyns handed Betty a sheaf of intel intercepts,
topped by a military order from the Japanese High Command describing dire
punishments to be inflicted on any soldier who surrendered in battle. Then there
was a morale report on the 18th Division in Burma, highlighting bad food,
depleted medical supplies, and the lack of mail or news from home. The resignation of Hideki Tojo was included with no explanation for Imperial troops eager
for news about the progress of the war. Betty mulled the possibilities. Perhaps a
single forged order, an official one, could suggest there had been a softening shift
in Tokyo's position on surrender.

"Washington still thinks Japanese troops in the field aren't a promising target for psychological warfare, and especially when it comes to surrender inducements," said Bill, sipping his tea.

"They are wrong," Betty stated flatly. "And besides, what is it we're doing
here anyway?"

"We're here because Donovan thinks the way you do," said Severyns. Betty
was alarmed. Severyns rarely supported her.

They began to review the whole surrender inducement idea. In addition to the Japanese soldier's adherence to obedience and abhorrence of disgrace, there remained a simple and increasingly well-known truth: in Asia and the Pacific, surrender was not a good idea for either side. Japanese fighting men often preferred death to surrender owing not just to pressure from their own side but also to the Allied disinclination to take prisoners.[2] Captured documents from Tarawa told of IJA soldiers attempting to surrender only to be mowed down mercilessly by Allied forces. Adm. William Halsey Jr.'s motto echoed across the Pacific islands and Asia: "Kill Japs, Kill Japs, Kill More Japs." Halsey was calling for "total elimination of the Japanese race," words the *kempei tai* repeated over and over in their propaganda. Allied men themselves did not surrender voluntarily, owing to the "kill or be killed" nature of combat, especially in the Pacific. There were frequent chilling reports of Japanese soldiers engaging in frenzied, ritualized dances in the line of fire, screaming both the emperor's name and outlandish phrases in English. The Japanese also booby-trapped the dead and made fake offers to surrender to lure American troops close enough for ambush. The escalating frequency of real and imagined battlefield atrocities on both sides presumably made the idea of surrender incredulous to a Japanese soldier.[3]

Betty did not believe all of this, at least not in its entirety. Bill shared her skepticism. Unlike the rest of the crew, the two of them had lived with Japanese, immersed themselves in the gentle rhythms of koi ponds and tea ceremonies, polished floors, and the almost silent sound of a shoji opening onto a garden. Betty could close her eyes and smell the peonies growing in Dr. Watanabe's garden, see the practiced hands of Mrs. Watanabe as she served their tea, hear their voices, never raised in anger. She knew every Japanese soldier, on some level, possessed a deep desire to return to his own version of that life. She just had to make him believe it was possible.

The British, on the other hand, had heard shrieks of banzai and had heard of men, women, and children bound and bayonetted in the occupation of Hong Kong. They had heard of decapitations and captured British and Dutch civilians doused with gasoline and set on fire. After at first dismissing Betty's musings, over the weeks the cousins began to grudgingly admit that their own perceptions, however grounded in reality, were stymying attempts to target either the Burmese or the Japanese. To them, the Japanese were brutal, invincible, inhuman beasts, and the Burmese were, well, worthless. British aspirations vis-à-vis Burma before the war focused almost entirely on making money from teak and oil, with precious little sympathy for any desire on the part of the Burmese to control their own economy, let alone their destiny.

The British began listening to Betty, finding themselves left with little choice when she talked shop on the dance floor or over cocktails. She wore them down, and despite themselves they began seeing the enemy as human beings. This helped them really see the target: one with pressure points of homesickness, hunger, resentment, fatigue, bitterness, even hopelessness.

As Severyns and Bill drifted off for more tea, Betty gazed out her window thinking back to a lecture in Washington the past spring. Standing at the head of an impromptu classroom in Que, Ruth Benedict told the assorted group of MO, R&A, and some shifty-looking SO men that for all the psychological pressures to avoid surrender, the Japanese soldier was even more conditioned to acceptance of authority.[4] Betty pulled her MO training notes out of a drawer and spent the rest of the day rereading them.

"Japs know their place," she shouted to Bill later that evening on the tennis court of the Gymkhana Club, causing him to overshoot his serve. "Orders from above trump everything. If a Jap is ordered to surrender, he will!" Knowing himself when to surrender, Bill declared her the winner of the set and led the way court side for gin tonics.

"There's another dimension here," he said. "The Jap soldier believes with his whole heart that to be disgraced by surrender is to be dead to his former life, never able to return to those he loves. To do so would disgrace them as well as himself. So getting home to tea with the family would not be part of the equation."

"It would be, if he were ordered to surrender," she insisted stubbornly. "Following orders, no disgrace."

"It would have to be an official order," he countered, "perfect in every detail. Any Jap field commander receiving such a thing will be incredulous, suspicious, disbelieving. We'd have to find a willing Jap, an officer, who could help us get it right. They don't exist."

"But they do," she said.

"Where?" he asked.

"I don't know," she admitted, "but they're out there." Whipping her notebook out of her bag, she read from her lecture notes. "When a Japanese was captured, the rules of life as they had known them were meaningless," she began. Bill settled back in his chair, thankful for the gin. "Benedict actually interrogated captured Japanese, Bill. They couldn't imagine returning to their homeland, no matter how the war ended. Some begged instead to be killed. One Japanese prisoner, having done that, announced, 'but if your customs do not permit this, I will be a model prisoner.' And he was better than model, and he wasn't the only one! They actually did things like revealing the location of ammunition dumps, remembering the most recent order of battle, even flying with bombing pilots to guide them to targets. Benedict had said, 'It was as if they had turned over a new page; what was written on the new page was opposite of what was written on the old, but they spoke the lines with the same faithfulness.'"[5]

In fact, even as Betty and Bill were sipping their cocktails, ten Japanese soldiers in southern Burma allowed themselves to be taken alive as prisoners, the first time for such a significant number. Before the end of the war, reports from all theaters would show the Japanese prisoner to be as cooperative as any European, and in fact to an even more extraordinary degree. Japanese POWs gave up military information, described the morale in their units, critiqued pamphlets and offered genuine corrections, made broadcasts, and even returned to their own lines to persuade their comrades in isolated units to surrender.[6]

Much of this was not known in 1944, and military experts were slow to get on board with the new thinking. Attitudes within SEAC and among theater commanders, along with the rest of the shifting chain of command in CBI, ranged across a spectrum. Publicly the Navy believed that the Japanese soldier could not be compelled, cajoled, or tricked into surrendering. Capt. Ellis Zacharias in the Navy Department wrote to the JCS that "the Japanese never surrender." Some in G-2 (Army Intelligence) argued conversely that the Japanese did surrender from time to time in the Russo-Japanese War.[7]

Betty sat at her typewriter and thought, "Who in northern Burma would know what sort of policy Kuniaki Koiso might have on surrender?" Perhaps he might favor the policy of conserving Japanese manhood for the hundred-year war ahead—the war the Japanese propagandists were promising in order to establish their Greater East Asia Co-Prosperity Sphere. Betty began typing a forged message from the Japanese government to the military high command in Rangoon and orders to distribute the message to all forward units. Old lists of penalties for surrender were thereby rescinded. "Henceforth, under certain stringent conditions—when soldiers were hopelessly outnumbered in battle, unconscious, too ill to fight or without further ammunition," surrender would no longer be considered a disgrace. The soldier should, in this extreme case, demand fair treatment as guaranteed by the Geneva Convention.[8]

Geography, among other things, continued to work against the Japanese. The field of battle was shifting from hilltops and jungle valleys to relatively level ground, where British tanks could gain the advantage. War in the Philippines and tension in China meant a continual withdrawal of IJA troops from Burma, further eroding the morale of those remaining. Stragglers lagged behind their units. The daily ration of rice was reduced to an eighth of that necessary to fuel even a minimal level of energy and focus. It is virtually impossible to "live off the land" in the jungle, which will not sustain a traveling human. The postwar account of a coast watcher in the Pacific reads, "The jungle is, in effect, a desert. At its best, the food the jungle can supply is only enough to sustain life, and under a prolonged diet of jungle food, mental and physical vigor decline until there is no ability to do more than barely support life itself. Even natives cannot live indefinitely on jungle products only, but rely on cultivated foods."[9]

Since the beginning of the retreat from India, there had been a shift into *jikatsu risen* mode—subsisting and fighting on one's own, giving up all expectation of support from Japan. To make things more desperate, Burmese collaborators were switching sides. The daily harassing presence of Allied Spitfires and bombers overhead made the successes of the British obvious. Retaining the hearts and minds of the Burmese, so recently accomplished with the enticement of independence, was a battle the Japanese were rapidly losing in the face of Allied reoccupation.

The search for a model, ready-to-turn Japanese prisoner—one who could not only write but write beautifully in the kanji *grass* style—meant a trip to the Red Fort. The Red Fort, located in the center of Delhi, housed the Combined Services Detailed Interrogation Center (CSDIC) and the Intelligence Bureau, both British. The interrogation of Japanese POWs had garnered the attention of Lord Mountbatten, who hoped for information on Allied prisoners. He visited one interrogation at the Red Fort and was amazed at the way the Japanese "readily, and indeed willingly, and almost enthusiastically, give away information on any point about which they are asked. . . . It appears that they can in no circumstances bear solitary confinement. 24 hours is enough to reduce the strongest Jap to tears."[10]

As a major drove Betty and Bill the seven miles to the Red Fort in his jeep, Betty felt centuries slipping away. She wrote later, "The old city seemed to effervesce, like a colorful composition of cellular activity under a microscope, and vibrate with dirt and smells and people who were going about their work unmindful of the war and foreigners who had brought it." The streets of ancient Chandni Chauk were tunnellike, with upper stories suspended out over the shaded shops below. The Red Fort was indeed red, a massive sandstone, mile-square, walled compound, complete with drawbridge. Within were beautiful marble pavilions and a mosque, all built by Shah Jahan, who also erected the Taj Mahal. These beautiful structures contrasted with drab mud and wood buildings housing the prisoners, yet even those were surrounded by banks of bougain-villea. Interrogators and prisoners walked together amiably, smoking and chat-ting along shaded pathways.

At the Red Fort, Betty, Bill, and the major were directed to a rather sullen Mr. Okamoto, a college-educated prisoner who had reportedly surrendered in disgust at the bungling of the Burma campaigns, which had led to "stupid" loss of life.[11] Okamoto possessed no great love for the Allies or democracy but just wanted to stop the slaughter. Although he had recently begun writing scripts for the All-India OWI radio programs, it was not clear if he would willingly sign on with MO. Betty, Bill, and the major entered his cell, a bare white room, sparsely furnished. The prisoner looked up and stared.

"You're probably the first white woman he's seen in years," the major whis-pered. Betty seriously doubted it. Okamoto stood, looking past her.

"Biru—Biru Magistretti?" He appeared on the verge of choking up. Bill too looked incredulous.

"Okamoto?" Bill asked.

It was a reunion of two old classmates from middle school in Japan.[12] Henceforth Okamoto became part of the MO family in Delhi. He learned fast and pronounced the surrender forgery idea, now designated JB-1, a real possi-bility. Before his surrender he had been assigned to Rangoon headquarters and was familiar with the necessary terminology and format for an official order. The first batch of copy was summarily dismissed as too stiff in translation. He made rapid corrections and then penned the order on a type of blocked paper used in Japanese print shops.[13]

Having obtained a compliant POW, special captured chops, special vegetable dye for the chops, and special rice paper on which to print and having perfected the language of a forgery, the most daunting task remained: for Betty and her team to obtain a press from their British allies.

"Put on lipstick and comb your hair," Bill ordered, "and I'll drive you over to the Council House where you will negotiate the use of Major Bicât's offset press!"

André Bicât had been an artist in peacetime. He convinced his superiors to put him in charge of tactical deception devices and worked out of the former quarters of the Viceroy's Royal Band. His success was such that his efforts resulted in a small network of factories turning out various camouflage devices, including one of his own invention, the Bicât Sausage, a contraption resembling a string of firecrackers with fuse that gave a beautiful imitation of small arms fire. The sausages were used along with dummy parachutists, fire simulators, chemicals reproducing the smell of cordite, and recordings of soldiers' voices. A single sortie by large airplane could drop enough such equipment to simulate a platoon-level firefight lasting up to six hours. Bicât Sausages were used to great effect in a bogus battle on D-day, diverting German troops. Bicât was very proud of his invention.

Approaching the chubby, ruddy-faced major, Betty felt like Theseus in pursuit of the Minotaur, and upon nervous completion of her well-rehearsed pitch, he leaned back in his chair. "You've come to the right place," he said. "His majesty's government pays me to forge documents and passports and odds and ends for those poor blighters they send behind the lines. In my spare time I make dummy paratroopers for deceptive warfare. Have to stuff them myself, it's so frightfully secret."

She handed over all the supplies, and Bicât brought the finished product over a day later. JB-1 was in a heavy envelope covered with red sealing wax and top-secret stamps. The MO crew decided to send up a trial balloon. Willie Clark slipped one of the forgeries into some captured material on its way to a nisei for translation. The boy rushed into the office minutes later exclaiming the presence of a new "surrender policy." It seemed JB-1 was a go.

It was placed in the hands of the first MO team to go into the field in Burma, code-named Gold Dust. The team included five men: a major, an Olympic broad jump medalist, a Seattle attorney, a writer, and an advertising executive—all in all a good representative cross section of OSS MO personnel. Betty later wrote that Gold Dust "roared through New Delhi in a great white heat of enthusiasm. . . . The lads were full of plans." Their field safe—a sort of chuck wagon box holding everything one needed for MO activities in the field—included mobile presses that they used to produce booklets on the Japanese mind and the Burmese mind and sheaves of projects to present to Colonel Peers as an "integrated program." She later learned that when Gold Dust roared into Assam, Peers promptly placed them on Kitchen Patrol (KP) for a cooling-off period.[14]

The question of how to actually plant the forgeries was solved by one of Gold Dust's Burmese agents, a "wiry little killer" who lived among the Japanese in an occupied village and secretly ranged far and wide, picking off Japanese stragglers or messengers. He enjoyed the reputation of single-handedly killing more enemy soldiers than anyone else in the area. Most of his victims were lone couriers, and so Betty plainly stated her request: kill a courier and plant the falsified orders on him so that his comrades will find them with his body. Courier duty in the IJA was hazardous, although it brought a degree of freedom. Couriers, enjoying no protection apart from their rifles, delivered messages between units. Some became veritable wandering ronin (homeless and masterless samurai who roamed the countryside during Japan's feudal years), making their way back to their home unit once a month or so, usually when they were hungry.[15]

The agent later reported the amazement of the Japanese company commander when he discovered the order in his dead courier's pouch back in the village. Encouraged, Betty ordered copies to be air-dropped through the jungles. A copy was mischievously delivered to the rather sanctimonious OWI white propagandists ("we print only the truth"), who followed the advice of their resident warfare psychologists and disseminated photostats of the "captured" order.[16]

Word filtered back from the field: an increasing number of Japanese were reportedly feigning unconsciousness, and a growing number of those captured agreed to let the Red Cross send their names back to Japan. The most gratifying news was that the Japanese who surrendered to Detachment 101 were carrying the leaflets.[17] After only four months in theater, having arrived with tennis balls, evening gowns, and orders to avoid the British, MO CBI seemed to be proving its worth. But as Betty later wrote, "When the man with the military mind hammers on his desk and demands a set of figures to prove what MO did in Burma, no one, not even the Japs themselves, can produce anything concrete for the Washington records." It was impossible to accurately assess the "casualties in thought warfare, and there are no grave crews assigned to count the doubts and troubles planted in men's minds that can make them lose the will to fight."[18]

Summer had begun to wear thin on the crew in Ceylon. No one was feeling very well, probably because they were eating slightly putrid meat. Cora made a flight to Madras to locate books she needed to supplement the two hundred something items in Detachment 404's library, and it was so hot there she spent the entire day barefoot. She arrived home exhausted and took a bath, and as she dried herself off, she wiped a giant cockroach across her face. Later, sitting on the edge of the bed, she opened an envelope and another cockroach dropped onto her thigh. Startled, she tried to slap the beast and succeeded in burying the tip of her fountain pen in her flesh, breaking off the point and covering herself with ink. Then she developed an itch, and her hands inexplicably began to look as if they had been dipped in scalding water.[19]

Paul contemplated the heat and tried to console himself with the idea that it must be hot in Washington too. He imagined Asian elephants having their hides scrubbed in the Potomac. Trips down the mountain to the MO shop in Colombo meant a ten-degree rise in temperature and unpredictable monsoon tempests, with slashing rain and howling winds. The ground in Colombo was regularly covered with palm branches, leaves, flowers, mud, and tree limbs. Tiles often flew off roofs.

Gregory proposed to Paul a crocodile-hunting expedition based on an experience in Sumatra. Being English, Gregory insisted on a technique giving both hunted and hunter a sporting chance:

> First one locates a muddy river infested with crocodiles, but the river must be shallow and not too wide. One then cuts enough bamboo pickets to form a palisade across the stream below where the crocodiles infest it. Next a floating island of grass sufficient to sustain one's weight is assembled. After removing one's boots one steps onto the island and allows the current to drift him down over the crocodiles. I must warn you, too, that if one is right-handed one must be sure to hold his Leica in his left hand, and the spear in his right or he may find himself, as I once did, trying to tickle the wretched beast with a camera. . . . A gun would be too beastly abrupt, my dear chap, and one can scarcely record the action without a camera, and how is one to know when he is over a crocodile unless he can feel it through the grass into his bare feet. . . . One then tickles him with a spear by plunging it down between ones feet. This causes him to thrust up his snout through the grass at which one nooses with a string.[20]

Gregory found no takers for his expedition.

Paul and Jane found the ever-present native workmen increasingly annoying. They gathered in silent groups and stared in the windows at the Americans, as though watching a movie. "As there is apparently no tradition of *not* staring, they all do it," Paul wrote to his brother. "They just stand there for ten or fifteen minutes, five to a window, stinking like weasels, staring and staring."

Paul came up with the idea of pretending they were Japanese agents and proposed to design and have built a special "spy" entrance for each building to make it easier for them to go in and out. Each "agent" would then be presented with a tin Rising Sun engraved in Singhalese: "Me Japanese Spy—you giving information please. Banzai!" When Paul realized even the Detachment 404 GIs were bored, he initiated a morale-building campaign and began giving judo lessons, even though the only exercise he had engaged in for almost a year had been riding a bicycle in Delhi.[21] Jane's contribution to the campaign was a spectacular pinup mural in the GI mess.

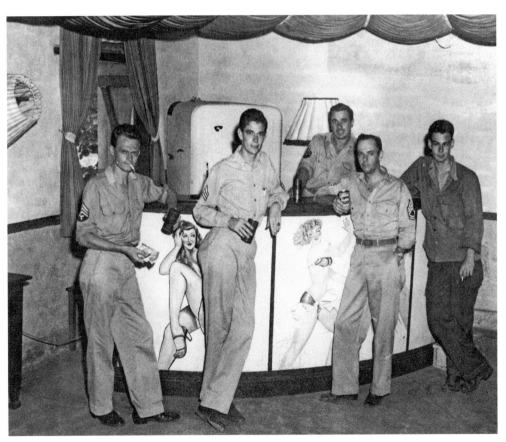

Enlisted personnel canteen in Kandy, Ceylon, with artistic contributions by Jane Foster
National Archives and Records Administration II, College Park, Maryland

In Delhi, Severyns was struck with a nasty case of amoebic dysentery and was removed to the hospital. Betty had recently endured her own three-day bout with Delhi belly and was tired, but she accepted a dinner invitation from General Fong, one of Chiang Kai-shek's visiting contingent from Chungking. The general speculated that postwar China would be faced with the possibility of an "American form of communism" but did not further elaborate on what Betty thought was an oxymoron. Instead, he bestowed on her a Chinese name, Bei Ti, a play on words meaning beautiful American. It was a rare night that a dinner invitation from visiting generals or foreign correspondents did not present itself, but the girl shortage was beginning to lose its charm. Betty determined to take a hiatus from partying that very night and turn in early.

NINE
A WOMAN IN
CHARGE

If your opponent is of choleric temper, try to irritate him.
If he is arrogant try to encourage his egotism.
If the enemy troops are well prepared after reorganization,
try to wear them down. If they are united,
try to sow dissension among them.

—*General Tao Hanzhang, Sun Tzu's* The Art of War

The fall of 1944 brought Capt. Oliver J. Caldwell to 32 Feroz Shah Road. Caldwell was an old China hand, or at least he was the child of missionaries who also had commercial interests in the land they loved. He had been born in China and was teaching at a university in Nanking when the Japanese made their major incursion in 1937. He eventually sent his family to the United States and tried to continue conducting classes, but at some point after Japan brought the war to America, Caldwell volunteered for Army service. He was thirty-nine years old and on his way to serve under Gen. Joseph Stilwell as a civil affairs officer. When Stilwell did not claim him, Caldwell found himself attached to OSS: yet another misfit with valuable gifts and graces to offer Donovan's family.[1]

Caldwell quickly took stock of the situation in which he found himself: "Much of the work was done at cocktail parties. Command responsibility was supposed to be given to the most competent person available for a particular job without regard to rank or other mundane considerations."[2] Having clear conceptions of his own place in the order of things, he placed himself in charge of the extremely competent women who had been carrying on quite nicely without him. Of Betty, Severyns, Joy Homer, and the others, he wrote, "My seven lionesses were nice girls, individually. Three of them were brilliant . . . [but] . . . none of them had any experience in psychological warfare, and therefore should never have been assigned to MO in India or anywhere else."[3] His lionesses studiously ignored him.

"Oliver was never in charge of anything," Betty stated flatly, many years later. "He was a *schnook*."[4] In fact, personnel records do not show him, in all his twenty-two months of questionable service to OSS, to have held any leadership position, at least not having to do with MO. He did, however, put himself forward for a Bronze Star in October 1945, for serving in the following campaigns: "China Defense" and "China Offense."[5] Captain Caldwell, having settled in among his lionesses, began poaching the local peacocks for his Saturday night formal dinners. In general he considered himself greatly burdened by the surrounding contingent of women, all of whom he felt to be "an intolerable obstacle to discipline." "I certainly did not fit in well with my young lionesses, their friends, and the savage intrigues in the headquarters of a large wartime army. I decided to do my best to help the colonel by bringing order out of the glorified cat fight which I had inherited from him. I hope we did do a few things while I was in charge."[6]

It was not long before the tide of war came and took Oliver away. No one knew exactly when it happened. Word was he was on his way to China, with big plans to lead Operation Yak, a daring MO infiltration of Tibet to counteract the "false Buddhism" being spread by the Japanese. As far as Betty knew, OSS had nary a recruit who spoke Tibetan, but she wished him well.[7]

Soon after Captain Caldwell left for what may or may not have been Tibet, Betty learned she had been appointed to fill the vacant position of Acting Head, MO CBI, until a more suitable (male) chief could be shipped from Washington. Grace Tulley, the secretary, read the special memorandum to her. Although acting chiefs had come and gone in SEAC and China, never had there been one for the entire theater. Betty's staff comprised the same people with whom she had been working, and no one, not even Angel Puss, seemed aware of her new title.[8]

In September 1944 MO Delhi sent a report of "outstanding achievements" to Washington:

1. Obtained use of British press facilities in Calcutta through Major Peter Glemser.
2. Indoctrinated four missionaries en route for China MO.
3. Produced three forged newspaper clippings; inserted faked Tokyo bomb-damage photographs in Jap soldier mail.[9]

Betty considered the winning over of Glemser a tactical victory for MO. Both the British and Americans considered him difficult. He was rumored to want to integrate British and American psywar efforts with the aim of furthering British postwar aims, or at least that is what the State Department believed. As always, MO Delhi needed more equipment to carry on with production. Glemser had it.

In preparation for her confrontation with the difficult major, Betty loaded up on Grace's perfume, put on a dress, clutched her carton of operational cigarettes, and headed over to the Maiden's Hotel. The dreaded Peter Glemser turned out to be a young man with an "elfin" sort of face. He emerged from a swimming pool, threw on a cashmere robe, and led Betty over to a table for sandwiches.

"What do the Americans want now?" he asked. She produced her list, simultaneously sliding the carton of cigarettes in his direction. "Now let me get this straight," he began sarcastically. "You want the use of our press, type, typesetters, translators—possibly our agent net—and in return, what? Your bright ideas?"

Betty bit back any remarks about reverse Lend-Lease and began lying. She described the vast shipment of the latest equipment, "new cameras, fast rotary and offset presses, fonts of Burmese, Siamese, and Japanese type, varitypes, newsprint, technicians, photographic supplies, inks, chemicals," all of which would arrive any day from MO Delhi and, of course, be placed at his disposal. He snagged the carton of cigs, tore it open to remove a pack, and asked just when all this bounty was to arrive. She was quick to assure him it had left the States, but owing to "so much secrecy about shipping," she did not have an estimated arrival time.[10]

True to form, Betty won over the major, and in fact they remained lifelong friends. She left that day with a date to play tennis and his promise to make equipment available. Peter Glemser eventually gave MO extensive help disseminating black propaganda throughout Burma, and Betty did manage to supply him with spare parts for a press, a large paper cutter, newsprint, and ink.

The second "outstanding achievement" was the indoctrination of a small band of missionaries who had arrived along with Oliver Caldwell. They were accompanied by former monk and trainer of Saint Bernards Robert Chappelet, who immediately decided everyone in MO was crazy. They arrived in Delhi with no clue as to their assignments, and when Severyns explained to them as a group what MO was all about, they collectively recoiled, aghast. It became immediately apparent that the missionaries needed to get over their scruples about black propaganda (lies, deceit, etc.), and so Betty and Severyns embarked on their own morale op to convince them. They concocted a document, attributed its "translation" to Bill Magistretti, and slipped it into the missionaries' required indoctrination reading, stamping it "Top Secret" to ensure they read it. This "captured" piece of fiction was supposedly written by Kenji Koinara, the notorious "Japanese Himmler of Occupied China." The Doihara Declaration outlined Koinara's program to "eradicate Christianity in Asia" and replace it with Buddhism for political expediency. Five years of Japanese occupation should "forever stamp Christianity out of China!"[11]

Betty and Severyns were gambling that the Doihara Declaration would be a waving red cape in the face of their target audience. Phase two of the operation involved circulating among the recruits actual intelligence reports about two of OSS's "finest agents of the cloth," Thomas Megan, the "Fighting Bishop of Hunan," and Father James Stuart, a Northern Irish priest who had spent ten years in Burma. Bishop Megan had set up his own intelligence network, supplied information to Tai Li, and been commissioned a colonel in the Chinese army. He became famous as an OSS sharpshooter and traveled by jeep with carbines strapped over his shoulder. He was worshipped by the Kachin mountain peoples, who considered him their own personal pope, and he hated the Japanese with a passion.[12] Father Stuart provided extensive aid to Detachment 101's operations, was not averse to combat in defense of his beloved Kachins, and led hundreds of their family members out from deep behind enemy-occupied territory to the safety of Allied lines.[13]

On October 9, as Acting Head of MO, Betty sent a memo to Detachment 101 proposing a threatening letter to a fictional Burmese headman, promising his imminent demise unless he stopped collaborating with the Japanese. "Attached are 16 blood stained paper notifications," she wrote. "We ran out of blood but I'm sure you can get some for the remainder." The certificates were purported to have been issued to the headmen as a testament to the aid rendered to Imperial forces. She continued,

Our idea is this: age and wrinkle these copies and distribute them to other headmen you wish to intimidate. Attach to the Jap certificates a threatening letter in Burmese, text of which reads thusly:

> To: (choose your name)
> We know you are helping the Japs. We know you carry a certificate saying so. Ritkuemu of Hodo Village (or Redonyemu of Onchyin Village) carried the same kind of certificate. You now hold it in your hand. You see his blood upon it. Unless you stop helping the Japs and refuse to give them food and help, your blood will be spilled as Ritkuemu's was when we cut his throat.[14]

The copies were printed, placed on the floor to be trampled for a day or so, then sent off to Detachment 101. William Peers later reported the messages had reached the hands of the *kempei tai*, with dreadful consequences for the traitor.[15]

When the initial Japanese invasion swept up from Rangoon in 1942, mountain villages were caught in the path of the massive British retreat and then in a tide of Japanese forces. Most of these indigenous people had little use for either side, and so they tended to go with whoever was on top. As the Japanese moved through, those village elders who swore their loyalty as "puppets" saved their lives and those of their people. When Detachment 101 became fully operational and turned its trained native forces back into the jungles of northern Burma, IJA forces were in retreat. Increasingly, the mountain peoples had a choice of three masters: the Japanese, with their bogus offer of coprosperity; the British, with their continued domination, however benevolent; and the American OSS, which seemed intent on actually winning the war and leaving the Kachins, Naga, Karen, and other inhabitants alone to govern themselves.

The choice was complicated by bribery on all sides, but at some point the real war became one of propaganda between empty promises of independence or inclusion in the Great Economic Co-Prosperity Sphere. Most mountain people had as much use for one as the other and were open to alignment with OSS. To win the battle of allegiance and thereby make continued occupation untenable for the enemy, OSS had to win over each village headman. Therefore, although MO continued to focus on demoralizing the Japanese soldier, it increasingly targeted these headmen as well.

Detachment 101 was on the ground in northern Burma and had the benefit of landing amid a needy population facing famine, the British having long since fled. The detachment's short-range penetration, Operation Knothead, greatly facilitated by Father Stuart, arranged for air-drops of rice, fostering much goodwill. Other, more Machiavellian tactics involved operations that caused the Japanese to carry out reprisals on the local population. Such brutality helped the Allied cause and discouraged collaboration with the Japanese.[16]

As Acting Head, Betty immediately pushed for more supplies. Her shop needed so much, starting with presses and Chinese typeface. She appealed to a fellow MO chief, Maj. Harold C. Faxon in China, for the material. He replied that a Mr. Brown of OWI had been able to get what he had needed in Chungking, so Faxon was willing to purchase her Chinese type there. She needed enough lead type for a four-page newspaper. This would weigh anywhere from 4,000 to 30,000 pounds, depending on the dimension of the pages, and was priced by weight: 250 China notes, with an exchange rate of US$1.00 = CN 280. The major shared with her that OWI not only had managed to procure Japanese type of all sizes but had hired a Chinese type cutter for US$1,400 per annum to work the lead into characters. He believed he could make the purchases for her, but the small problem of weight remained, since the material would have to come over the Hump.[17] Recalling sacrificing her dresses in order to make the weight limit in Miami, Betty tried to imagine the face of a transport pilot told he would be carrying 30,000 pounds of lead.

It was amazing what miracles could occur with the acquisition of a title after one's name. Supplies did arrive, and Maj. Harold C. Faxon, MO chief, China Area, turned out to be a helpful colleague with whom to exchange ideas. Someone had translated a Japanese propaganda leaflet for him, which he was sending along to her with the idea of using a reprint to point out how the Japanese army was doing exactly the opposite of what it had promised. This would be the truth, in point of fact, but he proposed making it "black" by having the leaflet purport to come from some fictitious anti-Japanese organization. Did she think they should let the OWI folks have it so they could keep it white?[18]

She did not, and so the Chinese received a flip-side version of the original leaflet. Betty smiled at the image of her counterpart in his Japanese MO shop seeing an edited version of his very own creation. She hoped he would have some grudging professional admiration.

"Sometimes when we got stuff the Japs put out, their propaganda," she remembered later, "I would see how they had bungled something, and just for a minute would imagine that if we could sit down together, I could straighten out his colloquial flubs and he mine, we could share typefaces and give each other the right kind of paper."[19]

By late autumn 1944, the Japanese were on the run all throughout CBI and Pacific theaters. A catastrophic defeat in Leyte Gulf meant their defensive line had pulled back to place Thailand and Malaya on the perimeter. U.S. submarine warfare meant the sea-lanes were closed to IJN supply ships. The Allies had over 1,300 aircraft in Burma while the Japanese were down to 64. In November 1944 the number of boys age 12 to 14 pressed into service in Tokyo reached 700,000; these were the replacements that made it through to Gen. Kimura Kyotara.[20]

The trickle of captured materials turned into a bounty when Japanese troops, turned at Imphal, started heading south across the Chindwin River down the Tiddim Road and jettisoned everything as they went: diaries, postcards, letters from home, family photos, cartoons depicting everyday life in Japan. The Japanese also had the habit of carrying into combat battle plans and marked maps, which when captured gave good indications of order of battle, especially the increasingly dire lack of supplies.[21]

Every Japanese soldier kept a diary. This was part of a long tradition dating from the tenth century, and each soldier and sailor was issued a new diary at the start of every new year. The diaries were inspected by superiors regularly, and so most were filled with patriotic statements and desire for glory in the name of the emperor. British propagandists had given them up as useless and stopped reading them, but Betty was intrigued. She found them increasingly easy to read as time went on, and by the end of 1944, they contained the simply worded musings of schoolchildren, leading her to discern that the IJA had been reduced to conscripting middle-school boys. The diaries' content was more heartfelt as well, describing extreme hardships and containing fewer and fewer references to the emperor. More and more poetry appeared. Now and then a passage, seemingly scribbled in secret, would emerge: "Whenever we make a major deployment, the *kempei tai* come and confiscate our notebooks, so I had to put my poems in my head; I'd write them later." To Betty, the soldiers all seemed to be crying out for their mothers.[22]

Postwar scholars examined many diaries, seeking answers to what motivated the Japanese. Donald Keene observed, "Reading diaries filled with the thoughts of men suffering from hunger and disease convinced me that those who professed to understand the Japanese psychology were grossly mistaken when they said that the Japanese were fanatics devoid of normal human frailty." "We are clearly being pushed back by the enemy," wrote popular novelist Takami Jun in Tokyo. "Why can't they write it plainly and appeal to the people? It's the same old story. That's why people are not taken in by reassuring, deceptive articles. They have learned to read between the lines." To record such sentiments courted danger. The *kempei tai* patrolled neighborhoods, randomly raiding homes and demanding to see all diaries and paperwork. Many Japanese were arrested for "thought crimes."[23]

Betty wrote to her parents that she was very healthy, weighed 125 pounds, was sunburned, and suffered only from the inconvenience of prickly heat and the occasional bout of Delhi belly. She could not remember the last time she put a fresh fruit or vegetable in her mouth, but like everyone else, she was diligent about taking vitamins. The weather had begun to cool, and that was helping very much. Alex arrived for a short visit from Chittagong, sporting a mustache and wearing shorts. Along with Severyns, Betty and Alex attended an arranged marriage engagement party for a nine-year-old boy. The child was dressed in elaborate brocade and had both hands painted cinnabar red. The ceremony, with a blaring brass band, was an explosion of color and sound. Looking like a little prince, the boy was placed on a horse for his ride to the temple.[24]

The day before, Betty and Alex had had dinner with the Maharaja of Givalior, who invited them for a weekend tiger shoot. Betty had no intention of attending, but her husband perked up at the prospect. She and Alex also went Christmas shopping, and the focus on family back home helped alleviate a sudden homesickness that threatened to overtake her. After he had left, she spent an afternoon lovingly wrapping her gifts—Punjabi slippers, an Indian bedspread, a silver pen, and ivory animals for her nieces and nephews—in brightly colored local newsprint. The October deadline for Christmas delivery had passed, but maybe a mail clerk would get in the spirit and send it on through.[25]

The censorship officer was not, as it turned out, in the spirit. He made Betty remove all the wrappings, as well as names on the gifts. He did allow her to explain what went to whom in a letter to be sent separately. None of these procedures made any sense to her at all. She enclosed her own wish list to her mother: stuffed green olives and angostura bitters as wampum for trade with the cousins and Castile soap for herself. Having learned her sister Marj had given birth to Art Jr., she added a baby blanket embroidered in Kashmiri wool, explaining that although it looked rough and primitive, it was actually soft and handwoven.[26]

News came that as CBI continued to fragment between SEAC and China, with Thailand and Indochina floating nearby, Delhi MO operations were moving to Calcutta. Marj Severyns was heading to China, Betty and Bill on to Calcutta. This was not entirely unwelcome news. In Calcutta a real print shop had been rented, equipment was expected weekly, and a team of translators slated to join the team as soon as a secure area had been established for them to live. Peter Glemser was worried about the translator situation. There would be ten issei, six Chinese, and one each Burmese, Thai, Malayan, and Annamite (Vietnamese). Glemser foresaw friction between the nationalities should they be crowded together in close quarters. The floor plans called for all of them to be housed on the second floor, but the Chinese could probably be housed in town since they posed no security risk.[27]

Rosie Frame was also ordered to China; she hoped to be the first girl to fly over the Hump. Betty's orders had her shipping out to Calcutta on January 1 of the new year. Lying on her cot the night before her departure, she looked at the moon through her bamboo shades and grew reflective, imagining that people all over the world were wondering if this new year, 1945, would bring peace.[28]

TEN

ON TO
CALCUTTA

Never before has there been such a predicament.
It is entirely the doing of the military.
Their crimes must be recorded for all time to come.

—*Nagai Kafu, diary entry, December 1944, Tokyo*

Dum Dum Airport in Calcutta was one of the busiest on the planet in 1945. It was the base for the ATC making regular flights over the Hump to Kunming, China, as well as the U.S. 10th Air Force and Eastern Air Command, a combined British-American force. The skies were filled with C-54s, C-47s, Hurricanes, and Spitfires, among others. When Betty arrived there in a C-47, she was disappointed to once again find herself in surroundings devoid of any hint of the exotic Orient. Angel Puss had been bounced from her flight, but a friendly young pilot promised to bring him along on the next one. Passing the ubiquitous Coke machine, she approached a clerk and asked quietly where OSS was located.

"Lady, OSS breaks out all over this city like the measles," he practically shouted.

OSS was variously located in R House, O House, G House, Buffalo House, Communications, the Girls House, and Headquarters.[1] Alex had been part of the advance team in Calcutta, charged with renovating and outfitting R House as MO Central before he transited to Chittagong. A memo from him, addressed to "Darling" Betty, warned of the unfinished state of her new office. Installation of the new facilities had been held up, probably by the British. Walls had been knocked down and new ones put up on the first floor, and wiring snaked everywhere to power the still-missing printing and photographic equipment.[2] As for Calcutta itself, it was a place "needing no war to be devastated" with crushing overpopulation and poverty, a miserable city reminding Alex of a Bruegel painting of hell.[3]

The Girls House was Harrington Mansion, a Victorian apartment house. Barely had Betty begun to unpack in her room when the head servant arrived, glowering darkly.

"Dog come," he announced. Angel Puss had arrived covered with grease, having tried to climb into the engine of the airplane on a layover from Allahabad. The young pilot was out of sorts.

"Traveling with that mutt was worse than leading a raid over Ploesti," he groused. "And as soon as Mahatma here lets us into your apartment the dog ate two love birds off that perch, beaks and all!"[4]

Traversing Calcutta invariably took one down the main thoroughfare. Chowringee Road originated as an ancient path for pilgrims trudging to the Hindu Temple of Kali at Kalighat. The guard shack at the entrance of the top-secret R House was graffitied with chalk: Spies Keep Out. As warned by her husband, Betty found the equipment, which had been damaged in shipping, for the most part nonoperational. The top of the Webendorfer offset press was knocked from the ink-feeding apparatus, and fixing it would require scouring all of India for welders and parts. The only thing working was the multilith press, but its chemicals had spoiled on the Hooghly docks.[5]

The first complete MO staff meeting for Detachment 505 Calcutta took place amid Indian carpenters, painters, and sweepers. Present were Betty; Bill Magistretti; Dr. Ina Telberg, the Russian expert on Japanese order of battle and many other things; Edward Hunter, assistant cable editor of the *New York Post*; Victor Beals, commercial artist; and Jack Gilmore, a former private detective from Denver who had been given the rank of lieutenant and sent to India to spy on the British. It was quickly established that no MO would happen in Calcutta at that moment without the help of the British, who once again had all the operational equipment, along with a net of native agents in place along the Arakan coast of Burma. Most up-to-date workable intelligence would have to come almost entirely from Force 136, an arm of British intelligence combining guerrilla activities, intelligence, and black propaganda operations. The latter function was a bit lacking, however, so Major Glemser more than welcomed a joint effort with the Americans and was glad to be reunited with Betty to resume their games of tennis.

Anxious to get to work creating MO projects for dissemination in Burma, Thailand, and China, Betty fired off a series of letters to her formerly helpful colleague Harold Faxon, Acting MO Chief for China (Detachment 202). Her requests included complete descriptions of agent setups, the extent to which propaganda could be distributed, and the type of material specifically needed for each region. On behalf of her husband, she wanted to know if China MO had sent a series of cartoons into Thailand. She stressed all information would be kept top secret, especially the agent network details.[6] She received a stern refusal. Faxon wrote it was "quite impossible to supply the desired top secret information due to the necessity to maintain the most perfect cover possible for agent activities." Furthermore, Thailand was not considered part of the China theater, and since there were no disseminating facilities, China MO had sent nothing.[7]

Betty turned her attention to a request from Alex to provide Gregory with materials for his Bittersweet operation in support of Detachment 101, specifically her DT-10, a surrender inducement theme, and DT-17, one of her best threat letters targeting Burmese headmen who had been collaborating with the Japanese.[8] In exchange for the Bittersweet materials, Betty wrote Alex, she wanted the kind of information Faxon had told her she could not have.[9] Covering all bases, she also wrote directly to Gregory with the same demand, thereby reinforcing her theater-wide reputation as "indefatigable."[10]

Having sent out her requests for top-secret agent network information, she began another series of requests for samples of Chinese government stationery with letterhead and crest, as well as any stray puppet documents, publications, and forms, in order to build up a library for the production of forgeries and reprints.[11] She also began pestering Washington to send Japanese nisei or issei personnel, particularly typesetters. Lastly, she asked Severyns to find someone, anyone, who could obtain or steal a Japanese cyclostyle unit for Peter Glemser. The Japanese army used a cyclostyle, a mimeograph device with a camera, to copy orders. The orders were then sent to forward areas. Obtaining one would allow virtual foolproof duplication.[12]

꙳

The Arakan was a stretch of coast along the western part of Burma, a thick swamp of mangrove trees infested with gigantic man-eating saltwater crocodiles. The British asked Detachment 101 for help making an amphibious attack there, and in February Detachment 101 Arakan Field Unit commenced Operation Bittersweet. Brainstorming for projects to undercut the *kempei tai* in the Arakan began in earnest at that time. The Go Native Campaign worked off intel reports that Japanese soldiers had begun deserting their units and taking to the hills with local Burmese women, melting into the indigenous population. False surrender orders, increasingly popular, could be inserted into the Japanese telegraph network. For the Good-bye Campaign, a number of agents in Rangoon and other southern cities marked the houses of collaborators with the word "Good-bye" and spread rumors and leaflets expressing various frightening interpretations of the word.[13]

One apparently successful angle was the "devilish trick," as remembered by William Peers, of forging letters in a Japanese soldier's handwriting purporting to be offers to work for the Allies. The letters would then find their way into the hands of the *kempei tai*, and the unfortunate traitor summarily executed.[14]

Conjuring up rumors was challenging. The following were rumors suggested to target the Annamites: Japanese overseers were feeding Annamites working in the mines a new odorless, tasteless stimulant famously used in Germany to keep workers on the job sixteen hours a day, with the unfortunate side effect of sterility. American planes were dropping explosives to Annamite saboteurs, and one hiding place in a mountain contained over three tons of Bastignite, the newest of the plastic group, a single pound of which could level a large house. Japanese officers in Hanoi and other places were printing money and using it to buy up scarce commodities to ship home. The Japanese were rushing construction of airfields to allow for quick escape when the Allies landed, but only high-ranking officers would be allowed to escape by plane. The bodies of three Japanese soldiers were taken from the river below Hanoi, each with a similar red cord tied tightly around his neck.[15]

Bill Magistretti became severely ill with dysentery in January and was ordered stateside to San Francisco. Betty knew she would be bereft without her fellow "Jap lover," whose dry wit made monsoon rains bearable and whose expertise had served as ballast when her ideas became too flighty. He was at once a tonic when her conscience at the pain her black arts were causing began to weigh and a reminder that they were in the long run trying to end the war sooner, saving lives on both sides. Bill continued serving MO in San Francisco, playing a key role in Operation Blossom, which used black radio transmissions. The new Detachment 505 chief, Lt. (jg) James Withrow, had put Magistretti's name in for promotion, but it was kicked back because the lieutenant failed to use the proper theater letterhead.[16]

Meanwhile, Alex submitted an Arakan report filled with insights from the field and suggestions for future MO projects in Burma. His Burmese newspaper, printed in Calcutta, was a big hit and completely accepted as the genuine organ of the Anti-Fascist League. He wanted cartoons to add to the copy. He cited the great value of the few Japanese POWs who had been captured, especially those who could be persuaded to work with the nisei. One POW was so embittered he wanted to "change his nationality."[17]

Alex came through Calcutta full of energy and ideas for MO. He picked up the surrender leaflets from Glemser and arranged for a low-flying Spitfire to let them go in a pinpoint drop over three hundred Japanese trapped outside Ramree Town on the Arakan coast. The leaflets had a safe conduct pass in English and Burmese on one side and on the other a Japanese-language appeal to give themselves up to hasten their country's "rehabilitation." The British, as always, were dubious about the operation, but Alex turned on the charm and persuaded them that they needed more intelligence from prisoners and that the conditions near Ramree were conducive to surrender. He argued for a full field unit and team to be sent down to the Arakan.[18] Orders arrived directing him to proceed to Akyab for the advance on Ramree Island, and when he left, Betty realized they had spent the entire visit talking about black propaganda. Waving him off at the airport was like telling a colleague, "See you later."

The Battle of Ramree Island, fought January and February 1945, provided ample justification for continued MO operations in Burma. Ramree, an island sixty miles long and twenty-five miles wide, was inhabited by a few Burmese and Arakans. It was an important staging area for the Allies to expand into southern Burma and block the road used by Japanese forces to resupply sea routes. Seizing the islands of Akyab, Cheduba, and Ramree would bring Allied air bases within range of Rangoon. British and Raj Indian troops retook the island off the southern coast of Burma after six weeks of fighting a Japanese garrison, a battle often remembered for anecdotal reports of nearly a thousand Japanese soldiers being eaten by the resident saltwater crocodiles. The British trapped the Japanese as they tried to escape to the east, and the Japanese commander elected to make the breakout through ten miles of mangrove swamps. The troops were wounded and diseased going in, and only five hundred emerged on the other side. The story grew with each telling until the enhanced version became "The scattered rifle shots in the pitch-black swamp punctured by the screams of wounded men crushed in the jaws of huge reptiles, and the blurred worrying sound of spinning crocodiles made a cacophony of hell that has rarely been duplicated on earth. At dawn the vultures arrived to clean up what the crocodiles had left. . . . Of about 1,000 Japanese soldiers that entered the swamps of Ramree, only about twenty were left alive."[19]

Historian Frank McLynn could find no surviving veterans on either side who had heard of the "Great Crocodile Massacre," but the story is a case study in how conditions in Burma, real or imagined, became nothing short of nightmarish for the Japanese, making them vulnerable to psychological warfare. Ramree did prove to be a test case for surrender inducement. Alex, Edmond Taylor, and Gregory Bateson were the field MO officers supporting SI and OG teams.[20] First Lt. James Hamilton composed an eight-page summary for the Planning Staff back in Washington in which he dwelled heavily on implications for psychological warfare following Ramree. He had heard various stories of "begging, starving, and thirsty Japs," and this was perhaps the perfect laboratory situation to test some black propaganda ideas, mostly having to do with surrender inducements. Hamilton ordered up some posters and leaflets on the spot, and his efforts were a beautiful example of a project that had been neither defined as an operation nor cleared as such. The lieutenant simply ambushed a British major after several operational drinks and gained permission.

"Hell yes, it probably won't work, but there can be no harm in trying," said the slightly drunk major.

Somewhat sobered the next morning, the major brought the idea to his general. "These Americans have suggested that some Japs might be persuaded to surrender by a leaflet or some-such thing," he said cautiously. The British general was unexpectedly enthused by the idea and skipped his lunch hour to design his own leaflet.

"He was so excited in planning the thing that the Brigade officer didn't get a chance to say OSS had already undertaken to produce posters and leaflets," Hamilton wrote.[21]

The general managed to get his leaflets dropped even before Alex could disperse his. Both batches made their way to the enemy, and on March 13 a small contingent of bedraggled Japanese showed up at the house of a Burmese MO agent to beg for rice. After listening to their hardships, the agent launched a sales pitch describing the good treatment Japanese prisoners were receiving in Ramree Town (no such prisoners existed) and presented them with a leaflet. Additional copies were given to a small boy to pass to more Japanese, and by the next morning, fourteen men and one wounded officer were ready to surrender to a British unit.[22]

William Peers considered the MO surrender campaigns "sophisticated . . . if not Machiavellian," and pronounced the leaflet "authentic enough in tone and appearance to fool a number of Japanese. Following its instructions, they surrendered." He pronounced MO a vital part of the Detachment 101 unconventional warfare effort.[23]

Hamilton agreed with the British when it came to surrender inducements: No need to worry about the soldier's mood and emotions. Convince him of the existence of a much-implemented protocol and suggest that many, many Japanese have already surrendered. If he is going to surrender, he is already in the mood to do so. Give him a specific list of actions to take in order to be safe.[24]

Demoralized Japanese soldiers were still for the most part opting out of surrender, but their growing desperation was reflected by instances of group suicide. In January a cadre walked into the Irawaddy to drown, and in February a troop of fifty survivors of the Battle for Mektila did the same in a nearby lake.[25]

In Calcutta it was decided that someone should head down to Ceylon to "find out how the other half of MO lived." Betty drew the short straw to her intense delight (she later admitted the game was rigged). Her task was to get some coordination going with the group in Kandy. Over the course of a weekend, she was to determine how much actionable intelligence had been extracted from the Brits there and to collect samples of the kind of MO propaganda being sent to Sumatra, Java, and Thailand. This would be the first of several trips. Getting useful intelligence from Ceylon to Calcutta was a persistent problem. For some reason, probably proximity to SEAC and Supremo, Ceylon enjoyed channels of communication seemingly blocked in Calcutta and Delhi. Cora DuBois and Julia McWilliams found it impossible to send bulletins to the staff at Detachment 505, let alone try to include personal letters in mail pouches. People in Calcutta had to travel to Ceylon to get their mail.[26]

Before Betty's departure on her fact-finding trip to Ceylon came a visit from General Donovan and the "Flying Circus," his entourage of branch chiefs from Washington, their aides, and various and sundry Far Eastern theater officers, all fresh from a jaunt through China. This presented the classic challenge: how to look busy when no presses in the press room were operational. Printing MO material was what they were supposed to be all about. What to do? Betty sent a Mayday to Peter Glemser.

"We have the same trouble with our big fellows too," he sympathized. "Always have to dress up the old shop. We lose all sorts of valuable time that way." He offered up his own Sergeant Farnsworth to carry a hand-cranked proof press to R House, and while one person inked the rollers, another could pull off "operation leaflets," which could in fact be anything from a list of the ranking officer's favorite cocktails to the ingredients for a pound cake. Since the leaflets would be in Japanese, no one would know the better.[27]

It was a good plan. Essential to the plan, however, was getting set up in time to spirit all trace of the very British Sergeant Farnsworth off the premises. As bad luck would have it, the Flying Circus landed early. When the General and his bemedaled and beribboned entourage made their unexpected entrance, Betty and her helpers were still struggling to align the British press stand with the uneven floor. All scrambled to their feet, leaflets flying, and snapped to attention. Sergeant Farnsworth, with his "unmistakable salute of the British soldier, with concave back and rigid hand twanging at his forehead like a broken string," could not have been more conspicuous. His presence did not, however, faze the General, and only the bevy of Far Eastern colonels appeared frosty about the unwelcome presence of British unfriendlies.[28]

The circus pulled out. Betty had met Donovan before but was once again struck by the way his very presence seemed to electrify everyone around him. Suddenly the presses rolled, and the still-wet leaflets were passed around to be admired. They said, in Japanese, "Greetings to General Donovan. This leaflet comes to you through the courtesy of the British Psychological Warfare Branch. It is printed on Lend-lease equipment. Welcome to our theater!"[29]

Betty landed on the tarmac in Colombo and was greeted by Jane's smiling face. They immediately set off for an evening of champagne, dinner, and dancing at the Silver Prawn, after which Betty was dropped by Jane and her coworker Howard Palmer at a European-style house where Detachment 404 stashed its native agents. Entering the house, Betty found a single dried squid hanging from the dish rack. Moving to the bathroom, she found four distinct rings around the bathtub. A small white owl clawed at the bedroom screen most of the night, and Betty would have let him in but for the mosquitoes. She passed a sleepless night until early the next morning when Jane and Howard reappeared in the MO jeep. They raced to catch the Toonerville Trolley up to Kandy.[30]

Betty had packed for every contingency, including social events at the mansion of Lord Mountbatten. Receipt of an invitation to one of Lord Mountbatten's parties was the envy of most everyone in Detachment 404 who loved a party. His wit and ebullience made the war seem very far away indeed. Not even "Vinegar Joe" Stilwell, who called Mountbatten "Lovely Louis," was immune to his charm. Jane referred to Kandy as "the Land of the Lotus-eaters," and Betty did find it a cool and beautiful respite from Calcutta.

"War is not hell here," Jane informed Betty.

Dr. Carlton Scofield was the civilian director of MO in Kandy. He gathered everyone at 7:00 a.m.—Detachment 404 operated on a "tropical routine," whereby work started early and ended at 2:30 p.m.—in the *cadjan* to conduct business. The first day's highlight, after a quick discussion covering the proposed implementation of ongoing black propaganda schemes in Kandy and Calcutta, was a demonstration arranged by Jane. She brought in a young sergeant carrying a large knife and what looked like a loaf of brown bread but was actually a brick of opium. The sergeant, who was a theological student in civilian life, deftly demonstrated the slicing of proper loaf sections for use as currency when paying Burmese agents. Betty took her turn and subsequently in China doled out her share of opium in the service of her country. Only years later did she allow herself to ponder how many addicts she had been responsible for creating.

Business concluded, jeeps were commandeered for expeditions into the mountains and then to the Kandy Klub, where various improvised versions of gin martinis and sherry flowed freely, for dinner and dancing. Present were Edmond Taylor, Jane, Paul, Julia, Cora, Dillon, and Gregory—the band was back together. Betty knew with certainty these wartime friendships would continue beyond "the duration and six months." She was amused to observe that Jane and Paul were on more than friendly terms by this time, at least in Paul's mind. Julia hovered, waiting for Jane to exit the picture so she could make her move.[31]

Betty was subsequently ordered down to Kandy on a regular basis, and Alex made an effort to meet her there for conjugal visits. She found herself with increasingly distant feelings for her husband, and when he came to meet her in Colombo, she watched wistfully as her friends left to go ride elephants in the hills. The marriage was dissolving, and she knew it.[32]

While "goofing off" in Ceylon Betty found herself struck by a lightning bolt of inspiration. She wanted to act on it immediately, especially once she had located a press, this one owned by the Navy. She sent a courier message back to Calcutta:

> Salaam Severyns:
>
> Marj . . . is it possible to get in touch with that cartograph artist Drew mentioned? I wanted a job done for the strip of photo-cards to be used in China. The Navy can do the job here if we get a map. The idea . . . is a time table, and the pix are labeled thusly . . . 1942—kicked out of Kiska; 1943, Mauled in the Mariannas, 1944, shoved off Saipan, 1945, nudged off Nippon! (or something corny . . .) A map should show the Chinese in occupied China, with Japan quivering in the center, with US armies closing in from the Pacific and Aleutians, the Chinese from China etc.[33]

Severyns located the artist, and Jane supervised the printing before sending all the materials to Calcutta, where Betty cajoled a Hump pilot into taking them to Detachment 202 in Kunming.

ᚾ

Alex and a little MO radio team were operating out of a British RAF camp at Chittagong, near the border between India and Burma. The camp was a base for pilots flying inland to drop supplies to Allied forces fighting in the jungles to the south. Alex and his helpers took over a *basha*, or shelter, where they found an abandoned half-ton generator. One of the crew members explained excitedly that it was a Model AXL 1150MW, which was powerful enough to broadcast into Thailand. Alex's helpers were three Free Thai college students, Nik, Lek, and Prayoon, whom OSS had spirited out of Bangkok. The boys had been listening to and analyzing Thai-language broadcasts over Radio Tokyo by Thai collaborators and convinced Alex that his Radio JOAK could simulate broadcasts with subliminal anti-Japanese propaganda.[34]

JOAK was snugged up next to a Tokyo frequency, only a "hair's-breadth turn of the dial." When JOAK made its debut broadcast, it worked so well it tricked British direction-finding units in Burma into thinking there was an enemy station operating in the jungle. A test program beamed into Thailand described bomb damage in Tokyo and the resultant instability in Japanese markets. Intel intercepts confirmed the broadcast was received in Thailand as the real deal. Meanwhile, Radio Tokyo was broadcasting that Japan was, of course, winning the war; therefore, Thailand, which remained nonaligned with either Allies or Axis, should join the empire in the Co-Prosperity Sphere. Moving slowly and subtly, Alex and his boys began introducing slivers of real news about regrettable Japanese setbacks in the Pacific. Nik came up with remarks and pronouncements he knew would be resented by the Thai—boasting of Japan's goal of subduing all of Asia, for example.[35] In addition to radio scripts coming from Betty and Jane, Alex began receiving musical recordings he had requested from Washington for use in broadcasts.[36] Music was an effective hook in a black radio transmission.

OSS got a jump on the British in the race to Thailand by establishing direct radio contact with Bangkok in a highly secretive mission, Operation Hotfoot. The details were kept secret not only from the British but from others within OSS who might leak them to the British. John Holladay, the reluctant MO missionary, volunteered to jump into Thailand and set up a shortwave station on Doi Angka, the highest mountain in the country. Holladay was familiar with the area and spoke the northern Thai dialect. He was to be accompanied by fellow Presbyterian Herbert Deignan, who was one of Dillon's ornithology colleagues. Holladay was held back at the last minute, and just as well—the team was captured after landing. A gloomy Dillon nixed further schemes to drop people into the jungle until he knew they would be greeted by friendly agents.[37]

჻

Jane had managed to get some of her material out by submarine when the British went on their "snatch sorties." During these sorties the British would lurk off the coast of various islands until a hapless fishing junk appeared. They would then sink the boat and snatch the survivors to be questioned back at the OSS Special Operations training base at Trincomalee. The Allies hoped the survivors could be trained as agents and set loose again, but this did not always work out, in which case they were interned or employed. Jane conceived a brilliant scheme to enclose her propaganda inside inflated condoms that could be loosed from the deck of a submarine as it submerged. The condoms would then wash up on the islands' shores with the tide. Her infamous "condom caper" went down in MO history when General Donovan and his Flying Circus came through just as Jane, Paul, Gregory, and her helpers were hard at work inflating hundreds of condoms.[38]

Jane was becoming increasingly frustrated with her work, and Betty recognized the symptoms of MO blues, a condition suffered by black propagandists who labored daily without confirmation that their work was of use to anyone. Betty conceived of a way to put her friend's talents to work: an exhibition of Jane's artwork, laced with subliminal messages, could be made into booklet form and disseminated as the work of "one of the leading artists of Japan." Jane found the idea excellent and promised sketches within the week.[39] Barely had she gotten to work when orders arrived from Col. John Coughlin, head of Detachment 404, informing her she would be shifting to Calcutta.[40]

ℵ

The last week of February, Betty sat through a tense meeting between psychological warfare representatives from P Division, Major Glemser, and MO Detachment 505 Calcutta. During the meeting everyone grudgingly accepted that cooperation between the British and OSS MO was actually accomplishing something and should, therefore, continue. Henceforth there would be open, above-board coordination in order to produce and disseminate black propaganda. No more sneaking around and pretending not to "deal with the British." Nor was there need to bribe the cousins with cigarettes and scotch. Everyone at the table felt a strange sadness. It was the passing of what? An era?[41] Then the orders came to report to CO, OSS Detachment 202, for temporary duty (TDY). Betty was going to China.[42]

ELEVEN

CHINA

China Is No Place for the Timid
—*Welcoming sign, Kunming Airport, 1945*

Betty clutched her lucky Gremlin as the C-47 flew between—not over—the snowy, needle-sharp peaks collectively referred to as "the Hump." They were approaching 18,000 feet above sea level, and mountaintops were sliding by her window like icebergs. Below was a scattering of black crosses in the snow, which she knew was the "aluminum trail" stretching from Mandalay to Kunming—planes downed so recently they remained visible in the whiteness. Twenty-six Hump flights had crashed within a ten-hour period on New Year's Eve, but those airplanes had long since vanished from sight.

The Hump was a 581-mile flight through a jagged and often mist-shrouded gauntlet of spikes at a bone-cold average altitude of 23,000 feet. The spine of the Hump passed over the nexus of the Mekong and Salween, two rivers ribboning through steep canyons as they rushed in descent from Tibet. The Hump was remembered by some as its own major battlefield of World War II, "a three-year siege of the Himalayas." In their *Thunder out of China*, Theodore White and Annalee Jacoby wrote that the "Skyway to Hell" was "the most dangerous, terrifying, barbarous aerial transport run in the world"; it "drove men mad, killed them, sent them back to America with tropical fevers and broken for the rest of their lives." More than 3,000 American, British, and Chinese planes were lost over the Hump during the war, with at least 500 American bailouts in the area. Many who jumped were never recovered and were thought to have frozen to death before they hit the ground. One of Claire Chennault's Flying Tiger pilots recalled maneuvering his lumbering DC-3 through a mountain pass at 16,000 feet when an updraft yanked him like a puppet up to 28,000 feet. Within 2 seconds he was slammed back down to 6,000 feet. He never understood how the wings stayed on his plane.[1]

When Betty reported to the ATC Hindustani Building at Dum Dum Airport at 6:15 a.m., March 14, 1945, she was ushered to her transport, a venerable C-47, on whose nose had been scrawled, "Is this trip necessary?" She shrugged into the leather flight jacket recently retrieved from the bottom of her A&F duffle, where it had resided since she had left steamy Miami. Sewn to the lining was a "blood chit," a rectangle of white silk covered with Chinese characters and the Chinese national flag. Also called a rescue flag or identification flag, the chit was designed to elicit assistance for downed fliers seeking refuge from enemy forces. A topographical map—with the regions of CBI displayed in lovely sepia-toned pastels—was also sewn inside the jacket. The Japanese, she knew, were offering reward money and other prizes for captured Americans—top money for pilots, lowest prices for "observers" such as OSS civilians.[2]

One of the pilots conversationally told her that deadly crosscurrents of air often sucked airplanes down from an altitude of 8,500 feet to 2,500 feet in 10 seconds, and during one such dive, the black paint on his flashlight had been completely skinned off by an electrical charge reaction to the drop. Fortified with this useful information, Betty looked carefully at her fellow passengers, trying to gauge whether or not they considered this a suicide mission. A staff car was strapped to the center of the fuselage floor and surrounded by crates of food and ammunition. A sergeant, sound asleep with his parachute as a pillow, was stretched across the hood like a dead deer. Next to Betty, two GIs were playing a harmonica and guitar, and two Flying Tiger pilots dozed next to them. Julia sat blissfully reading a book, casually turning the pages as though sitting in a beauty salon rather than hurtling through space in a ship of death. Betty hated her intensely for her sangfroid.[3]

Betty recalled that the Indians considered the Himalayas to be the roof of the world, and despite her fear she could not help appreciating the awesome spectacle. After the war she reflected, "Perhaps it was from these vast reaches of silence

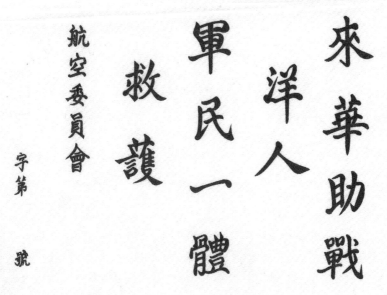

A "blood chit" was a rectangle of white silk sewn to the lining of flight jackets in Asia. Translation of the Chinese text: "Foreigners coming to China to engage in the war. All [Chinese] military and civilian people have to rescue and protect [the foreigners]."
Author's collection

that Indian mysticism flowed—embodied in the sacred rivers which were born of these snowlands."[4]

The plane began to toss, the lights went out, and the Flying Tiger pilots began whispering about the number two engine. Betty ran her hands over her parachute and wondered which cord she was supposed to pull, as no one had instructed her, or maybe someone had. Her mind flashed to her cabin on the *Republic* and the mysterious tangle of straps and toggles crisscrossing that life jacket. Then the pilot miraculously found a hole in the clouds. They dived through it and leveled off over Kunming Airport. Col. Richard Heppner, CO for OSS Detachment 202, was waiting anxiously for the overdue flight. Betty had been less than impressed by him when they were in Washington. Now in China, he seemed different. Perhaps it was the air of authority, or maybe, for the first time, she was struck by his handsome face and the muscles he still had from rowing crew. Maybe she was in the mood to be rescued.

The OSS jeep sped across the countryside to the walled city of Kunming, through ornately carved gates through which Marco Polo had also passed. To the west of the city lay the deep gorges of three rivers running parallel and close to each other: the Yangtze, Salween, and Mekong. To the south Lolo tribesmen—headhunters and opium growers—occupied the hills stretching to Indochina. Kunming was a frontier town in 1945, swollen with refugees and incoming Americans spreading the population beyond its ancient walls. It was the terminus for a one-track railroad coming north out of French Indochina, which before the Japanese shut it down had served as a conduit for French merchandise. The railhead south of the city remained surrounded by a compound of French offices and residences, with elaborate homes and summer villas. Lush gardens ran to the shores of the lake, which was called "the Pearl on the Plateau." French bread could still be found in some Chinese bakeries, but most Americans now paid exorbitant prices for contraband soup and bad champagne in restaurants.

Seeing laughing children herding their ducks between brilliant green rice paddies, Betty once again had the impression that the war must be very far away. The war was in fact very near. Kunming sat behind enemy lines. Japanese forces surrounded all the provinces of southeastern China, leaving a peninsula of land approximately six hundred miles long, from north to south, and three hundred miles across. It was bounded on the north by the Yangtze River, on the west by the Hankow-Canton Railway, and to the south and east by the coastline of the China Seas and Formosa Strait. This preserve inside enemy lines was mostly hills and mountains, dotted every fifty to one hundred miles with a village hidden in a deep valley. Still, it was an oddly tranquil place given that the war was lapping at the base of the six-thousand-foot plateau like a tide. Japanese raiding parties surged into the countryside to conduct "rice campaigns" to replenish supplies and then retreated rather than deal with the burdens of occupation. Likewise, Chiang's forces melted back with each offensive and then returned. Their dance was predictable.

Passing through more massive wooden gates, Betty and Julia saw their home for the next eight months: an imposing stone house with tiled roof and balconies overlooking formal Chinese gardens. The driver told the women that the house was called Mei Yuan, which meant "Beautiful Garden." The Beautiful Garden had a leaking roof, an inadequate number of rooms for the occupants, and toilets that worked sporadically. Just before the jeep's arrival, the house cook had asphyxiated himself with one of the open potbellied charcoal braziers used to heat the building. Lee Ming, a young Chinese man, greeted Julia and Betty in English. "I learn English at the YMCA in Canton," he boasted and, thereafter, understood not a word they said.[5]

The weary travelers were rescued by Mary Hutchinson of R&A, who gave a quick command to Lee in Chinese, sending him diving for their luggage, and led them up to a temporary dormitory-style room, where they would sleep until they could be paired with roommates. Betty ended up with Hutchinson, who had been a POW at Weihsin. She was one of the few to be sent home, despite her protestations at leaving behind those older and more frail to the tender mercies of the Japanese. Hutchinson had subsequently joined OSS with a fierce determination to help end the war. Her job was the implementation of target studies for the 10th and 14th Air Forces.

As they settled in, Betty was delighted to be reunited with Rosie Frame and Paul Child. Rosie had taken it upon herself to oversee a refurbishment of the men's quarters. She used her Mandarin to direct Chinese workers in the purchase of materials and negotiated for the loan of domestic servants and furniture. Paul had lost his "Janey" when he left for China and she for Calcutta, and he was in the process of renewing his interest in Rosie. By his own admission, Paul did not like to be alone.[6]

It was time to officially report in to their CO, who having seen them safely on the ground had sped off in his own jeep from the airfield. Col. Richard Heppner had been a junior partner in Bill Donovan's law firm before he was called to active duty in June 1941. He was swept almost immediately into OSS, snagged by Donovan from the 35th Field Artillery as a first lieutenant. Heppner was sent to the highly secret British Camp X in Canada, directed sabotage efforts in London, and participated in Torch, the North African invasion that did much to prove the worth of OSS. His dress uniform was a fruit salad of ribbons, including the Legion of Merit and campaign bars and battle stars for the European, African, Pacific, and Middle East theaters of war. He also sported the golden wings of the first Chinese parachute regiment in history.[7]

Betty was again struck by his youth, then by the fact that he was very handsome. She came to see him as the sort of man Claire Chennault told Donovan was necessary in China, where "imagination, resilience, cool reserve were essential for working with our strange and sometimes reluctant ally [Chiang], and for fighting in territory which was not far different from American frontier country in the days of Daniel Boone."[8] Paul did not share Betty's admiration for their commander. Possibly tainted by a bit of jealous envy, Paul found Heppner "highly nervous and tired, not very effective, slightly disintegrated, makes snap decisions not all of which are good."[9] Heppner sent them off to meet their MO boss.

Mr. Ronald Dulin, chief of MO China, was a bit stunned by Betty's enthusiastic desire to get to work. She observed in him a tendency to stare into space. He appeared to have "stepped right out of the fifth dimension" and had "a detached way of talking. His words floated down, tinkling, unsteady, bearing fragments of thoughts, never welded together into complete sentences but made the more melodious by a mixture of Irish and southern accents." Mr. Dulin told her to go meet her Chinese helpers, Ma and Ting; then, as though fearing she might come back too soon, said, "Go on down, all of you, and have lunch at the Peiping Cafe. Relax. Absorb atmosphere. Let China come to you. Don't be eager beavers. There'll be plenty to do later on."[10]

The MO production office was a tent pitched next to a mud-brick printing shop on the edge of the OSS compound. Ma Guaoling was a young, thoughtful magazine editor from Shanghai, and Xiao Ting was an ebullient cartoonist, brilliantly talented. Betty sat patiently as Ma, waving his hand over a map that may or may not have been China, explained at length that everything in Washington's MO school curriculum having to do with "emotional appeals" and "patriotic stimuli" were worthless when dealing with the Chinese. Black propaganda was supposed to be guided by certain JCS assumptions about the Chinese character,

Col. Richard Heppner, chief of
OSS Detachment 202, China
*Reproduced with permission
of Elizabeth P. McIntosh*

but "God, fatherland, flag, and government" meant little to the Chinese, who valued a good joke and mischievousness above all else.[11]

"You tell a ferry operator in Kowloon to sabotage his boat for the glory of China and he'll laugh at you," said Ma. "But offer him a certain amount of money to pour salt water into the machinery, and he may listen." The best method in dealing with the Chinese was to appeal to their sense of humor, suggesting it would be a great "joke," for example, to throw a lit cigarette into a Japanese fuel dump.[12] When experienced OSS veterans of the European theater—SO and OG men—arrived, they had a hard time working in China, being used to organized and motivated French Maquis and other resistance forces. Chinese conscripts to Chiang's army were entirely different. Chinese officers commonly obtained "recruits" by surrounding villages, rounding up men and boys, and shackling them together with steel collars and chains.[13] Needless to say, such "soldiers" felt scant loyalty to the Nationalist cause and, by extension, the Allies' cause. Most deserted at first opportunity, which usually coincided with the completion of training and granting of leave. They disappeared, along with their weapons, which typically added to the stock in Mao Tse-tung's arsenal. American GIs found the behavior at first strange and then as an indication the Chinese were hardly human.[14]

Betty hit the ground running when she arrived in China in March 1945. Allied focus had finally shifted from "Europe first," and this shift meant, at long last, a steady stream of supplies and personnel arriving over the Hump. From

Betty McIntosh with a helper, MO
print shop, Kunming
*Reproduced with permission of
Elizabeth P. McIntosh*

Kunming, the hub, MO sent teams into all corners of China to disseminate materials and in some cases set up their own mobile presses. Main field bases were established in Chihkiang, Hsian, and Chungking, which in turn ran field missions extending the tentacles of OSS MO to all important target areas in China.

Before any operation could be launched, a team needed approval from first the Operations Committee of OSS Kunming and then from the Theater Planning Staff in Chungking. In practice this chain of approval functioned remarkably well, mainly because Betty and her crew piggybacked their ideas onto already approved OSS missions, usually SO, not unlike Jane's bribing British pilots to drop her material over Burma.[15]

Back in Washington, the official objectives of MO in China were summarized by the JCS as follows:

1. Convince Chinese residents of occupied areas to bomb strategic targets, such as munitions factories.
2. Persuade laborers in such places to desert their jobs and flee with their families.
3. "Deceive, misdirect, and confuse" the Japanese as to any intended targets and operations of the 14th Air Force.
4. Give "false, misleading, and confusing" directions to disrupt Japanese shipping.
5. Discredit Japanese engaged in coastal military and shipping operations.
6. Encourage friendly Chinese to passive resistance and eventually active sabotage and revolt.
7. Harass, confuse, and demoralize Japanese troops as well as civilians, especially in isolated locations.[16]

There was a meeting every Wednesday morning in the Washington office of the OWI's overseas director. Always present were representatives from the War, Navy, and State Departments, as well as someone from the British Psychological Warfare Mission. OSS was always welcome, by invitation, but continued to enjoy the status of redheaded stepchild and had no vote. Following this meeting was a more informal gathering during which OSS and the representatives of War, Navy, and State came up with a weekly OSS MO directive for field outposts. The British were not invited to this smaller meeting. Directives were sent to the field but were invariably so general and nebulous that they were easily ignored. MO China usually received actionable intelligence long before Washington, and so Betty and her team fell into a familiar habit of crafting their own material, sending it into the field, and only later submitting a report either asking permission or presenting a fait accompli. It was an agreeable relationship of mutual indifference, and rarely if ever were there recriminations.[17]

One shockingly bright beam of reason came to them from Washington in the form of a directive lifting the prohibition on releasing individual names and photographs of Japanese POWs. MO had long fought a losing battle on this front, arguing that a major obstacle facing surrender inducement attempts was the Japanese soldier's belief that he would be the first in his race to willingly lay down his sword. This new policy sought to "condition the Japanese mind to the view that the Japanese people as a whole can surrender unconditionally without fear of reprisal." The hope was that a release of photographs along with surrender leaflets might induce surrender in local groups and even have an impact on the home islands. In the Pacific one of the first pictures to be released was that of a Japanese officer at Santo Thomas by a *Life* magazine photographer.[18] Betty, along with the others, was happy with the development but slightly cynical. The "unconditional surrender" mantra had been drilled into all Japanese since Roosevelt had announced it in 1943. She believed this new policy to be too little too late, and its implementation would be seen for what it was: a blatant propaganda ploy.

By the time Betty had arrived in Kunming, Nimitz's Central Pacific offensive had reached the Marianas, and MacArthur had made his big return to the Philippines. Whereas earlier Allied strategy involved pinning down the Japanese to prevent them from shifting forces to the Pacific Islands, now the goal was to prevent the return of IJA troops to defend the home islands. In Burma MO continued to work to demoralize and deter Japanese forces. In China the target was expanded to include motivating the Chinese to sabotage and actively resist Japanese forces wherever they could be found.

Barely a week had passed when a fluffy golden cocker spaniel bounced into the tent, dropping a thoroughly slobbered tennis ball at Betty's feet by way of introduction. Sammy, whose formal name was My Assam Dragon, belonged to the handsome Colonel Heppner but came to prefer Betty's company and made himself at home most days thereafter in the MO tent. Angel Puss had been denied passage over the Hump and was now the companion of a young pilot back in Calcutta; the dog accompanied him on banking runs over Burma. Sammy's official translator was Sgt. William Arthur Smith, who explained that although Sammy was fond of Betty, it was the proximity to the war dogs (whom he worshipped), several tents away, that kept him near.

Bill Smith was a slightly plump young man with full lips and a kind smile who showed up one day, entering the MO sanctum sanctorum with pens, paints, and sketchpad. Although unassuming, he was an artist of some repute whose work had been published in *Cosmopolitan, Life*, the *Saturday Evening Post*, and *True*. Smith originally hailed from Toledo, Ohio, and had been something of a child prodigy, winning prizes soon after he began sketching at age nine and establishing his own studio in New York City when he was only nineteen. He was hired as an instructor at the Grand Central School of Art, became fascinated with Chinese art and culture, and eventually illustrated Pearl Buck's *The Chinese Children Next Door* and her two-volume *Folk Tales from China*. This work showed up on the OSS recruiting radar in 1944, and Donovan himself ordered Smith sent to China.[19]

The MO team soon bonded, and the four of them—Betty, Bill, Ma, and Ting—became inseparable companions, moving as a little pack through the back alleys of Kunming. Because of dysentery, many restaurants in Kunming were designated "out-of-bounds," as had been the case for many restaurants in India. Americans were to eat only base food or food from the few approved places known to follow minimal vague sanitary guidelines. Sooner or later, everyone ventured into one of the restricted places, in search of succulent chicken with black bean sauce, garlicky eggplant and red-devil peppers, crispy sweet and sour carp, and bright green crunchy and steamed bamboo shoots—knowing they would pay for it later with the Chinese version of Delhi belly. The Flying Tigers, who were also stationed in Kunming, were partial to a place referred to as the Hoc Shop, where diners spat chicken bones and watermelon seeds on the floor. An unexpected treat was delicious mint ice cream. Upon examination the flavoring agent was revealed not to be fresh mint but Vick's VapoRub.[20]

It was reassuring to see the dashing Flying Tigers—by that time more accurately known as the 14th Air Force—around town; they gave everyone a sense of protection. They were funny and carefree on the ground, but Betty knew once in the air they were deadly. The Tigers lived in a former university administration building commandeered from the Advancing Intelligence Society, a fraternity of Chinese students and their professors. The beautiful two-story building with redbrick walls and a dragon tail dormer over the entrance had been whitewashed inside and turned into a hostel. On her first visit, Betty found the building not unlike a college dormitory, with clean showers and toilets on every floor and two busy bars, one for the enlisted men and one for the officers, despite Chennault's expressed desire to ignore differences in rank. A softball diamond, tennis courts, and a basketball hoop occupied a rear courtyard, and a recreation room housed a ping-pong table, hand-cranked record player, and books. After Burma, Kunming, with its small plots of green winter wheat, clumps of pines, and a winter climate rivaling Florida's or California's, was for Chennault's men nothing short of luxurious.[21]

The Tiger pilots liked to celebrate their successes at the Chinese version of a Western restaurant that had steaks and genuine whiskey in abundance. The only other recognizable dish on the menu—fried chicken livers—was consumed by the hundreds. Conversation at the bar inevitably turned to tactics, with much weaving of torsos and swooping of hands to tell tales.[22] Betty and her friends became regulars just to eavesdrop and watch the retellings.

A cable from Jane caught Betty up with the goings on outside China. Gregory had gone missing down in Burma, causing much anxiety among his friends. They should have been used to it by then: Gregory regularly wandered into the jungle to observe and document the cultural practices of native peoples. He reappeared on this occasion in time to be put in charge of a rescue mission organized by Jane. She was still in Kandy when OSS inadvertently received information about three Indonesian agents who had been missing for some time. The information came in the form of a scribbled note in Malay on the back of a captured report on rice supplies in Sumatra, taken by the British from a sunken patrol boat. Jane had become familiar with the area while researching her master's thesis on stone sculpture of the Batu Islands. She translated the report and refused to let the matter rest until a rescue mission had been launched, arguing to Colonel Coughlin that native agents would never work for OSS again if an effort were not made on their behalf. Just such grumblings—that too many indigenous agents were being abandoned to their own fate—had been overheard by everyone in the Ceylon Trincomalee Training Camp.

The British agreed to ferry the rescuers on a destroyer, and Jane lobbied hard to go along. But to no avail—the British would not allow women on board their destroyers. Jane poured over depth charts of the waters around the Batu Islands and briefed the team, which as yet had no leader. The only other person fluent in Malay was Gregory. So it was Gregory, who could get lost in a closet, who led a team of a dozen commandos in an amphibious island landing. The agents were not found, unfortunately, and Gregory again disappeared off among the natives, taking notes and pictures. Much to Jane's relief, he eventually surfaced and sauntered into the office.[23] Not long after that, Gregory was transferred to China, and Jane made her move to Calcutta.

Once again, Paul Child led the advance across the theater, arriving in February, which is spring in China. The artist in him delighted in his surroundings, and he sketched bright green seedlings being set in wet fields by men and women in palm-fiber rain capes. Bamboo water wheels creaked as they turned in the nearby river current, lifting canisters of water to troughs spilling into irrigation ditches. Other irrigation arrangements involved chains of buckets hitched to a horizontal wheel turned by water buffalo. Here and there a woman peddled a rickety bamboo bicycle contraption to raise smaller buckets. Baby fish were also placed in the flooded fields to grow fat by the dry season.[24]

The MO tent in Kunming was a nice place to work in the spring. Each morning a weapons carrier showed up at Mei Yuan to pick up the girls and an odd assortment of dogs. Usually Sammy, having spent the night with Betty, would sit in back with her; a fat Chinese puppy rode shotgun up front with Dorothy Martineau, the MO secretary; then there was Mortimer Snerd, a large Irish setter, Marj Kennedy's Alsatian Tai Tai, and a "dog-faced dog" named Merry who lived in the truck with his stash of bones and belonged to no one in particular but just liked to ride.

In May a mobile printing van showed up off the Burma Road. It had no room in it for MO equipment until the cases of beer that had made the trip through Burma were consumed. As the weather got hotter, tables were set up outside in the shade of the print shop, where the work of sketching and typing and brainstorming took place until the sun chased Betty and her team inside the building, which was cool and dark, lit only by a dim bulb and a shaft of sunlight. At 5:30 the transport returned, and they bumped along the back streets to home. Evening entertainment ranged from movies to tea dances to twilight sampan rides on Kunming Lake. Someone always managed to barter for something fermented; there were various imaginative concoctions and home-brewed offerings to keep the gatherings festive.

TWELVE

THE LAST SUMMER

Nobody could have believed that these men
had once possessed the strength to
survive a series of intense battles.

—*Staff Sergeant Yasuma Nishiji, Burma*

Jane arrived in Calcutta in a black mood the evening of March 3, 1945. Not only had she been uprooted from her eclectic little MO family in a beautiful setting, but the paperwork listed her as a CAF-9 rather than a P-3, ignoring her promotion to P-4, which apparently had not yet taken effect.[1] She quickly concluded that Calcutta was the seventh ring of hell, the hottest place she had ever lived, and as she later wrote, "the cesspool of the world." It was dirty and "artificial," full of "huge, hideous incongruous Victorian buildings." The air reeked of death: close to three thousand people died each week of cholera and other by-products of the 1943 Bengal famine. Everything was made worse by the location of OSS headquarters in the Kalighat District, close to the river and the site of ritual cremations. When rare Indian Ocean breezes wafted through, Jane spent her off-hours outside sketching and painting colorful street hawkers delivering daily necessities to doorsteps, people lowering baskets from their verandas to purchase wares, boys maneuvering their "fighting kites" on strings coated with glistening cut glass. When word came of the German surrender,

Jane thought briefly of her husband, George, who last she heard was in Germany. This led to thoughts of her first husband, Leo, and she wondered if he had gotten out of Batavia or been interned with other Dutch citizens. Then she put them both out of her mind, something that was becoming increasingly easy to do.[2]

Removed from her network of British pilots and submariners, Jane once again could not get her materials into the Netherlands East Indies. However, after their smashing success in the Arakan, MO products were suddenly much in demand in Burma. Detachment 101 wanted some airdrops into their Japanese battle zone within ten days. These deliveries would include various captured articles considered irresistible to the average Japanese soldier: helmets, knapsacks filled with personal items, food packets, medical kits, and ammunition pouches. All these items were stored in Delhi, so Jane arranged their transfer to Calcutta. In Calcutta she had them stuffed with black propaganda designed to alert the *kempai tai* that the soldiers carrying them had entertained dangerous thoughts, been subverted, or were actual traitors. All of this, approximately two hundred items, was to be dropped by Allied air forces into heavily occupied areas and yet dispersed enough to prevent a deluge in any one place.[3]

Within thirty days 101 wanted to distribute five hundred captured Japanese rifles, also stored in Delhi, that had been "repaired" by R&A so that they would explode in the operator's face when fired. After the rifles had been dropped and enough time had passed for them to blow up, rumors would be circulated that "Japanese war production has reached such a sad state that Japan can no longer manufacture serviceable weapons, and that they care so little for the men who will use those weapons that they are producing quantities in spite of imperfections." Detachment 101's memo concluded with a note that more project requests would be forthcoming.[4]

To transport five hundred booby-trapped guns into Burma, Jane knew she would have to approach the boys in British Detachment 136, which would go as it always did when she met her friend Alec at the Silver Prawn:

"Did you bring any operational scotch, Jane?" he would ask. She would then pass it over.

They would have a drink and then she would ask, "OK, Alec, let's get it over with. When are the bombers going over?"

"On the twentieth."

"Would you drop some of our leaflets?"

He would usually agree, and with business concluded, they would move on to dinner and dancing.[5]

Jane was putting a great deal of effort into Project 113, a fake underground newspaper, *Akatsuki no Katsudan*. Japanese POWs were finally being used extensively and were a great help. Her feature article in *Akatsuki no Katsudan* described an editorial conference between two Japanese soldiers serving in Burma. The soldiers were shocked by constant withdrawals, retreats, and disappointments and by the degree to which they, their comrades, and their families back home were being misled by Tokyo. In accordance with army instructions, the two soldiers had been propagandizing a Burmese couple regarding the Co-Prosperity Sphere, only to become propagandized themselves with the "truth" about Japanese setbacks and disasters. The Burmese couple were members of the Anti-Fascist League and had given the soldiers refuge after they had become convinced Japan was losing the war and a new Japan was needed. As true patriots, the Japanese soldiers were now willing to sacrifice everything to get the truth out, which was the policy of *Akatsuki*. The leading headline for the first run on July 15, 1945, was "The Only Way to Save the Country: Stop the War!" The article read, "Some of us Japanese are taking this dramatic step of getting out this little stenciled newspaper for the following reason: At present Japan has reached the most critical stage since the creation of the empire during the glorious history of 2,600 years. We, men and officers of the army, are dragged into this most critical situation by our blind leaders. The continuation of this war can only mean the liquidation of Japan. We do not want this war . . . we want to create a new Japan."[6]

The article went on to describe the shifting of Allied forces from Europe to the Japanese mainland, two thousand bombers from each base. Saipan, Tinian, Guam, Iwo Jima, and Okinawa had already fallen. The population at home was described as increasingly antiwar, despite crushing reprisals from the *kempei tai*. Page two carried a directive against national suicide:

> It is necessary to have people to cultivate, to build houses, and to organize the nation. To commit suicide because they had lost in battle may be welcomed during the last century, but we know today that those who commit suicide now will be treated as traitors who do not think of the future of Japan. At present, Japan is losing war and each time national suicide is attempted, this decreases the power of the nation. Do not think that loyalty is such sacrifice. By all means, do not die. Have hope for the New Japan. Let us live.

Jane's cartoon on page two shows the country Japan carrying Blind War Lords of Japan on its back and stepping into the abyss of National Suicide. From the abyss, in upside-down characters, comes the warning cry, "Danger!"[7]

Takami Jun, a popular novelist in Japan, had written in his secret diary two months earlier: "We are clearly being pushed by the enemy. We are losing. Why can't they write it plainly and appeal to the people? It's the same old story. That's why people are not taken in by reassuring, deceptive articles. They have learned to read between the lines."[8] Jun lived in constant fear of the *kempei tai* but was assiduous in recording his observations throughout the war.

July 1945 found 27,000 men of the Japanese 28th Army beginning the long march to Thailand, only to bog down in Burma during the worst monsoon of the war. The men were desperate for food and had been reduced to eating bamboo shoots, snakes, snails, and lizards. Taking rice from the villagers by force had driven the Burmese farther into the Allied camp, and IJA troops grew terrified when Burmese hill people began falling on wounded soldiers, bashing their faces open to extract gold teeth while the soldier was still alive. Cholera and plague were rampant. Soldiers became delirious, breaking into wild song and wandering off into the jungle. Increasingly, the sound of a grenade indicated the suicide of someone unable to continue. More and more were opting for surrender; 740 allowed themselves to be captured.[9] Jane's propaganda targeted those shattered souls, urging them to relinquish a hopeless cause, planting rumors of Japanese officers receiving secret shipments of food and comfort bags from home. Her work was also now in support of Lord Louis Mountbatten's Operation Zipper, aimed at retaking Malaya and Singapore.

Germany had surrendered May 8, and Donovan wanted to ramp up MO operations in China going into summer 1945. Field units working in tandem with SO teams rushed to establish themselves in the most strategically vital parts of China. The Schools and Training Branch in Washington, always two steps behind, updated its OSS Organization and Functions Booklet to reflect the expansion of operations, finding "limitless opportunities" for organizing and supplying resistance to the Japanese. Donovan was optimistic that OSS China would benefit from lessons learned in Europe and in the MO successes of Detachment 101. He hoped that OSS China would "be able to coordinate all its weapons against the enemy as never before, and will operate through the air, on water, and on land."[10] Washington did manage, at long last, to acknowledge the wisdom of sending more Japanese Americans to the theater to make much-needed use of their skills in linguistics and calligraphy. After more than three years of reticence, the Army admitted the need for people who "think as Japanese soldiers think. . . . It takes soldiers to live in the field with soldiers; it takes soldiers to interrogate prisoners of war at front echelons; it takes Japanese soldiers in the uniform of the United States Army to be fully effective in the Far East." Nisei soldiers were pulled from Camp Savage in Minnesota and rushed to OSS detachments in China, Burma, and India.[11]

Donovan had begun aggressively recruiting from among many nationality groups in American society—those who knew the culture and language of their native countries—from the beginning of his appointment as COI. However, he did not recruit Japanese Americans until November 1943, when he sent one of his Asian experts, Daniel C. Buchanan, to select an initial group of four nisei lieutenants and fifty enlisted for OSS training. Nisei had been attempting to enlist in all branches of the U.S. armed forces since early 1941 but were rejected by all except the Army Military Intelligence Service. When war erupted and citizens of Japanese and German decent (and some Italians) were forcibly removed to internment camps, men of other nationalities were training to parachute behind enemy lines and work with resistance groups, as well as infiltrate German forces. By 1944 there ranked among OG personnel in the field ethnic Norwegians, Frenchmen, Italians, Greeks, and others, but none of Japanese descent were released for service in the Far East. The reluctance to put Japanese Americans in the field was not overcome by the performance of the all-nisei 442nd, which distinguished itself by rescuing the Lost Battalion of 230 men. When FDR rescinded the prohibition against nisei in the military, volunteers, including fifty women of Japanese and Chinese heritage, were sent to Military Intelligence Language School in Camp Savage, so Donovan had a trained and ready pool of recruits from which to pick.[12]

If CBI had been a kaleidoscope of shifting and overlapping authorities, China was a crazy quilt with no seams. Betty struggled to make sense of the OSS mission there and the "factional jealousies, political upheavals, wars-within-wars which fomented in China's pockets of resistance, those little islands of chaos between the relatively peaceful Jap-held coastal areas and so-called Free China." Warlords pitted Chinese against Chinese and traded favors with the Japanese. Anyone could be bought for a bag of rice. OSS guerrilla operations, intelligence networks, and MO activities worked to stiffen whatever resistance could be mustered against the Japanese.[13] After Pearl Harbor Chiang responded to the invasion of Southeast Asia by attacking Mao Tse-tung's 4th Army instead of the Japanese, and he kept that priority throughout the war. His real enemy was the Communists.

Donovan's people were engaged in a "sting-and-run" harassment campaign of irregular warfare against the Japanese-held strategic land corridor stretching from Nanking to Singapore, a corridor from which troops and supplies could be moved rapidly. OSS sabotage teams were given animal code names: Elephant, Spaniel, Goat, Mink, Alpaca, Lion, Leopard. Although there were many successes, training Chinese guerrillas produced mixed results. The Chinese, for example, persisted in detonating explosives whenever they felt like it, for the simple pleasure of "hearing them go *Boom!*"

Gregory was given the task of contributing to a sabotage project worked up by Edward Hunter of the Intelligence and Projects Committee in Calcutta. Hunter compiled a veritable textbook that could be used anywhere, anytime, covering machines, vehicles, industrial mechanisms, and changes that could be made to adjust to different locales. What he wanted from Gregory was a more complete listing of "household hints" for pointed sabotage of specific industries, such as sabotage of locomotives in railway yards, ships in repair yards, and stationary machinery in mills. Gregory tapped everyone—R&A people, Severyns, Paul and Julia, Betty. They came up with useful ideas, such as bending an insulated wire until it broke without tearing the covering, removing cotter keys and replacing them with whittled toothpicks, holding a lighter under a rubber belt until it had weakened almost to the point of breaking. The brainstorming was a nice change of pace from the usual schemes to sabotage the Japanese psyche.[14]

The MO tent buzzed with activity. In addition to newspaper and pamphlet production and the ongoing altering of postcards and other mail, MO black radio had come to take center stage, requiring daily scripts. Gordon Auchincloss had arrived in Kunming almost a year before and set up a radio transmitter that was powerful but still only able to send a signal as far as southern China. His broadcasts were designated Operation Hermit and targeted Japanese troops and their collaborators in occupied China, despite the fact that for the most part only wealthy people or officials could afford radios. MO hoped there would be one radio in most villages in the Chinese countryside under Japanese occupation. Scripts were written in various dialects for transmission through short wave in Kunming, then directed at Canton, the Wuhan cities, and the area in and around Nanking. Four programs ran simultaneously, produced in Kunming and then transmitted from various mobile units to elude detection.[15]

Betty was by this time an old hand at black radio script production, having made a complete transition from newspaper reporting. She often started her day helping Gordon come up with ideas for Hermit. Their radio announcer purported to be a prognosticator named Wua Yan Chu-he, aka the "Hermit of the Clouds," who based various predictions on a combination of the Chinese calendar, the Japanese calendar, the Zodiac, and any other astrological cosmological fiction Betty and scriptwriter Sy Nadler could conjure. The Hermit typically predicted things that had already happened and then congratulated himself.

"It was a Walter Winchell technique," Auchincloss said in an interview years later. It worked because of the time lag in getting information from Japan to various places in China. Hermit was one of the programs beamed to Nanking on a daily basis.[16]

"The key to black propaganda," Gordon explained to Betty and the others, "is to do as much truth as possible, and just bend it a little at the end. Just put a little hook on it." For one of his operations, he cast his Chinese characters as Yangtze riverboat captains chattering on their ship to shore. The piece was complete with a sound that simulated the whistles on the riverboats, a sound achieved by blowing on canteens partially filled with water.[17]

Other Kunming broadcasts, Charlie, William, and Jig, went on the air several times a day in addition to Hermit. Charlie, a broadcast beamed to Canton, from where it purported to originate, was the first. It claimed to be operated by an anti-Japanese resistance movement headed by Liang Tin Han, a self-made guerrilla fighter embittered since the death of his wife and child. William broadcast to the Wuhan cities of Hankow, Hanyang, and Wuchang. The voice of William was Wang Chu Mien, who called himself the "business counselor of Wuhan." He dispensed advice on hiding valuables from looting Japanese soldiers and hoarding goods until U.S. troops arrived and would purchase them with gold. Jig was begun in the last days of the war as a series of seven scripts written by Auchincloss and translated by multilingual Chinese students. Jig was never aired because the translations were considered inaccurate. The Kunming station also monitored Japanese short-wave propaganda and prepared reports for OSS, OWI, and China Theater G-2 (military intelligence).[18]

The days settled into a familiar routine. After brainstorming with Gordon and Nadler, Betty oversaw the layout of her newspaper, with all the attendant challenges arising from faulty or missing equipment, lack of language-qualified personnel, and the myriad little issues that arose from trying to work in China. Editorial production in the MO tent was of a long-range character. The propaganda was created to have general applications and not be limited by definite time factors. It could be used in a variety of situations. Newspapers were printed on a schedule to be disseminated, but postcards and letters were altered as the captured material became available. At the main field bases, however, production took on short-range characteristics, with direct application to specific military tactical situations. Two or three Americans were usually at the base supervising a group of Chinese agents in the production of materials in Japanese or Chinese. The Americans would organize the missions to disseminate the products throughout the countryside. Chinese agents also set up cells in cities, garrison towns, and communication centers, usually in a basement, and produced material clandestinely on the spot. By the end of the war, seventeen field missions were operating under three field bases at Chihkiang, Hsian, and Chungking. MO field missions adopted reptilian names: Bushmaster, Viper, Mamba, Rattler, Python, Copperhead, Boa, and so on.

Betty found herself happy that summer of 1945, not only with the work but with the surroundings. She took long walks with Dick Heppner and Sammy and enjoyed the sight of boys swimming in the hyacinths in the canal separating the compound from surrounding rice fields. She watched Chinese soldiers as they sat on the bank and soaked their feet while kerchiefed women washed cabbages and then filled jugs with water before heading home. She wrote home to ask her mother to send clothes. Hers were wearing out.

"I didn't realize how shabby my clothes looked until some gals arrived from the states with new raiment," she wrote. "Could you please airmail some simple cotton or chambray shirt waisters . . . red, green, pink . . . size 14?" Other urgently needed items were bobby pins, a good comb, slips, and shell or pearl earrings. Betty's sudden interest in fashion coincided with an undeniable growing attraction for her CO. She would always care for Alex, but it had become increasingly clear that their mutual marital affection was mostly a memory. This caused an ache in her chest—nostalgia mixed with some guilt and loss. Uncharacteristically, she pleaded for letters from home to assuage the growing sense of disconnection from that past life.[19]

Mei Yuan, with its balconies and open rooms, was big enough for parties. At least once a month the MO press put out formal invitations to a dance. The men took turns cranking the Victrola, and Big Band music wafted across the compound late into the night. Dick Heppner continued accompanying Betty on her walks with his dog. He was feeling the strain of responsibility and found her an understanding listener. They liked the same books and movies. The walks became longer, and they fell in love, but unlike most wartime romances, theirs remained chaste. Both were people of deep conscience, and neither wanted to hurt Alex. Also, Betty never felt the nearness of death that compelled many during wartime to "live for the day." She simply did that as a matter of course; there was nothing urgent about it.

Other romances blossomed. At last Julia's efforts were paying off, and Paul took to spending most evenings in her room, reading poetry out loud. Paul had actually fallen hard for Marj Severyns when she arrived from Delhi to help set up Kunming's intelligence office, but her head was turned by another and, after he had lapsed into a lonesome sulk, it suddenly seemed that wherever Paul turned, "Julie" was there. They hiked the hills, visited the Black Dragon Pool temple, frequented the flower market, and took many a twilight sampan ride on the lake. Paul enjoyed exposing Julia, with her "meat and potatoes palate," to genuine Chinese food. He came to respect her organizational skills and willingness to be a good sport when encountering inconveniences like leeches and tropical downpours. As the two spent more and more time together, Betty and the others silently cheered them on.

Meanwhile, Alex sat in a C-47 as it droned over the Burmese jungles toward a drop zone in Udon, near the Cambodian border. He had only recently completed jump training in Trincomalee and now sat silently with his team, each man dealing with the excitement, apprehension, and fear in his own way, occasionally glancing at each other with tight smiles of encouragement.[20] OSS was flying weapons, radio, and personnel into Thailand in support of the Free Thai guerrillas. Everything from bazookas to radio tubes was pulled off C-47s on hidden jungle runways and stashed in small shelters built in thickets surrounding the field. A sole American OSS officer had been operating in Bangkok for a month, hiding in plain sight under the noses of the Japanese. He coordinated the replacement of arms and equipment for the Free Thai guerrillas by radio, operating with a noisy gas-powered generator for up to eight hours a day. He was teetering on the edge of a nervous breakdown and needed to be exfiltrated.

OSS got the jump on Britain's Force 136 by parachuting the first guerrilla training team into Thailand on the night of May 26. A second attempt on May 29 claimed the life of the only American to die in OSS operations in Thailand when his B-24 crashed in the jungle.[21]

Cpl. Frank J. Chisari had set up a cozy billet for himself on the Kunming Airfield in the fuselage of a junked C-47, where he arranged his sleeping quarters and a fine radar workshop. He was kept busy repairing equipment for Chennault's fliers, and no other duties were imposed on him. Driving from the field to the mess hall one night, he stopped to give a lift to a Chinese coolie. They were sitting at a railroad crossing, the passing train, like all Chinese trains, overflowing with humanity fleeing from the fighting. Chisari heard a splash in a nearby rice paddy, and his passenger pointed at a barely noticeable ripple. The corporal waded out and took hold of a woman's legs near the surface, pulling her to safety. She was a pretty young peasant but clearly dead. Turning away, he spotted a bundle laying between the rails of the tracks and assumed it was the woman's belongings, which might identify her. Chisari picked up the bundle and was shocked to see a baby's face gazing silently at him.

"Ding how, ding how!" the coolie declared—very good, very good!—nodding vigorously.

The corporal carefully opened the neck of the little jacket and saw the baby was pitifully thin and undernourished. Cinders had been ground into her face and blood pumped steadily from a nasty gash running from her cheek to her throat. With the coolie driving madly, they sped to the air medical center. There Chisari was told bluntly that it was against regulations to treat a "native." An officer gave the baby's neck a quick swab and handed Chisari a container of sulfa powder.

When Chisari finally returned to the jeep, the coolie was no longer there. The corporal drove with his left hand, holding his fingers on the baby's wound to staunch the bleeding. The baby was turning pale, and Chisari was frightened. He screeched to a halt at the Catholic mission school, only to be told by the good father that only boys were being accepted, not girls. Desperate, Chisari began stopping people in the street. He was directed to another mission, where Chinese women waved him away, scolding "boo how, boo how" (no good, no good). The tiny girl had begun murmuring the Chinese word for water, which was Chisari's first clue that she was older than her malnourished body suggested.

Just then his buddy Howard Fenner rounded the corner, and the two of them rushed to a French mission, where they begged in high school French for aid. A sister reluctantly agreed to take the child, who was still bleeding and murmuring softly, in exchange for a promise of money and parachute silk. With grave trepidation, Chisari left the girl. When he returned to his makeshift home, he stared at his workbench, which was covered with equipment needing attention.[22]

The next day he walked into a deserted courtyard at the French mission and was taken to a dismal room where the little girl was lying alone, her face still covered with dirt and blood. Snatching the child up, he drove to the nearest Chinese hospital, hitched his .45 up high on his hip and kept one hand on it as he pushed his way to a doctor. When the doctor went to wave him away, Chisari slammed him up against a wall. The corporal was standing in a sea of Chinese, a bullying American with a gun and a bleeding baby girl. The doctor relented and, in perfect Yale-educated English, motioned to the nurse to stitch and treat the girl. They sent Chisari and his charge away, with no assurances she would survive. He settled her in his quarters, named her Ann, and began feeding her a concoction provided by the mess tent: soup, rice, and goat's milk. She ate heartily, settling in on Frank's cot while he got busy crafting diapers out of his supply of shorts.

Ann received a visitor almost immediately. Tony was a large proud German shepherd, one of the more famous of the war dogs much idolized by Sammy and known for tracking down and ruthlessly mauling Japanese snipers to death. Accompanied by his handler, the wolf-like creature silently approached the tiny child, observed her briefly, bent his huge head over her and licked, his tongue covering her face. As he nuzzled her with his nose, she laughed for the first time. Thereafter, no one, not even Frank, dared to pass Tony if he had been given the command to "watch" Ann, until his handler told him to stand down.[23] Ann's diet was now supplemented with water buffalo steak, chopped finely and mixed with greens, eggplant, and boiled potatoes. When Frank read sections of his hometown paper, sent by his wife, Ann studied a section in imitation. Then came the news that General Donovan was arriving for an inspection.

"You've got to get her under cover," Chisari's lieutenant informed him. "But don't worry—I've found a place."[24]

Kun Wei Orphanage, part of the China Inland Mission, was directly across the road from Kunming Airfield. Chisari had passed the walls a hundred times without knowing it was an orphanage run by German Lutheran sisters supported by wealthy Chinese women. Every bed was full, of course, but more promises

One of the "G.Is." was going along in a jeep and he saw a bundle thrown out of a train window in a lake. He was curious enough to stop and fish the bundle out and unwrap it. He found this little Chinese girl inside.

William Smith's sketch and Betty's description of "Ann," a rescued Chinese orphan
Reproduced with permission of Elizabeth P. McIntosh

of blankets and parachute silk bought another bed. Chisari left reluctantly as the deaconess led an unhappy Ann away. The next day he picked Ann up in the jeep, drove her to town, and bought her a doll and dress; then they dined at the mess hall and watched a movie at the post theater before he finally deposited an exhausted but happy child back at the orphanage. Chisari had a special seat built in his jeep, and each day he picked her up for a ride to the airfield, where she patiently watched him work.[25]

The MO crew learned of Corporal Chisari's mission and set to work on a campaign to fund Ann's education and upkeep at a reputable local orphanage. Bill Smith sketched the little girl, Betty wrote up the story, and they ran off a hundred leaflets on the offset press. Over $300 was collected in one lunch hour from OSS personnel, enough for Ann's board, education, and even a Chinese marriage dowry. The funds were promptly stolen, but in a twist of OSS fate, the thief was caught and found to be a Japanese agent. His interrogation yielded vital intel.

The reality of war outside the MO tent was becoming apparent in the faces of recent arrivals from the European theater. Thin-lipped and perpetually frowning, most of the arrivals were OGs—highly specialized guerrilla fighters who had been dropped by parachute behind German lines to blow up bridges, capture documents, and wreak general havoc on the enemy.[26] For young officers who had parachuted into Serbia, the contrast was disheartening. OSS captain Walter Mansfield wrote, "In Serbia there had been a strong sense of patriotism and duty which permeated all and gave rise to a fervent espirit de corps. Here in China, individual bravery is the exception rather than the rule."[27]

One day Charlie Fenn invited Betty to lunch at one of the out-of-bounds restaurants where he was meeting with some of the OG guys and a Vietnamese man he was trying to recruit to OSS. The two OGs arrived with a frail and wispy-looking Asian with sad eyes and a soft voice. His name was Nguyen Ai Quoc. He had rescued a downed American pilot and transported him through the jungles to Kunming, where he refused to accept any monetary reward for his efforts, asking only for a meeting with Claire Chennault, whom he admired greatly. Betty found herself feeling sorry for the small man, as he was largely ignored by the OGs, who told him Chennault would not be joining them and thereafter concerned themselves mainly with the food. Fenn began asking him questions about his group, the Vietminh. This recovered the OGs' attention, and they listened as he spoke quietly but passionately, first in French, then Russian, then English, striving to be understood. If only the French could be extracted from his country, he almost pleaded, democracy would have a chance. Betty and Fenn listened intently. It would be years before Betty would understand much of what was happening around them and how close they had been to a turn of the wheel of events when they listened to a thin man who would come to be known to the world as Ho Chi Minh.[28]

THIRTEEN
A GREAT
CATASTROPHE

If I am obliged to take up a bamboo spear, I will go
where I am told to go. But I will definitely not kill an American.
I will voluntarily become a prisoner. I curse those
who have swelled the ranks of our people's pride.
This is the source of all our unhappiness.

—*Diary entry of Watanabe Kazuo, March 1945, Tokyo*

Betty was in the new habit of waiting on the stone steps of Mei Yuan for Gordon Auchincloss to arrive on his motorcycle each morning. She would climb into the sidecar, and off they went to the radio hut, where she began her day sharing ideas for radio scripts. Often she woke in the night and recorded them, so she rarely arrived empty-handed. On the first morning of August, Betty and Gordon arrived to find Sy Nadler stomping up and down in a too-familiar pique of MO frustration.

"We gotta do something to get into Japan!" he almost screamed. Nadler was convinced that if the Hermit could predict something truly alarming, something to really rattle Japanese forces in China, word of it would get to the home islands almost by mental telepathy.

"Why don't you just tell them they're going to have a huge earthquake or something, maybe some sort of fire-from-the-sky kind of cataclysmic event?" Betty offered. "You know, a Great Catastrophe! That usually gets good play."

"Nah, that won't do," he snapped, shaking his head. But she finally convinced him to bend his energies to writing a script predicting a catastrophe for Japan the first week in August. Her work done, she headed down the road to the MO tent and coffee.[1]

⚒

Rain was drumming heavily on the roof of the MO shop where Betty had been working for several hours when Bill Smith remembered that Dulin, their boss, had been looking for her—"most urgent." Betty knew that "most urgent," in the OSS universe, could mean anywhere from an hour to three years but stopped what she was doing and walked to the administration building. As usual, Dulin was gazing out the window. He greeted her absent-mindedly and listened as she told him that the Hermit was going to predict a Great Catastrophe for the first week in August. He continued gazing in silence but then seemed to remember her presence.

"I'm sending you to Chungking for a couple of days to take some material to Lt. Laird Nagle and the Koreans he's working with," he said.

"Where should I find him and how will I know him?"

"You won't have any trouble spotting him," Dulin said, waving her concerns away. "In the first place his uniform won't match. He'll probably be wearing a French beret, British trousers, and an American shirt." Apparently whenever generals passed through for inspection the CO simply gave Nagle a wad of cash to clear out of the compound until the brass had departed. Dulin described Nagle as "possibly bewitched . . . likes little kids; they follow him like the pied piper . . . takes long walks in the hills . . . unpredictable . . . was negotiating to buy a little Chinese girl so he can send her home and educate her"—all this convinced Betty that Lieutenant Nagle was definitely an MO prototype.[2]

When the Chungking shuttle plane lowered itself below the cloud layers, Betty caught her first sight of the city. "I saw what appeared to be a flimsy city of matchboxes, flotsam snagged in the fork of the Yangtze and Kialing rivers," she wrote after the war, "a little less romantic than I'd imagined; but still it was China's courageous wartime capital belligerently facing east as if defying the Jap to push it back another li."[3]

China's wartime capital perched on a cliff high over the Yangtze, the first large city above the sheer rock gorges pinching that mighty river down to the width of a large creek. Chungking dominated the province of Szechwan, from which the republican revolution that overthrew the Manchu Dynasty had originated.

The city had a reputation for notoriously bad weather year-round. Fog and rain slicked the streets and alleys with slime during the winter months; summer brought a glaring sun and replaced the slime with equally thick dust. Bugs swam in the drinking water, and spiders four inches across crawled the walls.

When the Japanese first bombed Chungking in 1939, the leadership of Chiang Kai-shek and the courage of the people were nothing short of heroic. Foreign correspondents saw a city united against the Japanese onslaught and carried that image to the outside world. But when the curtain of censorship dropped down after Pearl Harbor, the West remained ignorant of the divisiveness and corruption that simultaneously descended on Chungking.

Betty walked out of the terminal building and spotted what had to be Lieutenant Nagle asleep at the wheel of a jeep. She tapped him lightly, and he awoke and smiled at her dazedly before welcoming her to Chungking and heading for OSS headquarters. On the ground, Chungking revealed itself in shades of camouflage gray, with occasional splashes of color appearing in the mist. Tibetan ponies pulled heavy carts, their bells jangling. Nagle pointed out that the rain-slicked road they were driving led through the Green Gate to T. V. Soong's mansion (Soong was the brother-in-law of Chiang Kai-shek) and to their destination, the Red Gate, staff house for OSS, which lay farther on just off the road. The OSS staff house was rumored to be richly decorated in teak and silk, with a steady supply of electricity since a "wily" OSS operator tapped T. V. Soong's private power line.

Betty and Nagle climbed steps winding along a mountain stream until they reached a stone building backed up against a gray-green cliff. Peach trees, bamboo, and willows graced the sides of the stream. A waterfall splashed into a rock pool. Inside the front door, a Chinese amah stood with a silver tray and two glasses of ice water to greet them as they settled themselves on a screened veranda, and Betty handed Nagle his documents. Before she left Kunming, Ting had taken her to the railroad yard to demonstrate the art of train sabotage. He produced diagrams for Nagle, who wanted to help some Koreans sabotage trains in the north. As they sipped ice water, Nagle told Betty about his Korean project, Mission Adder, which would take him to Linchuan to help Korean minority groups launch a sabotage campaign against the Japanese and their puppets. He tried without success to explain the complexities of working with minority groups in Chungking who, when not fighting the Japanese, fought each other. Nagle broke off abruptly and stared at Betty, leaning forward.

"Now here's an MO job that should have the woman's touch—sob stories on the Comfort Kittens," he announced. The term "Comfort Kitten" was derived from Comfort Kit, a package sent by Japanese families to their soldiers in the field. Each kit contained soap, toilet paper, cigarettes, and postcards. The coordinating agency was the Special Services unit, a Japanese version of the United Service Organizations (USO) charged with lifting the morale of troops in the field. One of the special services offered was obtaining, clearing, and authorizing prostitutes who were circulated among troops from Burma to the Pacific.[4] The Chinese captured some of these "Comfort Kittens" and learned that they were Koreans. Nagle wanted Betty to go interview them in the hospital and gather intel. With memories of the whorehouse in Honolulu, she set out that afternoon with an interpreter. She talked to five of the kittens, who were "of peasant stock, dull-looking but well-fed." Their focus at the moment was cadging cigarettes and borrowing lipsticks from the nurses. Two of the more demure ones said they did not like the work. All had been captured and sold to the Japanese. The three others shrugged and indicated "it was a living."

Betty asked the translator to clarify what was meant by "a living." After the war she recounted the interview:

> There followed a rapid exchange of brittle Korean with one of the Kittens, and finally the interpreter came in on the English wavelength with a proper snub:
> "She wants to know how much you American girls make."
> "Tell her the American Army doesn't have camp followers."
> More Korean.
> "She wants to know why not?"[5]

Pressing on, Betty learned the girls were sent out on circuits from coastal staging areas and rarely went to the front, although a few had come under fire. The kittens declared they would be glad when the war was over. They did not like all the traveling. Nagle was pleased with Betty's report.

"Let's whip up a true confession from one of these sweet girls," he gushed. "She was snatched from her home in Korea on the eve of her marriage to a fine, upstanding Korean; sold into the Jap army; disgraced. They have treated her beastly, but in moments of drunken abandon have admitted they are afraid of Korea. They admit the war is lost. People of Korea, strike back. What do you think, Mac?"

"Shades of William Randolph Hearst!"

Encouraged, Nagle ran with the idea, proposing that Betty should "dash off a sizzler against the Japanese troops: Mitsu's diary or something. Split the officers and men. Tell how officers pay Mitsu to spy on enlisted men, to find out if they're thinking dangerous thoughts." Betty liked Nagle and was sad to see him leave several days later, bound for what he called the "Chosen Land" with bales of MO material. Then she met up with Rosamunde Frame, whom she had last seen in Delhi early one morning in a fur-lined jacket, slacks tucked into boots, carbines strapped over her shoulder, preparing to load five trunks of operational party gowns into an airplane headed over the Hump. As they enjoyed chocolate sundaes in an out-of-bounds ice cream parlor, Betty listened as Rosie described being told she might have to be evacuated from Chungking as the Japanese closed in.

"So I ordered a complete escape outfit from Abercrombie & Fitch—including a collapsible bath tub!" she exclaimed.

Rosie was hired by R&A to compile target studies for the China air forces and fit pieces of intel on Japanese order of battle into whatever puzzle of battle reports she already had in order to hand over a more complete picture of what was happening in various places in China. Like Joan Bondurant and Maureen Patterson, Rosie was ordered to embed herself in the party circuit, where she trolled for information among rich Chinese in Chungking. She explained to Betty, "After all, men can't slip into a frothy party gown and listen to a lot of chitchat, especially if it's in Chinese. There are so many barriers between our two civilizations yet, and the well informed Americans in Chungking feel it's part of their job to know how the Chinese think and what they are doing. It's fun, you know, being a snoop. You can tell by the tables some Chinese set just who is trafficking on the black market. The other night I ate a lobster that never swam up the Yangtze."[6]

On August 6, 1945, Betty killed time waiting for Rosie to pick her up for a ride to the airport by writing to her parents. She chatted about Sammy's amazing progress in obedience class and described a quiet Sunday spent shopping for coolie coats and shoes with the fellows. She enclosed embroidered hankies for which she had traded a pack of cigarettes each and sealed the letter just as Rosie pulled up in an OSS jeep. Before walking to the shuttle, Betty remembered to pass on affectionate greetings from Paul Child, who was in Chungking earlier in the summer, and still carried a small torch for Rosie, Julia notwithstanding. Paul had been struck with the maudlin thought that he would not see Rosie again and worried about her. Betty thought Paul tended to cast the women in his life in something of a Pauline-in-Peril role. Rosamunde Frame, a determined woman carrying out real-life espionage and prepared for any contingency armed with the knowledge that a warm bath required a simple unpacking of her A&F bag, bore little resemblance to Paul's description: "I can almost hear, coming from the center of her hurricane, a gentle voice saying, 'Love me, for I too have something to give.'"[7]

On the ground in Kunming several hours later, Betty strolled into the MO tent, where no one glanced up to greet her. The staff was clustered around an OWI release. Finally Bill looked up.

"Did you hear the news?" he asked, an anguished look on his face. "It's awful, simply awful—we just dropped an atomic bomb over Hiroshima and wiped the whole God-damned city off the map!"[8] Betty was stricken. Her Great Catastrophe had fallen on the city of Hiroshima.

ᘏ

On August 7 the JCS received a memo from OSS officer Charles S. Cheston on "Morale Subversion Activities Directed to Japanese Resistance to Unconditional Surrender." It was still too early to know just how Japanese in the field would react to news of the atomic bomb devastation. There had been no noticeable weakening in Japanese determination to fight, and therefore morale subversion took on a new urgency. Ways had to be found to help the enemy surrender while "saving face." Above all, this mission had to be "black," with all operations "so conducted that they will not be traceable or chargeable to other than enemy sources, and thus the United States Government will be in a position at all times to disclaim and disavow any connection with the operations."[9] After spending most of the war discounting much of what Donovan's MO Branch was doing, suddenly everyone was interested in black propaganda and the possibility of a Japanese soldier being induced to surrender.

The problem remained, as stated by the JCS, that Japanese propagandists had been wielding Roosevelt's unconditional surrender pronouncement like a cudgel, reminding the population that there was no alternative but to continue fighting and that to cease resisting the enemy would bring on them "terrible catastrophes" such as "eternal enslavement, practical extermination, suppression of the Shinto religion, starvation, and a general reign of inhuman cruelty." The new task of MO was to "undo" the work of Japanese propagandists by somehow associating surrender with "desirable rather than feared prospects." The Japanese had to be convinced that further continuation of the war would bring down on them "all the evils they have been told would follow unconditional surrender at this time."[10] The Joint Chiefs had decided OSS MO should now commence doing what it had been doing all along.

In the interests of time, radio broadcasts were deemed to be the best way to conduct the new surrender inducement campaigns. Black radio could offer conjecture on the advantages to Japan of no invasion, such as retention of certain islands and continuation of the status of the emperor. Another proposal had Stalin presenting the Japanese leadership a secret peace proposal at Potsdam, offering to spare the home islands in return for giving up the rest of the occupied territory. An added commentary boasted that Japan had forced the Allies to set forth new lenient terms, declaring that such concessions will "ensure Japan's existence for 3000 more glorious years, etc., etc." Betty had to admit the schemes had merit.[11]

The suggestions continued to flood in from Washington, especially regarding rumors. The Japanese government could be described as planning to impose martial law to prevent workers from fleeing factories targeted by Allied bombs. Government priorities had become so bungled that whole warehouses stood full of airplane wings and fuselages while no motors had been manufactured, and workers sat idle in some factories while other vital industries could not meet quotas because of labor shortages. Perhaps the fear of starvation could be increased among the Japanese populace. Huge fires and bomb concussions might affect climate, causing unseasonable rains and consequent loss of crops. Along those lines, why not incite hoarding by "quoting" authorities advising families to store food in order to avoid future starvation.[12]

MO's fictional *Minshu* (The People) underground newspaper, ostensibly originating from the New Japan Party, cited Italy, Finland, Romania, Bulgaria, and Germany as proof that the Japanese militarists were liars. There was life after surrender. Unconditional surrender applied only to "the war leaders who have misled the Emperor . . . *not* to individual soldiers and civilians." Japan's industrial base would not be destroyed because it was so necessary for the rebuilding of Japan. Lastly, the Japanese people were to be "guaranteed the same freedom of religion that has been granted to every other nation which has surrendered." Rather than devastation, surrender would bring an end to the destruction of factories, railroads, and shipping; a return of the workforce from the war zones; and a liberation from the militarists' yoke.[13]

The MO shop printing presses hummed around the clock, putting out issues of newspapers, pamphlets, and cartoons that were then rushed to field bases for distribution. The work was hampered by monsoon rains deluging Kunming soon after the first atom bomb was dropped on Japan. The worst flood in twenty-five years ensued, driving swarms of rats, hungry for anything, out of ditches and drainpipes into the buildings. Shredded packs of Lucky Strikes littered the floors. A young major took to killing the creatures at all hours with his .22 hand-gun, collecting the corpses of his victims so as to prove they really were as big as he had been telling everyone. His largest kill to date measured twenty-two inches long without the tail; it looked more like a beaver than a rat. The doctors made him soak his rats in gasoline to kill fleas and lice.[14]

The compound, surrounded by a wall with no drainage, soon filled with brown water, and three generators ringed by sandbags chugged away around the clock, powering three portable pumps. Army engineers rigged pontoon-plank bridges between buildings, and bright orange airplane life rafts were being towed in the streets. The floors of all the buildings began to buckle, and the walls cracked. Water streamed through the barracks, floating foot lockers and dissolving clay walls. Every wall of the bachelors office quarters fell in, leaving a skeletal frame of wood holding up the roof. The fringe of the city became crowded with refugees from the countryside, many digging down under the water for cabbages and onions to eat as they moved over flooded fields. Occasionally the sun broke through briefly, and people scurried to spread rice and wheat on the rooftops to dry. On isolated islands of high ground, peasants continued to hoe their rice paddies, seemingly oblivious to the rushing water all around them.[15]

Betty and the others rowed to and from Mei Yuan and the MO tent in inflatable rafts. When the tent washed away, they transported their supplies to the mobile printing van that was perched just above the water line. Floating flotsam piled up on the bumpers. Betty was riding piggyback on Bill Smith when he stepped out of the print shop just as it dissolved into the mud. Halfway to the van, Bill stopped.

"Remember when I made staff and you sewed my new strips on upside down? And the MPs picked me up? Hm-m-m?" he asked, leaning backward. She did not believe he would actually dunk her. He did, to the cheers of her team members watching from the van.[16]

FOURTEEN
MERCY
MISSIONS

I knew the Japanese had not broken the spirit of
this Marine Sergeant. He paused at the door,
slapped a battered Marine Corps cap on the back of
his head and marched erect down the gangplank.
—*Elizabeth P. McIntosh, Kunming, 1945*

Alex McDonald's plane was crossing into Thailand on August 15 when a pilot burst out of the cockpit, his eyes wide, waving his arms.

"It's over!" he yelled. "The goddam war is over!"

Headquarters in Calcutta radioed that Hirohito had surrendered. The shouting and back pounding began, and the sergeant miraculously produced a case of beer, as only sergeants can do. The Free Thai boys sobbed openly as the plane banked and headed back to Rangoon. For all his desire for action, Alex was relieved not to be plunging into darkness and possible death. He would forever take consolation that he had been willing to do it at all. After only a night in ravaged Rangoon, he was airborne again, this time part of a contingent of OSS officers, including Jim Thompson and Howard Palmer, heading for Bangkok.[1]

Betty struggled with her conflicting emotions. There was the awfulness of the atomic bombings and the joy mixed with relief that the war was over. But the overwhelming feeling for her was one of loss. She was bereft. Her life as she had known it the last two years was over, and she wanted to stop time, absorb everything around her—all the intensity and purpose and beauty, even the devastation. She knew with certainty she would never again live each moment as fully. When someone pressed a celebratory highball into her hand, she had trouble drinking it. After the war Betty wrote of the irony of her anguish:

> Suddenly I didn't want to drink. I was glad, like everyone else, that it was over, because the people who might have been killed tomorrow in action would be alive now for the rest of their natural lives. But there was a sudden vacuum which peace had brought. Up to now there had been purpose, urgency, importance in doing what we were doing. Now suddenly things had no meaning. The jeeps outside were relics of a former age. The men in uniforms were now suddenly just civilians who would go home and try to find lost threads of an earlier life. They would never go out again and blow bridges or count Japanese convoys rolling along the dusty roads of China. . . . I was depressed about the sudden collapse of this exciting war world, and I kept telling myself not to be an idiot because there was so much to be done to win the peace. The world had to be patched up.[2]

Paul experienced a sudden exhaustion. "Everyone had themselves nerved up for another year of concentrated toil," he wrote his brother, "subconsciously for the most part, I guess—and we all suddenly feel as though our legs were made of rubber hoses, and as though almost nothing was worth the effort." He was refreshed, however, by the return of the irrepressible Gregory Bateson, who was instantly enchanted by his surroundings and who enlivened dinner conversations with his observations of the breastfeeding rituals of Chinese peasants as compared with those of the Burmese hill folk. He was invited to speak several times at the local university and managed to get lost en route each time, along with whoever had been charmed into accompanying him.[3]

Betty's sense of purpose also flickered back to life when, as she was walking with Sammy, Dick Heppner's staff car screeched to a halt beside them. Heppner told Betty and his dog to climb in; they were needed back at the compound. Not only was it the best thing that could have happened to her that night, but she also became part of what was arguably the last truly important operation in OSS history.

Douglas MacArthur had made his promised return to the Philippine Islands in October 1944, just as Betty was being elevated to Acting Head, OSS Morale Operations CBI. By January he had, with JCS approval, formulated a plan for the occupation of Japan at the end of hostilities. Blacklist called for complete disarmament and demobilization of the Japanese military and the restoration of law and order under a military government. It also called for the immediate rescue, relief, and repatriation of all Allied POWs and civilian internees being held throughout Asia.

The American public was as yet largely unaware of the terrible conditions being endured by those imprisoned in Japan. According to the *New York Times*, "Japanese are not invariably cruel to their prisoners." Probably without Mac-Arthur's blessing, the War Department invited OSS to spearhead the rescue effort. Edward Stettinius, U.S. secretary of state, charged Donovan with finding out what was happening to the Allied POWs. Colonel Heppner was by then chief of OSS in China and received his orders from Lt. Albert Wedemeyer, head of military operations for China. Heppner ordered the establishment of an OSS field unit in Hsian, located a thousand miles west of Seijo, which is now Seoul, South Korea. The field unit was to be a staging area for operations into Japan's "inner zone" of occupation.[4]

At Weihsin Internment Camp, where fifteen hundred civilian families were imprisoned, one dirty Chinese coolie, slow of mind and body, had been allowed outside the walls of the compound each day to remove pails of refuse from the latrines. Father Diego, a Catholic priest, volunteered for the unwanted job of cleaning the latrines and passing the buckets to the coolie. In actuality, the coolie was an OSS agent and Father Diego was his contact. Through the coolie and Father Diego, Heppner was able to monitor conditions in the camp until the end of the war. In mid-1944 Arthur M. Hummel and a British friend climbed the walls of Weihsin and escaped to join the band of guerrillas that was keeping Kunming apprised. A new Japanese commandant had taken over the camp shortly before the escape and provided a rare glimpse at the humanity of the enemy. When the men were reported missing, he assembled the camp and tearfully begged that no more escape attempts be made, as the episode had caused him to lose face with his superiors. Should it happen again, he would be forced to commit hara-kiri, and he had a family and did not want to die.[5]

Betty became a runner, carrying messages from Heppner's headquarters to the men in the communications center, who in turn flashed word to units in the field that OSS had been tasked with liberating American POWs from camps in

China and Indochina. It was back to rolled-up sleeves as cease-fire orders were sent out to field units and logistics for the Mercy Missions, as the overall operation was dubbed, were communicated to OSS officers.

Chennault's men provided staging facilities for sorties to rescue Maj. James Devereux and the Wake Island Marines and the Doolittle fliers in Peiping. The mission to free Gen. Jonathan Wainwright in Mukden received top priority. American civilians interned in Shanghai, Hanoi, and Hainan Island needed immediate medical aid. It quickly became apparent there was a shortage of qualified paratroopers but no shortage of volunteers, so the missions went forward.[6]

OSS Mercy Mission "bird" teams were code-named Magpie (heading to Peiping), Duck (to Weihsin), Flamingo (to Harbin, subsequently canceled and joined to Eagle, going to Keijo, Korea), and Cardinal (to Mukden). Personnel included SI, SO, Medical, and Communications (COMMO) officers with interpreters, and all except Cardinal were slated to fly in C-47s. Cardinal took a B-24 Liberator. The bird teams were tasked with locating the camps, assessing the condition of the prisoners, radioing out for needed supplies, and clearing an airstrip. Secondary concerns included securing Japanese documents and establishing an agent net to secure intelligence on Russian and Chinese activity, along with taking the temperature of political unrest and secret organizations. The worst POW cases were evacuated within three days of the bird teams' arrival. The teams could tell the prisoners that they were being rescued by OSS personnel, and treatment of all Japanese was to be "official, courteous, and impersonal."[7] Bill Smith learned he would be a member of Team Duck and gathered his pens and paint.

The Soviets invaded Manchuria on August 12, which put Operation Cardinal squarely in their zone of occupation. Team Cardinal, which included a Russian linguist, survived a near miss from a kamikaze Zero and received a tepid welcome from the Japanese on the ground. It took forty-five tense minutes to confirm the war was over.[8] Contact with the prisoners was allowed, but future landings and all evacuations had to be cleared with the Russians. Technically, all activities on the part of the United States at Mukden were a violation of Russo-Japanese treaty terms. Russians were flown in, and evacuations began on August 21. The Russians further delayed Wainwright's evacuation by refusing to furnish fuel for the planes, complaining of the arrival of too many U.S. planes and personnel, and restricting the amount of airstrip available, which meant a longer haul for supplies.[9]

The Russians eventually relented. They allowed the use of a northern strip nearer to the camp and promised to obtain permission for evacuations through the Port of Darien. But the fact remained that the evacuation missions had gotten off to a rough start between OSS Cardinal and its erstwhile Allies. Dick Heppner received a communication: "*DO NOT* plan on any Russian cooperation in any respect." Cardinal found 1,673 prisoners at Mukden, including 1,325 Americans. General Wainwright was being held at Xi'an, a hundred miles north of Mukden. Maj. Robert F. Lamar was dispatched to retrieve him, but the Russians insisted an armed guard accompany the train from Mukden, which delayed the operation several more days. When the general finally flew out on a B-24, he was followed by another plane with more VIPs: British lieutenant general A. E. Percival, who had surrendered Singapore; Sir Benton Thomas, prewar governor of British Borneo; Major General Calaghan of Australia; and A. W. L. Tjarda von S. Stachower, the last governor of the Netherlands East Indies.[10]

Back in Kunming the POWs began arriving on stretchers to the airfield, and their boils, shrunken limbs, and haggard faces brought the true darkness of the war into the OSS compound. The haunted weariness of the rescued men was almost too much to witness. Paul Child described them as the "hideous jetsam of bestiality" and observed that most were clutching "some symbolic connection with safety, a battered tin cup, a ragged hat, a dirty shawl." Most looked minutes from death.[11]

Bill Smith was initially flown to Xi'an on Heppner's special order. He was met by a dilapidated truck containing enthusiastic members of the Chefoo Boy Scout Troop. Some of the Doolittle fliers who had been captured after the 1942 Tokyo raid were being held at Xi'an, and Bill was sent to sketch them. He sat before George Barr, a pilot who had been rescued by OSS team Magpie when it jumped into Peiping. Barr had endured three years of solitary confinement and was gaunt with beriberi, too sick to be flown out by plane, greenish and pale. He stared vacantly at the broken knuckles of his hands.

"I was so overwhelmed I couldn't draw him," Bill confessed to Betty upon returning to Kunming, "but the sight of that man is still so vivid in my mind, I could sketch him now—or ten years from now—in every horrible detail."[12]

Team Duck landed safely at Weihsin on August 17 to a rather hostile Japanese reception. Colonel Nobuhilo Jimbo, CO of the entire Shangtung Peninsula, held Duck as prisoners in the POW compound, his reasoning being that he was required to cease fire, not allow the Americans to make use of his airfield. General

Wedemeyer had to intervene in order for evacuations to begin. Duck had still more troubles when the Chinese Communists, who had moved to within five miles of the camp, gained control of the railroad and cut off food supplies from Tsingtao. The Japanese began fighting the Communists, taking back the railroad and protecting the town from takeover by the Communist Eighth Route Army. Supplies began to arrive from Okinawa, and it soon became apparent that if the Japanese helped unload the planes less material disappeared than if the Chinese pitched in. Duck worked hard to raise the morale of the inmates at Weihsin, ordering a movie projector with film and magazines and arranging through the Swiss consul to get letters out to the prisoners' families.[13]

Weihsin internment camp was a former Presbyterian mission that had also been the birthplace of *Life* magazine publisher Henry R. Luce. The brick buildings, surrounded by a high wall, had been converted by the Japanese to hold fifteen hundred civilians for two and a half years. Bill found long, one-story buildings where families—two or three people, including children—had lived in rooms approximately nine by twelve feet. He climbed a wooden ladder, startling a Japanese sentry at the top, who snapped to attention and presented his rifle. Bill inspected the firearm, gave it back, and descended. Hoping he had established rapport, he returned the next day to sketch and paint the soldier, who was strangely grateful and left a bottle of sake on Bill's bunk that night.[14]

After his anguished visit at Xi'an, Bill found Weihsin a bit of a respite. The inmates had made the best of their predicament with varying degrees of resourcefulness. Each family cubicle had a tiny backyard where residents constructed stoves and shanty-town furniture. Stovepipes were tin cans pieced together, and bamboo, bricks, and crates were made into furniture. Women who had never cooked or sewed found they possessed these latent talents, although finding material to make clothing was a challenge. OSS teams' blue, red, and yellow parachute silk was quickly snapped up and transformed into beautiful dresses and blouses. A woman who had been an interior designer before the war made the cubicle she shared with her husband one of the "wonders of the camp." Supplies poured in: GI combat jackets, fatigue caps and shoes, and types of food the prisoners had never seen, such as canned butter and stews and lemonade powder.[15]

Bill made his rounds, sketching people at their normal tasks, which went on for some time until evacuation could be arranged. Bakers continued baking, people waited in line to fill water buckets, cooking on the backyard stoves went on, albeit with better food. Everyone in the camp, including the Japanese, was fascinated with Bill's work and understood he was capturing a moment in their personal histories. He was asked to put on an exhibition, and when the doors opened, he was moved and humbled to see a long line of internees waiting. Upon carefully viewing the paintings, they patiently returned to the back of the line to be able to come through again. When the first group of mostly hospital patients were finally evacuated to Tsingtao, Bill followed shortly after. There continued to be problems. Ten thousand armed Japanese troops remained in the area, and Chiang's government was warring with four different guerrilla factions. All sides needed to agree to take a respite from blowing up railroad lines long enough to get the internees safely out.[16]

Team Magpie found itself interned at the Grand Hotel Des Wagon-Lits under the courteous "protection" of the Japanese, who did not allow contact with the Allied prisoners. They were permitted to send in cigarettes. Eventually the Japanese relocated the prisoners to hotels in the city. Other bird missions met with varying degrees of success. Flamingo was canceled and folded into Eagle, which was turned away by the Japanese at Keijo, in Korea. When it was decided that U.S. troops would soon occupy the peninsula, Eagle too was canceled. Team Sparrow was interned by the Japanese in Shanghai when it landed with an Air Ground Aid Section (AGAS) mission.[17] Pigeon, a joint OSS-AGAS mission commanded by Capt. Jack Singlaub, safely jumped onto Haiman Island, but the radio was smashed. The Japanese proved more hospitable on Haiman, providing the team with one of their own radios. The mission found four hundred POWs, many dying of malnutrition and disease, and moved them to Sanya, where it set up a two-hundred-man hospital. Quail landed outside Hanoi together with an AGAS mission on August 22 and was welcomed by POWs running onto the field. Team leader Capt. Archimedes Patti was an Italian American who bore a distinct physical resemblance to Benito Mussolini. He was put in charge of all intelligence operations in Indochina in April 1945. His Bronze Star citation at the end of the war noted that when Patti took over his duties, the Japanese had wiped out OSS intelligence networks, leaving Japanese dispositions and intentions largely a mystery throughout the theater. Patti was credited with quickly cobbling together an agent network, probably with liberal amounts of unvouchered funds, and learning of the existence of five U.S. airmen and twenty-nine American members of the French Foreign Legion being held in Saigon. The

Japanese refused to allow a landing and immediately interned the five Frenchmen of Team Quail "for their own protection." They were eventually released. A great deal of animosity toward the French remained and never really dissipated.[18]

By October the rains and floods had stopped, the cholera epidemic in Kunming was in its last phases, and there was a brightness to the days and coolness at night that hinted at coming frost. The ban on eating Chinese food was finally lifted, and Betty and her friends gleefully traveled to their favorite restaurants once again, binging on spring rolls with garlic (*jaodze*), duck (*yaadze*), sweet and sour fish, pig meat, green bean pudding, and duck windpipe soup. They walked past large iron pots containing chestnuts and pebbles hanging over charcoal fires, and the smell of roasting chestnuts filled the air as the mixture was turned and stirred with shovels. The first rain since the flood settled the dry yellow dust that had previously coated everything. The flower street was an explosion of color, crowded with marigolds, zinnias, and cosmos. Blue-jacketed, brown-legged women trotted into the city each morning with enormous baskets of fall flowers. War had come and gone, and China remained as it had always been.[19]

FIFTEEN
OPERATION
ICEBERG

The Dutch were truly clinically crazy.
Who wouldn't be, considering that they had all
been prisoners of the Japanese?

—*Jane Foster*

On the evening of August 20, Jane Foster was summoned to a meeting with Col. John Coughlin. En route, she began a frenetic review of her most recent indiscretions, trying to decide which one was to land her in trouble this time. Too much fraternizing with the British consistently topped the list, but it was always Dr. Scofield who did that reprimanding. Upon arrival at the bungalow, Jane was relieved to see the coffee table set for cocktails. Over drinks the colonel explained that he would like Jane to remain in OSS for one more assignment, a trip to Java following the formal Japanese surrender there. As chance would have it, the operation would be headed up by Bob Coke, an old friend who ran the Bali hotel where she had stayed before the war while she painted and waited for her divorce to finalize. Major Coke would take a group of four to Singapore and then on to Batavia (later Jakarta) by way of a Royal Navy cruiser. As a woman, Jane was not allowed on the ship and so would be flown in on the first postwar plane to land on Java.

The Indonesians were in full revolt against the return of Dutch colonial rule. The mission was dangerous and therefore voluntary, Coughlin explained, but Jane was indispensable because of her language skill and familiarity with the area, plus she appeared to be the only one to have kept pace with the unfolding political situation in the region. One obstacle to mission success was the strong possibility for encounters with hostile Japanese who may have to be convinced of the need to surrender. Word of the surrender had not reached many Japanese commanders in fields, jungles, and islands, so the theater was littered with pockets of IJA forces that remained unaware or in denial of the fact the emperor had capitulated. As the colonel refilled their glasses, he explained that Jane would wear a military uniform and carry a pistol.

"Get a uniform from the WACs and I'll get someone to give you shooting lessons," he said.[1]

The field assignment brought a promotion, a pay raise from $3,300 to $4,300—which Jane didn't know at the time—and a shift from MO to SI, since she would be gathering intelligence for the War Department. By the time Jane landed in Java, the OSS was coming to the end of its extraordinary run. Donovan's enemies now included the new president of the United States, who on September 20, 1945, signed Executive Order 9621, ordering OSS dissolved October 1. R&A was absorbed by the State Department, and everything else went to the War Department. According to the executive order, the secretary of war should liquidate OSS activities "whenever he deems it compatible with the national interest."[2]

Assistant Secretary of War John McCloy, a friend of Donovan's, preserved SI and Counterintelligence (X-2) in a new office, the Strategic Services Unit. Someone in the Budget Bureau conceded that "the secret and counterintelligence activities of OSS should probably be continued at a fairly high level for probably another year," and Truman himself quickly came to the conclusion that "strategic warning" should be the mandate for any continuing intelligence operation.[3] The Cold War was looming, and everywhere in Asia the removal of the scab of Japanese occupation revealed a great mass of festering inflammation. In the midst of a frenzy of U.S. military demobilization, Truman grudgingly grasped the need to understand what was developing on the ground in China and Southeast Asia, and no one had a more complete picture than the people in OSS. No one had a better understanding of Indonesia, it was judged, than Jane Foster. Jane learned of her new status when form letters went out announcing, "in accordance with General Order 93," the "liquidation of OSS." A subsequent memo detailed her assignments to Rangoon, Bangkok, Sumatra, Java, and "numerous other points within the Theater," along with the possibility of an official station transfer to one of those locations.[4]

The mission to Java was called Operation Iceberg and had five objectives: interrogate POWs, begin war crimes investigations, survey American property, gather information about the members of Operation Caprice, and gather information about both Ripley I and II. Caprice and Ripley were intelligence teams that were missing and feared lost. Jane was also to take stock of the current political, sociological, and economic situation.[5] The original plan was to put Jane up on the beaches of Java from a submarine, but women were as unwelcome below the water as above when it came to oceangoing warships. In another version of the plan, she and a team of wireless radio operators would join ten other OSS personnel, lift off in a C-47 from either Rangoon or the Cocos Islands, and land or, if no airstrip presented itself, parachute into Batavia "immediately upon the cessation of hostilities of Japanese forces." Yet another plan involved the team attaching itself to any military mission that might be entering the area, which likely meant jumping into occupied territory with armed soldiers.[6]

The Dutch, predictably, were not keen on Operation Iceberg. The team had discussed this fact; many were familiar with Dutch colonialists and had spent some time in the region before the war. Jane had even been married to one. Colonel Berno of OSS requested the inclusion of OSS operatives with the initial intelligence "assault" on Java. In response, Captain Perks of the Royal Netherlands Navy—ranking representative of the Dutch government with SEAC—emphasized that the Netherlands East Indies was not, in fact, an American sphere of influence. Colonel Berno then made it clear the mission was already approved at the highest levels, and he was asking only to be polite.[7]

The first Betty heard about Operation Iceberg was a communication from Jane asking for spare clothing to take to the internees on Java. Betty made the rounds and sent a full A&F bag on the next Hump flight to Calcutta. Jane received Betty's bag and ultimately left with three black body bags full of clothing. Coughlin told her there were an estimated forty-five American POWs on Java, including three civilians.[8] When war erupted, American journalists, businessmen, and professors in Europe enjoyed "friendly enemy alien" status, allowing them comfortable confinement while arrangements were made for their exchange. The East had no such tradition of polite confinement, and when the Japanese juggernaut rolled across Southeast Asia, all English, Dutch, and American civilians living there were declared "enemy aliens" and interned for the duration of the war.[9]

᳁

Betty was in her bed in the predawn of October 3, dreaming that one of her booklets, *Medical Order Number 4: Bomb Loneliness*, was on display in the window of a bookstore in Tokyo. Sales were brisk, and the little books were being snapped up by soldiers who, having read some of her pamphlets, had deserted and found their way home to their families. They knew her work. It was a pleasant dream about her first best seller, even though she was a secret author—the work had been credited to the Japanese Patriotic Society. What made Betty smile in this half-drowsing dream state was that General MacArthur had been duped right along with the Japanese when he not only approved the reprinting but provided her with a sparkling new offset press and lots of ink.[10]

Betty came fully awake when three Chinese commandos outfitted in bandoleers and helmets tiptoed past her bed, giving her not a glance. Sammy yawned, but then he tended to ignore most Chinese. She threw on a robe in time to hear a deep blasting boom and machine gun rapid fire, along with chattering Chinese voices on her balcony. Walking to the balcony door, she watched as the three Chinese and her friend Al Cox, an OG—where had he come from?—assembled their machine gun. The gun refused to stay propped, and the legs kept sliding apart on the marble floor. At this point a fighter plane roared over the house so close she could see the face in the cockpit.

"They're strafing," yelled Al, motioning violently for her to get inside.

"Who's fighting whom?" she called, backing into the room.

"The Chinese are fighting the Chinese," he shouted. "Get dressed. Tell the rest of them to get dressed. There's a revolution going on and we may have to evacuate the lot of you."

Betty ran from room to room waking the girls. Everyone reacted in their own way to news that Kunming was having a revolution. Some headed for the showers. The bathroom became a clearing house of misinformation.

"If anyone tried to rape me I'll kill him," a voice came from the showers.

"Who'll try to rape you?"

"Soldiers. They're beasts once they taste blood."

"Chinese wouldn't rape white women."

"Oh no? Remember the rape of Nanking?"[11]

The immediate scuttlebutt in the compound was that these were not *their* Chinese commandos on a training exercise but the forces of a local warlord making his move to gain control of the province. By 6:30 the compound was on full alert, and bulletins were coming over the radio. Mortar bombardment could be heard and soon felt coming from the northern part of the city, and rifle shots were cracking all around them. The central government's man on the scene, General Tu, rallied the OSS-trained Chinese commandos as shock troops. Many of these commandos were Betty's friends, and concern for them suddenly brought the reality of the situation home to her. How tragically ironic would it be to be killed after the war had ended? A call from one of them, Col. Sammy Yuan, explained that the excitement had actually been instigated by Chiang, to "reorganize the government of Yunnan!"[12]

From the upper stories of the compound, troops were visible in a nearby rice paddy as they set up a 37 mm gun, but which way the gun was aimed was unclear. Troops massed at the base of West Mountain, and newly trained Chinese pilots used the opportunity to make roaring swoops over the city in pairs and threes. The air smelled of crushed eucalyptus leaves and cordite.[13]

Sammy was missing. Betty pushed her way through men rushing in bearing stretchers piled with medical supplies and food. Outside, a cowering Chinese guard told her "Shammee" had kept to his usual morning routine, slipping out the gate to go pay his respects to General Aurand's black cocker spaniel. Betty rounded a corner and found Sammy barking at an indignant group of ducks. He ignored her calls. Out of the lull in gunfire came a zing, and a bullet ricocheted off the plaster wall directly behind her, with two more following within seconds. Betty froze and considered "hitting the dirt," like in the movies, but somehow this seemed silly while she stood all alone with no actual enemy in sight. Besides, the ground was muddy and full of bugs. Sammy finally responded when she pretended to race him back to the compound, and they made it in the gate unscathed.

Mei Yuan settled into lockdown. The sounds of battle came over the walls, at times from a distance, then seemingly from the street outside. Boredom descended over the contingent until after dinner a muddy and excited American soldier appeared at the gate. He downed a glass of vodka and recounted coming under fire in his jeep. He had dived into the canal and swam underwater to arrive at their compound, which he had mistaken for a brothel. As he was ushered off for a bath and prophylactic eye drops, a shot rang out and a body tumbled through the beam of a searchlight from the compound wall.

"Nice winging!" someone sang out.

Al Cox (right) with unknown friend. As an
Operational Group officer, Cox trained and
equipped Chinese commando units.
Reproduced with permission of Elizabeth P. McIntosh

Al Cox had run out of ammo up on Betty's balcony and was sitting in something of a sulk in the corner, chafing at the confinement. Al was a man of action.
He had been one of Donovan's first OGs who trained second-generation Americans to parachute behind enemy lines in aid of resistance fighters. In recent
months he had commanded 5,000 handpicked American and Chinese volunteers in 110 combat teams.[14] One of his fellow officers emerged from the kitchen
at one point with an apron fitted over both his uniform and a holstered pistol.
He was helping the girls in the kitchen beat a bowl of fudge. As night drew to a

close, Major Kubler, chief of security, came in to report that Agnes, a Doberman in the K-9 Corps and the love of Sammy's life, had caught and mauled one of the warlord soldiers skulking around attempting to steal American supplies for the revolt. With morning word came that the resistance had ended due to some magical Chinese face-saving negotiations between Chiang and the warlord Governor Lung.

On the island of Java, Jane paused at her typewriter when submachine gun fire erupted across the street. She ran outside in time to see two young Indonesian teenagers in a small old car, top down, take a round of fire from a fat Dutch sergeant wearing a straw hat and sitting in a rocking chair, laughing hysterically. The car veered off the street and crashed into a flagpole flying a big American flag. Jane ran to the boys and saw they were unarmed and dead, the car covered with blood. She stood in shocked sadness until she heard what sounded like a swarm of bees over her head.

"For Christ's sake, Jane! Hit the ground!" Bob Coke screamed at her. She did so, crawling her way to a Banyan tree, where she hid in full view of the Dutch madman who continued to fire mindlessly. She reversed course, crawled to a window, and heaved herself over the edge, skinning everything badly. Covered with blood and mud, Jane yelled for an ambulance for the poor boys, though she knew it was too late.

"We can't get mixed up in this!" exclaimed one of the officers in the room. At that moment a tall turbaned Sikh colonel rushed out of the house next door, where the British were quartered. Jane wrote later, "[He] ran across the lawn, ignoring the bullets and shouting, 'You damned bloody murdering bastard!' He grabbed the machine gun out of the Dutchman's hands and flung it into the bushes. The Dutchman stared at him with his little pig eyes, smiled a bland schizophrenic smile and kept on rocking. Shortly after, a British ambulance hauled away the bodies and a truck towed away the pathetic little car."[15]

This would not be the last time Jane witnessed violence at the hands of the Dutch. What little sympathy she felt for them evaporated quickly as each night filled with the sound of gunfire. One night she found herself unable to sleep through the noise and went out to crouch on her balcony with her pistol. She watched "another fat Dutch sergeant" shoot and kill a young boy riding his bicycle. She took careful aim at the back of the Dutchman's head, only feet below her. Minutes passed before she crept back to bed, feeling every bit the coward.[16]

When Jane's plane had flown into Batavia, terrifyingly low, Allied POWs swarmed beneath it wearing ragged shorts, naked from the waist up, barefooted, waving and screaming. She pulled out her canteen and began swigging hits of cheap Indian gin—liquid courage carried for just this sort of occasion. The pilot decided to buzz the POW camp. They were met by a surly crew of Japanese on the airfield, and later another group of Japanese took up guard at the entrance to her hotel. It was immediately apparent that the situation was a powder keg. Retaliation on the part of Indonesians began swiftly, not only against unwanted authority and a lingering Japanese presence but also against certain unpopular minority groups, specifically the Chinese, in response to rumored Dutch plans to allow Chinese participation in a postwar government. The city swirled with rumor, mostly centering on the intentions of three opposing forces: the Allies, the Japanese, and the Indonesian Nationalists.[17]

By all accounts, the only ones behaving themselves were the Japanese, who had been ordered to keep order and to facilitate any Allied demand. The Allies were completely dependent on the Japanese for the maintenance of law and order, causing Indonesians to look down on the Allies. Not all Japanese had surrendered. Some had "gone native" and, like deserters in Burma, assumed native dress, speech, habits, and religion. Japanese-sponsored organizations were believed to still be functioning underground, and of course, there were the Communists.

As for the Caprice and Ripley agents, search parties had been launched by OSS Detachment 404. Jane rendezvoused with the sole Indonesian undercover operative with whom contact had been made; his identity was so secret no one really knew who he was until he sought Jane out. Over drinks she learned how he had been put ashore on Java off a British submarine, made his way to Batavia, and secured a job driving for the *kempei tai*. "Humpy" was a nervous little man, and Jane understood why. He described at length the intense level of anti-Dutch sentiment among Indonesians; hatred of the Japanese came in a close second. The British were viewed somewhat more favorably, and the Americans enjoyed high marks but were considered impotent. The "great mass of people wanted nothing short of independence," he told her. The independence movement had "great strength and breadth" from momentum that had begun building before the war. The Dutch were doing nothing to meet the movement's demands, and in fact their heavy-handed tactics were causing the violence to escalate by the hour.[18]

Humpy told Jane it was rumored that Achmed Sukarno, the president of the as yet unrecognized Indonesian Republic, had fled to Singapore along with his vice president, Mohammed Hatta, when the Allies arrived. That rumor was false. Sukarno was even then addressing large crowds of supporters almost nightly all over Batavia, and mob violence usually followed. The Japanese stopped trying to contain it and retreated to the areas they controlled. The Dutch made no secret of the fact they intended to execute Sukarno, and the Dutch and British began ordering the Japanese to surround Sukarno's rallies with tanks, guns trained on the crowd. Humpy was certain the Japanese were supplying the Nationalists with money and arms, raising expectations that the Japanese would rise up against the Allies when full reoccupation occurred. Jane had herself seen Japanese riding around in Batavia in cars flying the Nationalist flag, leading her to believe they were playing a double game: promoting strife subversively while avoiding responsibility by appearing to satisfy any Allied demands made on them.

Jane wore the .32-caliber pistol and holster she was issued under her left arm, but being left-handed, she knew she could never wrestle it out in an emergency. Fortunately, she was assigned a Japanese army captain, Oshida, as her aide-de-camp, and he was a gentleman. Captain Oshida was fluent in Malay, as was Jane, which dispensed with the need for English or Japanese in their communications. Her every wish was his command; he procured transportation, arranged housing for Air Force personnel coming in to pick up prisoners, and in general made her life easier.

Two days after the Indonesian boys were gunned down by the mad Dutchman, Sukarno and his entire cabinet called on the OSS team. He told the Americans simply, "We like the Americans and have nothing against them, but we do want our independence." This began a series of meetings with Sukarno and his cabinet, providing Jane Foster with the best firsthand intelligence concerning the developing situation in Indonesia. She compiled "reams of information" and worked late into the night to type up reports. She sent many reports by radio, but they were not acknowledged. Was anyone reading them?

Abruptly, Jane was ordered out of Indonesia and sent to Indochina (Vietnam) to prepare reports on the political climate there. Her C-47 limped into Saigon after a flight to rival the Hump. The plane was full of refugees, mostly children and pregnant women, all of whom began vomiting as soon as they were airborne. Jane tried to minister by handing out paper bags. The pilot flew by the nap of the earth, one hundred feet above the rice paddies, owing to remnants of sugar in the gas tank. Jane was well aware that if they had to ditch, the Vietminh below would probably show no mercy.

Saigon was pretty much as she remembered it, only shabbier. She ran into Edgar Snow, author of *Red Star over China*, whom she held in high regard as a journalist, and he became her companion during the day. Not long after they had arrived, she and Ed were lunching in a café on the main market square when hand grenades lobbed by the Vietminh began to explode, sending the two of them diving under a table. One of the perpetrators was caught when he threw a grenade in the window of the French Information Service and was torn limb from limb by French women standing in line for bread. Jane wrote that the situation in Saigon differed little from that in Batavia. The British controlled the city, but the Vietminh held the countryside and its roads. The French, recently released from prison camps, were fearful, angry, and undernourished, and behaved no better than had the Dutch.[19]

John Coughlin received orders for Jane's transfer back to Washington in mid-October. Her last working day was December 17, to be followed by one month's leave plus terminal leave concluding at 3:30 p.m., February 15.[20] Jane left Saigon with Ed Snow, who balanced a tiny Hermes typewriter on his knees and clacked away at it the entire flight to Bangkok. Jane was on a mercy mission of her own now, hoping to locate her ex-husband Leo, who was reportedly being held in a POW camp in Bangkok. Howard Palmer met Jane and Ed's plane and informed Jane that he had gotten her an actual palace as her transient billet. OSS did indeed occupy palaces around the city. The Swiss consul general located Leo for Jane. He was still being held by the Japanese in a detention camp. She found him thinner but healthy and still the paternalistic chauvinist she had loved and left.

Dillon Ripley and Edmond Taylor had been en route to Thailand in a C-47 September 19. Word came back that the air strip at Pukio was too wet for a landing, which meant the passengers might have to make a jump. Neither Dillon nor Ed had ever parachuted, and Dillon was quite concerned the contents of his suitcase—dinner jacket, white suits, and three bottles of scotch—would not make the trip intact.

"If you're afraid of losing your clothes, we can unpack and you jump in your dinner jacket and I'll jump in my white uniform," Ed offered.

Dillon continued to fret about the scotch until the pilot spotted six flares and a blinking flashlight in the darkness below, the signal to land. Maj. Alec

Griswold was waiting for them with a group of Thai who were tending the bonfires. Although the Japanese emperor had publicly surrendered and ordered his troops to cease fire, in Southeast Asia the fighting continued. Allied planes were taking fire over Moulmein and the Gulf of Martaban, and the last of what came to be a multitude of surrenders in Burma was still two weeks away. The world was far from being a safe place. Just before the first bomb was dropped on Hiroshima, Japanese suspicions about the Thai underground had led to an intense search for hidden bases. Pukio received ample warning of the sweep: Griswold retreated into the bush with a Collette novel; the Thai offered the officers in a Japanese patrol teacups of muddy water and made references to a recent outbreak of cholera. The searchers moved on quickly.[21]

Ed and Dillon continued on to Don Muang Airport in Bangkok, landing "secretly" in full daylight. Planning to pose as Swiss or Danes if they were stopped, they changed into white shirts, fedoras, and dark glasses and were driven across Bangkok. Stashed in the car were several .45s and machine guns. Dillon watched out the window as the car passed canals crowded with boats of every shape and size and enormous water buffalo in paddy fields surrounded by lotus and white egrets. Golden spires and horn-shaped finials adorning monastery and palace rooftops gleamed on the skyline. The two officers joined Howard Palmer in his plush OSS palace and set up their command post in a large second-floor living room, furnished with red leather sofas and chairs and a center table covered at all times with Mekong whiskey, Indo-Chinese brandy, and leaded crystal scotch glasses and decanters.[22]

The first order of business was safe transport of twenty-six allied POWs, including six downed American pilots, British officers, and a Chinese army sergeant. Plans were laid: direct contact would be made with the POWs in their internment camp and trucks commandeered to transport the prisoners out of the camp and up to Pukio, where they would be flown out—all under the noses of the still unsurrendered Japanese. The Thai regent, also living in hiding, insisted the POWs be given a send-off banquet there at the palace, so that had to be arranged as well. Predictably, the plan went afoul when the banquet was scheduled a night early, and the truck with the POWs showed up in the driveway before the event could be moved. After a dinner of steaks, pork chops, ice cream, and multiple rounds of whiskey, the freed prisoners were told they had to go back to the internment camp for another night to await the arrival of C-47s from Rangoon.[23]

Dillon found the prisoners an interesting group. They were mostly pilots or crews of P-51s downed by Japanese flak who managed to fall into the hands of the Thai—who then smuggled them into their own internment camp. One of the men had landed on a beach in a rubber raft to conduct reconnaissance of the coastline and offshore mines in advance of a proposed invasion force. There were four in his group, but he was the only one who managed to escape to the Thai; the other three were shot.

An American colonel, with a Nambu pistol on his hip, turned up in the palace driveway. He was full of information about his forced labor on the Burma-Siam Railway, a slave labor operation that cut through the jungle and cost an estimated 12,000 Allied lives. Another American was brought in just as the OSS contingent sat down for their usual ten-course breakfast. Yeoman Flanigan was from the long-missing USS *Houston*, which had vanished in the Battle of the Java Sea. The yeoman had recently escaped from a Japanese prison camp and been smuggled by boat down the canals to Bangkok. As he tucked into breakfast, his story too mesmerized the Americans. The *Houston*, by grudging admission of his Japanese captors, had sunk an aircraft carrier and rendered seventeen other vessels inoperable. Flanigan's information led to location of the last remnants of the *Houston*'s crewmen who had made their way out of jungle captivity.[24] On another morning a British captain with side arms arrived by parachute, ready to join the search for POWs. These wandering and rescued souls were for the most part in good shape, but starved for news and American cigarettes. Above all, they were bewildered by the OSS men and their palace accommodations.[25]

One of the palaces was occupied by Alexander MacDonald, who ultimately accepted the Japanese surrender in Thailand. The returned regent of Thailand was himself an OSS agent and eager to celebrate the end of the war by throwing dinner parties. Alex, along with his friend Jim Thompson, took on diplomatic duties, taking turns dining at the British, French, Danish, and Dutch embassies.[26] He would soon realize that staying on in Bangkok meant more to him than his marriage.

SIXTEEN
GOING
HOME

For the war, the hated and perilous and mad, had been home
for a long time too; everyone had learned how to live in it,
everyone had something to do, something that looked necessary,
and now we were back in this beautiful big safe place
called home and what would become of us?
—*Martha Gelhorn, quoted in* The Women Who Wrote the War

T he Chinese in Kunming celebrated the final signing of the surrender with an exploding galaxy of firecrackers. Pine boughs were erected over the OSS compound gateway and hung with banners reading, "Thank you, President Roosevelt and President Chiang," "Hooray for final victory," and "Let us now fight for Peace as we fighted [*sic*] for war!" Sixty-foot-long dragons made of flowers and paper whirled through the streets and alleys, accompanied by gongs, flutes, and drums. Every storefront boasted a Victory sign in gold and red.[1]

Col. Richard Heppner sent all personnel under his command a heartfelt memo of commendation, officially informing them of the imminent dissolution of their agency. It was a wistful communication: "I know that you share with me a regret that the group which worked in such close companionship during the war is already breaking up. . . . I am proud of you, thankful to have been associated with you, and will always speak of you with friendship and gratitude in the years to come."[2] Heppner put Paul Child up for the Medal of Freedom in CBI, writing, "With great technical skill he designed and built the War Room of Headquarters, United States Forces, China Theater . . . almost single-handedly creating the War Room out of a glaring dearth of materials and assistance."[3] Heppner's request was denied, and Paul was not "favorably considered." Any disappointment he may have felt was offset by his delight in receiving the Medal of Merit and a set of gold parachute wings for the part he played in training the very first unit of Chinese parachutists in the history of China.[4]

Marj Severyns planned to remain in China and eventually married fellow OSS officer Al Ravenholdt. She was happy about her new job as a news correspondent on special assignment to write a biography of the "Gitmo" (Chiang Kai-shek), with a luxurious salary of $300 a month and the promise of travel throughout the country.[5] Gregory Bateson received the Asiatic Campaign Service Ribbon for his participation in "clandestine missions," as well as the Emblem for Civilian Service. Dr. Cora DuBois, his official supervisor, wrote in the commendation paperwork, "Mr. Bateson is a person of outstanding intellectual ability. He has shown personal bravery and devotion to the Mission. He does not, however, have much interest in subjects not related to his area of specialization."[6]

Julia McWilliams received the Emblem of Meritorious Service for her work as head of the Registry Section of the Secretariat of OSS in the China theater. Captain Dulin wrote the citation, noting the critical importance of "registering, cataloguing and channeling a great volume of highly classified communications and documents," all of which she accomplished with "exceptional speed and accuracy." Julia had devised her own filing system to keep all branches of the agency in CBI interfacing smoothly. Dulin wrote, "Her drive and inherent cheerfulness, despite long hours of tedious work, served as a spur to greater effort for those working with her. Morale in her section could not have been higher."[7]

꒰

Getting out of what had started out as CBI turned out to be more difficult than getting in. Two C-54s, the *Neptune* and the *Trojan*, made regular trips over the Hump. Julia was scheduled to depart in the *Trojan*. She made it as far as Calcutta, where she sweltered in a ten-by-ten-foot room with five other women, one bare lightbulb hanging from the ceiling and one sheet for each Army cot. Word came that their boat would be leaving within two days—good news—but space problems required eighteen people to share each cabin—not such good news. Then word came from two OSS women who had shipped out two weeks prior but were now stuck for a month in Casablanca. Gregory flew back on the *Neptune*, still fascinated with his surroundings, although rarely clear as to where they were on a map.

Paul's return home became a connect-the-dots as he hopscotched across China from Kunming to Peking to Shanghai. He embraced and ultimately enjoyed the odyssey, which began on a train overflowing with Japanese civilian families laden with possessions and sitting in the aisles, on the cowcatchers, on the roofs of all the cars, and on the steps. When Paul made it to Shanghai, he found OSS in possession of three Studebaker limousines and quarters for six men and one secretary in a "swank" modern suburban home, complete with a famous chef from the city. The rent was a dollar a month, which the owner charged in hopes of keeping his house out of the hands of either the central government or the U.S. Marines. When the Japanese finally surrendered, OSS operatives were either already on the ground in Peking, Mukden, Tientsin, and Shanghai or the first ones to jump in. This meant having first dibs on temporary housing, cars, servants, and so forth, before the rest of the military gathered its skirts and followed.[8]

October 31, 1945, came and went, and still Paul remained in China, rising each day to load his gear in a jeep, drive to the airfield, and wait for a plane that never arrived. Negotiations between Mao Tse-tung and Chiang Kai-shek had broken down completely, and a tide of chaos was moving inexorably to engulf the country. Trains were delayed for days at a time when entire sections of track were removed or blown up, and planes in northern China were commandeered to move Chiang's troops to troubled areas. There was little to do but wander the streets, shopping for jade, ivory, bronze, and other souvenirs, many undoubtedly lifted from museums. Chinese tailors were kept busy making bathrobes and pajamas out of parachute silk for Americans to take home.

While picking up some newly sewn silk garments, Paul noticed a hapless Japanese civilian wander into an intersection just as a parade of Chinese soldiers reached the same spot. Someone shoved the man, and he was seized, beaten, and torn to shreds within minutes. Paul watched it all, horrified and disgusted, from his seat in a rickshaw. The same night he was returning to his quarters after a fine meal of steamed dumplings and rice wine when figures became visible in the black street. He found himself once again caught up in a "whirlpool of thousands of Chinese, some with torches, lighting up the scene with a wild orange light, many with clubs and ropes." Forty Japanese had been rounded up and

Paul Child in uniform with CBI patch
Reproduced with permission of
Elizabeth P. McIntosh

were summarily clubbed to death in the street. Paul wrote his brother, "I suppose the sudden presence of thousands of their own troops has released the pent up hatred, fear, and vengeance stored like dynamite for six long years."[9]

OSS had agents and paid informants, including women of the night, throughout the country. With intelligence from these sources, counterespionage teams conducted raids on Japanese and German hideouts, collecting documents, charts, and photographs clearly showing who had been collaborating with the Japanese from early in the war. The loot included much top-shelf liquor and French wines, all considered booty. Getting the booze home did not pose a problem—it did not last that long. British and French agents stepped up their operations with most of their spying targeting OSS.[10]

On August 25 the OSS commander of R2S, a base that had been gathering intelligence in the Fifth and Tenth War Areas, was traveling on the Lunghai Railroad en route to Suchow. His name was John Birch, and his mission was to seize Japanese documents, occupy the town, and report on airport conditions. At Huang-Kow, twenty miles west of Suchow, Communist troops of the 12th Regiment of the 11th Army District fired on the train. Birch was killed and his three comrades captured, along with nine of Chiang's government officials. Birch's body was recaptured and buried by a general of Suchow's puppet troops. Wedemeyer lodged an immediate protest with Mao Tse-tung. The incident marked a beginning salvo in the Cold War in Asia. Betty received word of Birch's demise from Rosie Frame. She had met Birch several times and always found him to be unfriendly and acerbic, and he made no secret of his resentment at being attached to OSS. She believed he was on his own personal mission, one he considered far superior to that of OSS or the U.S. military.

Jane made her way from Thailand to Singapore in a C-47; from there she flew in a C-54 to Calcutta. She was fed up with military hops in shot-up airplanes, and when priority orders came through sending her back to Washington, she instead took the first troopship leaving Calcutta for New York by way of the Suez Canal. She found herself among four thousand male officers and GIs and forty nurses and Red Cross girls. The ship was barely seaworthy, apparently thrown together in a great hurry during war production. Jane never bothered learning the ship's proper name and instead dubbed it the USS *Unspeakable*. She spent her days sitting on the deck, working on her Indonesian report, which she intended to make into a book, and sketching the troops down in what had become the psych ward on D-deck—poor boys, half of them black, who had survived the jungles of Burma. Jane found them "as wounded in their minds as if they had stopped a bullet or stepped on a mine, but they bled where it did not show." Eventually she scrounged pencils, paper, and crayons and passed them among the patients, encouraging them to express themselves as a form of therapy.[11]

Jane stepped off the boat in a New York snowstorm wearing a khaki shirt and skirt, WAC shoes, no stockings, and a tattered sweater given her by someone because she had given all her clothes away in Java. She showed up thus attired to brunch at the Plaza Hotel. Her mother got wind of this all the way out in San Francisco and insisted Jane use her accounts at Bergdorf Goodman, Bonwit Teller, and Bendel to be fitted.[12]

𓅂

On October 23 Betty was flying to India in the *Trojan* on a number two priority with Sammy, whom she had cleverly gotten classified as K-9 First Class under transfer orders, "having discharged his duties as a guard at OSS installations." Her plans had changed radically. Originally having intended to be home in Hawaii for Thanksgiving, she was now headed the other way, to Cairo, then Casablanca, the Azores, Bermuda, and then Washington, where she would stay for a couple of months to "see what gives." She was melancholy.

Alex continued to serve as diplomat and intelligence agent in Bangkok, pending the arrival of U.S. State Department officials to open an American legation. This duty lengthened, and he came to greatly enjoy the rounds of dinners and receptions at the British, French, Danish, and Dutch embassies. The original OSS contingent winnowed down to fewer than a dozen, including Alex and his good friend Jim Thompson. The Kingdom of Siam came to feel like home, and both men began "falling in love" with the city of "gaudy Buddhist temples, innumerable klongs, the cheerfully raucous market places, and the people themselves, so hospitable and so unaffectedly gay in spirit." When Jim announced he was separating from the Army in order to stay in Bangkok and set himself up in the business of trading fine Thai silk, Alex gave serious thought to his next move. His Thai friends suggested he use his talents as a newspaperman to start an English-language daily in Bangkok, and this seemed a perfect solution.[13] Betty gave the matter little thought before she opted to return to the United States. Their marriage was over. The drift between them had been steady and unrelenting, and where Alex had once lived in her heart now resided Dick Heppner.

Betty tried to cheer herself up by looking forward to her first camel ride, probably in Cairo. The trip from Kunming over the Hump on a Sunday was bumpy but otherwise uneventful, much less harrowing now absent the danger of flak. In Calcutta Betty curled up on a couch outside the main mess hall until her flight to Karachi was called at 3 a.m. She spent a day window shopping in Calcutta until she could leave on a war-weary C-54 at midnight. Dawn was breaking when the plane landed at Abadan, in the middle of the desert. At noon it flew on to Cairo. Arriving in Cairo at 5 p.m., Betty was snapped up by a couple of OSS OGs and escorted to see the Pyramids. They climbed into the interior of the largest pyramid by candlelight, awed by the masterpiece of Cheops dating from 2000 BC. Outside they sipped cider and had pictures taken with camels before they headed back to town, where Betty bought her mother a bottle of Essence of Shalimar perfume. The next morning they lifted off for Casablanca, the Azores, Bermuda, Miami, and then Washington. The adventure of a lifetime was over.

SEVENTEEN

HOME

I felt a growing sense of loyalty to a brave and brilliant,
if occasionally erratic, organization which had suddenly
been disinherited by the government.

—Elizabeth P. McIntosh

The first real shock upon reentry to life stateside was the absence of servants. It could now take a week, not a day, to get one's laundry back. No one dived for baggage, nor was there anyone bringing tea in the early morning. Betty knew her aunt had rented out her room even before she crossed the threshold en route to India in 1944, and so she found herself lucky to be offered a small cabin in one of the houseboats on the Potomac. This amounted to a cubbyhole aft of the engine, referred to as the "bear's armpit." She shared an adjoining "head" with a lieutenant from Burma and his wife, as well as another OSS couple from the European theater of operations.

When she was stopped from entering Que because she had no badge, she began to feel the weight of an "I've been overseas, dammit" chip on her shoulder. The building itself was the same maze of corridors, but now it echoed like a mausoleum. She located three SO guys from CBI who were playing the fan game: The blades on a fan were numbered, and an arrow was chalked on the wall beneath. Whatever number came up nearest the arrow won the pot. Al Cox, the OG who had set up the machine gun on Betty's balcony in Kunming, was manning the switch of the fan. Instead of holding Chinese revolutionaries at bay, they were battling boredom. And losing. Betty moved off in search of coffee, and when she passed the desk of a secretary, a name on the top of a stack of papers jumped out at her. The woman behind the desk noticed her interest.

"Do you know Jane Foster?" she asked, then handed Betty a sheaf of Jane's reports on Indonesia.

The papers bore no "Secret" or "Top Secret" stamp. Betty took them off and sat reading. Sukarno had explained to Jane in detail the aims and policies of his new republic, the strength of his military, the way he planned to dispose of foreign properties, either returning them or selling them to Indonesians. He had presented Jane with a petition for speedy negotiations addressing Allied acceptance of his Nationalist Police Defense Force to maintain order and a timetable for withdrawal of all Allied forces. Jane repeatedly emphasized in her report that the Indonesians were not planning a revolution, but rather sought peace.[1]

On November 9 Betty penned a letter to Hawaii:

> Dear Mummy,
> I am unhappily located in Washington, not knowing what to do with myself. Mac is getting out of the Navy and is staying in Bangkok and I am waiting for Dick to come back. I don't know what is going to happen but I hate waiting . . . I only wish I knew what was to become of me. I hope Dick comes through so you can meet him. He's a wonderful person and I know you'll like him.[2]

Betty felt a weariness, as though everything vital had drained away overnight, and she was adrift and as vulnerable as a child. She could not relax or sleep. She did not want to go back to the reporter's life she had before the war but did not know which way to turn. And there was something else wrong—she did not feel well. There had been no time in China to seek a diagnosis for the pain she felt in her ovaries. Now, along with the sadness, anxiety, and lack of purpose, she was truly uncomfortable. In this scared and uncertain state, she wanted to see one person above all others: Dick Heppner. She wanted him to come driving up as she walked. She wanted Sammy to jump out of the car with his slobbery tennis ball. She wanted to get in the car and be taken with them, someplace safe, familiar, and above all, meaningful. She took terminal leave and boarded a flight for Honolulu.[3]

🏹

When Jane finally returned to Washington, she was called into the office of the undersecretary of state, Dean Acheson, who listened to a synopsis of her report before he sent her off to the North Atlantic desk. Since the State Department did not recognize Indonesian independence and still considered the islands a Dutch colony, Indonesian affairs were handled by the North Atlantic desk. Whereas Acheson had listened politely, the head of the North Atlantic desk interrupted Jane almost immediately.

"Indonesia can never be a unified nation," he pronounced. "There are about a thousand islands and they all speak a different language." Jane patiently explained that she had lived and traveled extensively through all of the larger islands, and the inhabitants spoke a common lingua franca, Malay. Again she was interrupted.

"Sukarno has always been a nationalist who has agitated against the Dutch all his life. To him, Dutch and Japanese overlordship is the same thing."

Jane felt her fury rising. "I've just come back from there," she insisted. "Are you interviewing me because you want me to tell you something or do you just want to be confirmed in your preconceptions?"

Jane left the encounter disillusioned and tired, torn between wanting to forget it all and go back to painting and wanting to write a book on the revolution in Indonesia. She decided to travel to San Francisco and see her parents.[4] In subsequent weeks her outrage over the situation unfolding in the Netherlands East Indies got the better of her, and she decided to make public the essence of her OSS report. She held a lecture titled "Revolt in Indonesia" for the Institute of Pacific Relations. At 4 p.m. on January 11, 1946, she began her talk by asserting that "trigger-happy Dutchmen, backed by Empire policy, started the shooting in Java by firing wantonly at any available Indonesian . . . shooting anything that moved." Jane predicted years of bloodshed to come, as the Indonesian freedom movement, given a jump start by Japanese occupation, moved inexorably against the Dutch. "Indonesia wants a government like that of the Philippines. They want economic improvement. They want a voice in their own affairs . . . they favor private enterprise. . . . The Indonesians will win."[5]

A transcript of the speech was published in the *San Francisco Chronicle* and drew a quick response from Julie Goss Lynch, deputy director of the Netherlands Information Bureau. She placed blame for any shootings squarely on "extremist Indonesians" who had been "attacking internee camps and even hospitals with the result that many women and children of Dutch and other Allied nationalities have been killed and wounded."[6] In the face of this reaction and the indifference of the State Department, Jane left for New York, determined to write a book about her experiences.

The war had been over more than a year when Betty and Jane reconnected in New York, moving into an apartment on Central Park West. Betty began her own book on her wartime OSS experiences. She wanted to be near General Donovan's office to seek his advice and, as important, to be close to his junior attorney, Dick Heppner. While Jane stayed at the apartment and attempted to pull together a manuscript describing the true situation in Indonesia, Betty got herself hired at the State Department as a radio information specialist, overseeing all programming for the Voice of America (VOA) and writing news and commentary. VOA's stated mission was to "reflect the culture of this country and . . . promote international goodwill, understanding, and cooperation." All those mornings spent brainstorming with Auchincloss and Nadler had parlayed into yet more propaganda work.

Betty was, in effect, still working for "the General," who had been instrumental in VOA's evolution. Donovan's COI began feeding war news and commentary to commercial American short-wave stations for use on a voluntary basis before Pearl Harbor. Direct programming began after the United States entered the war, when VOA became an official broadcast institution of the U.S. government. The first live broadcast to Germany was February 1, 1942. It was introduced by "The Battle Hymn of the Republic" and included the pledge "Today and every day from now on, we will be with you from America to talk about the war. . . . The news may be good or bad for us—we will always tell you the truth." But Donovan had no intention of telling the truth to the Nazis, and so OWI took over operations when it split off from OSS in 1942.[7] The Cold War mission of VOA, as Betty described it years later, was to find many different ways to broadcast the message: "The Russians Are No Damned Good."[8]

Betty took the subway each week to Donovan's office at #2 Wall Street for feedback on the pages of her book draft. At the office she also found Dick

Heppner, who was more and more available for companionship as he waited for his divorce to be finalized. Betty's own divorce had been swift and painless when Alex elected to remain in Bangkok. Giving serious consideration to divorcing her own husband, Jane agreed to hold off until he returned from Europe.

Jane found herself losing interest in the Indonesia book. She was becoming more and more cynical about the prospects for change in that part of the world, largely owing to the support the United States was giving to its wartime colonialist Allies. But instead of returning to her painting, she resumed friendships with members of the American Communist Party she had known before the war. One character in particular was responsible for Jane's life taking a bad turn. Jack Soble was a naturalized U.S. citizen from Russia who had left for Japan just before the war broke out; allowed to leave Japan, it later emerged, with the agreement that he would do underground intelligence work for the Soviet Union. Back in the United States after the war, Soble expressed inordinate interest in Jane's OSS experience, especially her Indonesian report. By this time she had given talks on her report in public and passed copies of it to the press. The report eventually made it to the floor of the United Nations, where it was delivered by Dmitry Manuilsky, the Ukrainian delegate, as his own. The Federal Bureau of Investigation (FBI) became suspicious of the source of Manuilsky's report, even though the delegate could simply have read about Jane's experiences in Indonesia in the morning paper.[9]

Betty and Jane enjoyed renewing their friendship. The apartment on Central Park became a gathering place for "all sorts of characters," as Betty remembered, "most of them grim and somber Communists. Jane made great fun of them behind their backs." Sammy moved in with them as well. Betty learned that Sammy, who was brought to China on the first truck across the newly opened Burma Road, had developed a liking for gin during that trip, thanks to a generous GI driver. Each evening Betty and Jane mixed themselves dry martinis, and Sammy had his own out of a saucer. If she expected to be home late, Betty slipped a note under Jane's door: "Please be back early this evening and fix the martinis. Sam does not like to drink alone." It was a sweet time, but Betty understood her friend had changed. Jane's ebullience had been replaced by a deepening undercurrent of sadness. The two friends took long walks and did a great deal of shopping, but on the streets Jane seemed to be forever checking over her shoulder.

In the absence of the intensity, urgency, and oddly life-affirming atmosphere of the war, life reached a turning point for many of Donovan's dreamers. Some would never recover the sense of purpose and belonging they found in OSS. Some never spoke of their experiences, honoring a pledge of silence they had taken when preserving security was a life-and-death issue. Others carved out new paths that allowed them to continue some version of the life they had as members of America's first intelligence agency.

Betty was in love and ready for new challenges. Jane's life began a slow decline. She eventually followed her husband to Europe, where she leveraged her OSS propaganda credentials into a job with the U.S. Information Service (USIS) as head of the Austrian radio station in Vienna. She had not written her book, was still not painting as she had before, and rarely exhibited her past works. The pay at the radio station was not good, and Jane had retained a lifelong affinity for the finer things, as did her husband, who forever yearned to recapture the aristocratic conditions of his childhood in Saint Petersburg. Jane's favorite slogan was "Give me the luxuries in life and I'll do without the necessities."

Betty MacDonald and Richard Heppner were married in 1948, in the springtime garden of Betty's grandmother's home in Clinton, Connecticut, surrounded by OSS colleagues from China; Sammy was also in attendance. Immediately after the ceremony, the couple boarded a train for New York, where they enjoyed shows both on and off Broadway before they continued on to the Greenbrier Hotel in West Virginia for a luxurious honeymoon. It was the beginning of Betty's second happy marriage.

Later that same year, the FBI began questioning Betty about her friend Jane Foster. She told them Jane was a patriot. By that point J. Edgar Hoover had directed his agents to root out the significant number of communists or fellow travelers Donovan had recruited into OSS. Dick began helping Donovan destroy papers and files in the offices at #2 Wall Street that might strengthen Hoover's case.[10] Julia Child was also questioned that winter about Jane. She gave the opinion that she did not "think someone that funny and scattered could be a spy."[11]

By the spring of 1949, Chiang Kai-shek had resigned the presidency of China, Senator Joseph McCarthy was accusing fellow Americans of being communists, Russia had manufactured an atom bomb, and the Berlin Airlift continued. In China the only advantage the Nationalists had over Mao's forces was in the air. The Communists waged their guerrilla warfare to control the ground, but the Chinese air force and three airlines could supply ammunition, reinforcements, and food from Nanking.

January 3, 1950, saw the arrival in Hong Kong of William J. Donovan of Donovan, Leisure, Newton, Lombard, and Irvine with his legal team of former OSS officers, Duncan Lee and Dick Heppner. Betty accompanied them. Claire Chennault and his business partner Whiting Willauer had hired Donovan to secure the release of ninety-four airplanes that had been appropriated from Civil Air Transport Inc. (CAT) by Communist China. The planes that were not being stripped for parts were corroding in the salty sea air on the ground at Hong Kong's Kai Tak Airfield, while British authorities dithered and refused the Americans access to their property. CAT had its origin in Lend-Lease. Claire Chennault and Whiting Willauer, an Englishman, had purchased Lend-Lease airplanes and equipment from Chiang Kai-shek's Chinese government to create a provincial airline to serve as a regional link to the outside world. Chennault wanted to make money, but by 1949 he had become alarmed by what he perceived as an increased Russian presence in Asia. He added his voice supporting a domino theory of unfolding events. George Kennan's proposed policy of "containment" was gaining traction, and John P. Davies, a foremost China expert, contemplated the "selective use of air power" in China to compel the Chinese to moderate their behavior. Thus began the role of CAT, and its airplanes, in a scheme to transport covert aid to anticommunist groups in China.[12]

A huge wrench was thrown into this plan when Chinese employees, soon to be referred to as "defectors," decided the airplanes and everything associated with them should be transferred to the Communist-controlled mainland from Hong Kong. Predictably, Chennault and Willauer protested and hired Donovan to help retain what they considered their property. Everyone turned to the governing authority, the British, to make a ruling. Britain balked and declared the matter should be hashed out in court. The Americans were shocked by Britain's reticence to help. Over time the Foreign Office had begun to concur with what was coming out of British ambassador Ralph Stevenson's office in Hong Kong: "British interests would receive better treatment in Communist regions than in those still loyal to the Kuomintang."[13]

This led to de facto British diplomatic relations with the Communists. Chiang had never made the British welcome in his country during the war, and Whitehall was concluding that foreign trade would be more likely to improve under a stable Chinese Communist Party bent on industrialization than in a climate of ongoing civil war. While U.S. businesses were divesting, Britain aimed to establish a beachhead in a new Chinese market. It became increasingly clear that "disputes over the disposition of Nationalist property" in Hong Kong would be problematic. The goal was to protect trade—this became known as Britain's "Foot in the Door" policy.

Arriving in China with Donovan, Heppner, and Lee, Betty was delighted with the hotel accommodations, high on the hill overlooking Victoria Harbor, reached by riding a trolley up the mountainside. She was not happy to be in the company of Duncan Lee, whom she loathed, and she avoided him whenever possible. Lee had become involved with one of Betty's dear friends in China; the woman later killed herself when Lee cavalierly broke off the affair.

Donovan met with Hong Kong's governor, Sir Alexander Grantham, and requested the immediate release of the airplanes, which by that time were being picked clean. Donovan did not charm the governor when he pointed out that "had it not been for the United States, Britain would have lost the war." Grantham not only denied the request but the following day announced Great Britain's formal recognition of the Communist regime of China.[14] The proceedings ground to a halt, and Donovan and the Heppners decided to take a side trip to India.

"General, let's go see the Taj Majal, the most beautiful building in the world," said Betty, and the three friends went to Agra. As they strolled through the famous mausoleum, Donovan and Dick talked about the case the entire time.

"Gee, wasn't that wonderful?" Donovan commented about the Taj when they returned to their car.[15]

Donovan held another press conference criticizing Hong Kong officials and then turned the stage over to Chennault and Willauer so that they could air their complaints.[16] Afterward Gen. "Wild Bill" Donovan asked Betty if she would like to go shopping and maybe stop for a cup of tea. In the days to follow, Betty came to know a side of her former boss few others enjoyed, as they roamed the silk markets between courtroom sessions. He was a wonderful shopping companion; he truly enjoyed their outings and put a great deal of effort into examining different silks to purchase for his wife, repeatedly soliciting Betty's opinion on color and texture.[17] Donovan was still in the cloak-and-dagger business, however, and repeatedly excused himself to step out on the balcony and talk with lurking figures. When he came back in, he would explain it was "someone from mainland China who had come to bring me up to date on what was going on . . . still in touch with the underground folks."[18]

On November 7, 1947, a matronly, middle-aged woman, well-dressed in a dark suit and matching hat, had walked into the FBI building in Lower Manhattan and been escorted to a small room where she met with agents Ed Buckley and Don Jardine. Her name was Elizabeth Bentley. Jardine was the resident expert on communist espionage and had been putting together a file on a writer for the Communist *Daily Worker*. Both men were curious about this woman, Bentley, who had asked for an appointment to talk about information regarding un-American activities. Bentley began describing her background, emphasizing her growing hatred for fascism and her idealistic desire for a better world, to be a part of something greater than herself. The men listened as she rambled nervously, at times wondering if they had a nutcase on their hands. Then she began to offer details about her life as a Communist spy. The agents began taking notes. She described a complex web of relationships making up a Soviet espionage apparatus that had inserted agents into all levels of government agencies, including OSS. She began to name names. Jane Foster was one of them.[19]

EPILOGUE

We fought a stupid war, didn't we?
—*Torpedo factory worker, Nagasaki*

Betty was working on a children's book, *Inky, the Seeing Eye Dog*, at her and Dick's home in New Jersey when the doorbell rang and she was confronted by two FBI agents with pasty faces and black suits.[1] They flashed their badges and asked to come in for a chat. Foolishly, as she later recalled, she invited them in. Brushing past her, they immediately began searching the house, focusing on the study. Asking no permission, they pulled two volumes off the shelf, Hitler's *Mein Kampf* and Mao Tse-tung's *Little Red Book*. When they left, with her books, she found herself shaking and called Dick. He was predictably furious, as was Donovan. The war was over and OSS had been disbanded, but still Hoover pursued the former employees of his old nemesis. The harassment was more unnerving now in the poisonous atmosphere of McCarthy's madness, and the OSS could no longer protect them, although Allen Dulles was doing his best to shield those who had found their way into the CIA. Sixty years later, Betty was still indignant she didn't get her books back.[2]

After the war Paul Child became one of those OSS officers who found themselves absorbed into the State Department. He eventually came to work for the same agency as Jane Foster did, the USIS, and he and his new wife, Julia, were posted first to Paris, where they thrived, and then Bonn, where they did not. By the time they had moved to Germany, Julia was a graduate of Le Cordon Bleu and was working on a French cookbook for Americans with her collaborators Louisette Bertholle and Simone "Simca" Beck. Paul, who was fluent in French but spoke no German, felt himself a fish out of water. He turned to his artistic interests of painting and photography.

As books were being pulled out of the Heppner home library, Paul was watching the FBI remove books from the shelves of the USIS library in Berlin, including Dashiell Hammett's *The Maltese Falcon* and Theodore White's *Thunder out of China*. Many of Paul and Julia's former OSS colleagues from China had already been forced out of the diplomatic service and labeled as either communist or communist sympathizers or simply blamed for having "lost China" to the Reds. Paul was summoned to Washington, where he faced a security investigation based largely on guilt by association with Jane Foster. No, he did not believe she was a communist, and in fact he thought she was "too disorganized to become interested in any organization."[3]

Soon after the Childs arrived back in France, a lengthy letter from Jane arrived. She described an ordeal suffered in the States when she flew home to be with her mother, who was scheduled for stomach surgery. Four days after she had reached San Francisco, she received a visit from State Department security personnel who confiscated her passport without explanation. What ensued was the beginning of the unraveling of Jane's life:

> I got a lawyer in Washington (who was an ass and I later had to fire him). He had me go to Washington (I criss-crossed the continent four times in two months!) for an informal hearing before a hideous creature who looked like a tarantula—Ashley Nicholas—Deputy Director of the Passport Division. Out of seven charges that they came out with against me only two were correct (that I belonged to the Washington Bookshop and that I had picketed the White House for peace, in 1941). To show the nightmarish quality of it all . . . they accused me of such things as being an active communist at Mills College in 1934–35, and of having joined the Communist Party in the Indies . . . although I didn't go to the Indies until 1937! They also accused me of having circulated a Communist petition around the Queen's hotel in Kandy, Ceylon [during the war]![4]

Jane went on to describe five months of "unadulterated horror," during which she and her family were subjected to unremitting surveillance and harassment, terminating with an eight-hour interrogation. Her request for the return of her passport was denied. She languished in New York, missing her husband and dog, Maggie, back in Paris and feeling betrayed by the country she had served. After she had spent five weeks in a New York psychiatric hospital, a new judge found in Jane's favor and her passport was returned.[5]

Her letter to the Childs concluded, "They took practically a year out of my life, uselessly and senselessly—wrecked my health . . . and for what? My dear grateful country." Paul and Julia never saw Jane again and remained unaware of her virtual house arrest with George in Paris, where the couple was harassed and surveilled relentlessly. The constant surveillance contributed to Jane's paranoia, and she spiraled into despair and alcoholism. Just before Christmas 1956, she attempted suicide by taking an overdose of Nembutal.[6]

On July 8, 1957, Jane Foster was indicted on thirty-eight counts of espionage, almost entirely on the basis of the word of Boris Morros, a man whose credibility was challenged by many, but not the FBI. The main charges were that Jane and her husband, George, had been giving American military secrets to an international Soviet espionage ring since 1940. The FBI asserted that a "report on Indonesia," a copy of which Jane had wearily handed one of her French interrogators, provided solid evidence that she had been gathering intelligence for the Soviets on that country throughout the war. Betty, of course, had told the FBI that Jane could not get anything *in* to Indonesia during the war, let alone *out*. The indictments against Jane and George, which carried the death penalty, led Jane to another suicide attempt and the two of them, bickering to the last, barricading themselves in their small Paris apartment. Letters sent to Jane by Betty and other friends were intercepted and never delivered, exacerbating her isolation.

Paul ultimately became convinced of Jane's guilt, inexplicably believing she must have been a spy for Russia during their time together in Ceylon. His "Janie," a "messy, wild and funny girl, always in trouble, always gay, irresponsible and liked by everyone," he wrote, nevertheless "turned out to have been a secret agent for the Russians and caused endless trouble to all her former associates because suspicion naturally fell on us. Some of us went through Kafka-like investigations trying to throw off the guilt-by-association which stuck to us like glue."[7]

Betty lost touch with Jane even before the indictments, and the loss of her friend deeply saddened her, as she did not know the reason for it. Betty was one of those souls for whom a relationship, be it a friendship or a marriage, rarely soured—probably because she never demanded more than others could give. She cherished people, and they knew it, and she stayed in their lives the way a soft light fills all the corners of a room without being an intruder.

According to Susan Tennenbaum, Jane's niece by marriage, Jane "willed herself to die" on September 24, 1979. She was suffering from macular degeneration, which made it impossible for her to paint. She was sixty-seven years old.[8]

Alex MacDonald remained at the helm of the *Bangkok Post* for eight years before he returned home to New England. He and Betty remained dear friends until his death. Al Cox went on to serve as president of CAT Airlines. In her eulogy for Cox, Betty said, "In the years between 1949 and 1955, he was, beyond any question, the indispensable man, a figure of heroic proportions, with a list of achievements that will never be quantified."[9]

In May 1949 a reporter for the *New York Daily News* was granted entrance into the New York home of Mme. Chiang Kai-shek, at 4904 Independence Avenue, in Riverdale. She listened carefully to the story of a six-year-old girl who was living in an orphanage in Kunming, China, and pledged on the spot to help reunite the child with Cpl. Frank Chisari, by then a $70 a week technician at the New York Naval Ship Yard. In June Ann was released from the orphanage into the custody of two waiting agents of Generalissimo Chiang Kai-shek. She was reunited with Frank Chisari and welcomed into his family within weeks.[10]

Dick Heppner took leave from his partnership in Donovan's law firm in 1957 to assume a position in Washington as deputy assistant secretary of defense for international security, appointed by Dwight D. Eisenhower. The Heppners rented a lovely little garden house on the Potomac River in Alexandria, Virginia, where Betty worked at home on *Inky* and volunteered at a seeing-eye dog school. Their family had grown to include two Siamese cats. This happy life came to an abrupt end on May 14, 1958, when after collapsing at his desk in the Pentagon with a burst aorta, Dick perished in Walter Reed Hospital. He was forty-nine years old, and Betty was forty-three. For the first time in her life, Betty was emotionally devastated. She remained in a daze for some months, when finally Al Cox and other friends convinced her to go see Allen Dulles.

Dulles was still in his old office on E Street, as the new marble and glass CIA building in Langley, Virginia, was not yet completed. He sat with his pipe, slippers on his feet, a map of the world covering the entire wall behind him.

"Well, are you ready to get back to work?" he asked Betty.

"Yes," she said simply.

"Alright, here's what we're going to do," he began and outlined an operation tailor-made for her. At the time Betty was completing another book, this one based in Turkey, where she spent some time with her mother after she and Jane had been evicted from their New York apartment. *Palaces under the Sea* centered on the scuba-diving adventures of the young son of an American Army colonel. The boy uncovers ancient treasures in the Mediterranean Sea and in the process encounters nefarious smugglers, very much in the Hardy Boy tradition. Dulles had the book translated into Japanese, and it became the focus of an extended working book tour in Japan, where she was assigned to the CIA Tokyo Station, handling agents as a case officer in what was by that time the Cold War. Betty felt she had returned home.

Communism had begun gaining strength in a shattered postwar Japan. More than 6.5 million Japanese were stranded in Asia, the Pacific, and Siberia at war's end. Many were held more than four years by the Soviets to offset their labor shortages. As soldiers and sailors made their way home, they bore little resemblance to the heroes who had left to fight for Yamato, the divine spirit of the Japanese people—"one million hearts beating as one." When soldiers returned unkempt and unshaven, they were often loaded down with loot from military warehouses, provisions that had been withheld from a ravished and near-starving civilian population. The public reacted with disgust. One historian observed, "The Emperor's loyal soldiers and sailors seem to have metamorphed overnight into symbols of the worst sort of egoism and atomization."[11]

Japanese veterans suffering from battle shock were shunned; the disabled were stigmatized, suffering the double humiliation of losing not only the war but also their physical wholeness. Homeless orphans lived in railroad stations, in abandoned ruins, and under railroad overpasses. They were regularly rounded up and taken to militaristic detention centers. War widows were left to fend for themselves and resented returning veterans who received severance pay, rice rations, and clothing. Wartime demonization of "devilish Anglo-Americans" was almost seamlessly redirected to "militarists," "ultra-nationalists," and *gymbatsu*—"military cliques." There was great enthusiasm for war crimes trials.[12]

Some adapted the *akari* attitude—"bright and new"—and embraced recovered hope for their lives. They removed blackout paper from their windows and abandoned mindless obedience to an authoritarian state. Sword makers began producing kitchen knives; machine gun plants made sewing machines; steel helmets became cooking pots. GIs bought "Baby Pearl" cameras created by optics technicians who had produced lenses for the military. Designers of Nakajima fighter planes made motor scooters from tail parts of the Ginga bomber. Liquor manufacturers marketed a "Special Six-Year-Old Brandy," distilled especially for the occupation forces.[13]

ℷ

Decades after World War II, the living members of OSS formed the Office of Strategic Services Society, and like siblings separated at birth, Donovan's dreamers began to find each other. People who had served within fifty miles of each other in China, or even in the same city, had never met while the war raged. This held true for those who went on to work for the CIA, such being the nature of compartmentalization and clandestine operations. While working undercover in Japan, Betty Heppner met her third and final husband, Fred McIntosh, who served there as a fighter pilot. When they retired, they enjoyed a large country home in Leesburg, Virginia, where Betty tended all manner of wildlife and doted on her dogs, cats, and goats. At age eighty she was regularly seen flying across the grounds on a dirt bike.

When Fred passed away, she was bereft once again and moved into an upscale assisted living facility, which turned out to be a veritable nest of retired spies. The old OSS warriors began to set aside their sworn secrecies and come together, comparing experiences and remembering "the General." Jedburghs described parachuting into France; Marine Unit sailors showed pictures of piloting fast boats in operations off the coast of Burma; a Communications Branch radio operator recalled being set down in the Chinese backcountry, where he lived off the land and transmitted coordinates by suitcase radio. The world began to hear of OSS, and the accolades, interviews, and feature stories began.

Dillon Ripley served for many years as the director of the Smithsonian Institution in Washington, D.C., and Gregory Bateson continued his career as a noted anthropologist and husband to Margaret Mead. Bill Smith, already a well-known artist before the war, enjoyed continued success and a wonderful family. He maintained a lifelong relationship with Betty McIntosh, as did Peter Glemser and Bill Magistretti. Julia Child's fame as a celebrity chef eclipsed her role in OSS for years, but she remained close friends with Betty until her death. Late in the summer of 2004, Betty sat watching the geese on the pond outside her window,

Betty with one of her beloved collies
on her Leesburg estate in the 1980s
Reproduced with permission of
Elizabeth P. McIntosh

listening to her old friend Julia describe the scene outside her own hospice window in California, where she was watching her cats. Julia died within two days of her ninety-second birthday.

Friendships forged in war are often lifelong, but people who served in OSS held another bond that came from being part of greatness. When he gave his farewell address to the men and women of OSS in 1945, William J. Donovan said, "This experiment was to determine whether a group of Americans constituting a cross section of racial origins, of abilities, of temperaments and talents could meet and risk an encounter with a long-established and trained enemy." Donovan's experiment helped win a war and in the process changed lives.

On Memorial Day in 1994, Betty had the honor of introducing President Bill Clinton, during the fiftieth anniversary celebration of D-day, before he placed a wreath at the Tomb of the Unknowns. In her book *Sisterhood of Spies*, she recalled that day in Arlington:

Elizabeth McIntosh introduced President
Bill Clinton on the 1994 anniversary of D-day.
Reproduced with permission of Elizabeth P. McIntosh

Elizabeth McIntosh inscribing a copy of her
book *Sisterhood of Spies* for the director of
central intelligence, George Tenet.
Reproduced with permission of Elizabeth P. McIntosh

Beneath the bright sun, I could see again the shadows of friends long gone: General Donovan lying next to his wife Ruth; OSS comrades, resting nearby in their final underground; my own husband, Col. Richard P. Heppner, who headed OSS in China, buried beside his best friend, Russell B. Livermore, an OSS colonel who fought with the resistance in Italy. Beyond another hill are the ashes of William Magistretti, the man responsible for the surrender of hundreds of Japanese in Burma. There are many, many more. The names, the faces, are blurred with time, but not those memories of a half a century ago.[14]

NOTES

PREFACE

1. Peter Mandler, *Return from the Natives: How Margaret Mead Won the Second World War and Lost the Cold War* (New Haven, CT: Yale University Press, 2013), 33–34.

2. Dr. Cora DuBois also rose to a position of leadership when she was made head of R&A for Detachment 404 in Ceylon. See Elizabeth McIntosh, *Sisterhood of Spies: The Women of the OSS* (Annapolis, MD: Naval Institute Press, 1998), 42.

INTRODUCTION

1. MO—Morale Operations Washington MO Drafts OSS, Box 7, E 116, RG 226, National Archives and Records Administration, College Park, MD (NARA II).

2. James Grafton Rogers, *Wartime Washington: The Secret OSS Journal of James Grafton Rogers 1942–1943*, ed. Thomas F. Troy (Frederick, MD: University Publications of America, 1987), xxvi.

3. Bradley F. Smith, *Shadow Warriors: O.S.S. and the Origins of the C.I.A.* (New York: Basic Books, 1983), 159. See also Thomas F. Troy, *Donovan and the CIA: A History of the Establishment of the Central Intelligence Agency* (Frederick, MD: Aletheia Books, 1981), 192. Troy notes that although the military "generally cared little for OSS," it nonetheless wanted control over any psychological operations directly affecting military strategy.

4. John W. Dower, *Embracing Defeat: Japan in the Wake of World War II* (New York: W. W. Norton, 1999), 218.

5. Lafcadio Hearn, *Glimpses of Unfamiliar Japan* (Boston: Houghton, Mifflin, 1895; Internet Archive, 2009), https://archive.org/details/glimpsesunfamil 09heargoog.

6. Haruko Taya Cook and Theodore F. Cook, *Japan at War: An Oral History* (New York: New Press, 1992), 42–43.

CHAPTER 1. VOYAGE BEFORE THE STORM

1. According to U.S. National Archive records, in 1951 all copies of passenger lists, manifests, logs of vessels, and troop movement files of the U.S. Army Transports for World War II were destroyed. Memoirs and newspaper accounts like those Betty filed provide the only verifiable information.

2. The U.S. War Department had a working defense strategy in place for the Philippines, Orange Plan 3, which involved an immediate retreat to the Bataan Peninsula in order to defend Manila Bay and await rescue. The plan hinged on a quick and early exit, with adequate supplies of food and medicine on hand for the holdout. MacArthur in fact rejected Orange Plan 3, which he believed amounted to sacrificing the Philippines to the Japanese, however temporarily. He believed, in sharp disagreement with his naval colleagues, that the key to success was a buildup of airpower and reliance on his nascent army of indigenous soldiers.

3. Elizabeth MacDonald, *Honolulu Star-Bulletin*, May 8, 1941.

4. Ibid.

5. More than five hundred black nurses served in the Army Nurse Corps during World War II in segregated units in the United States and abroad, including in Burma. See Carolyn M. Feller and Constance J. Moore, *Highlights in the History of the Army Nurse Corps*, rev. and expanded ed. (Washington, DC: U.S. Army Center of Military History, 1996).

6. *The Oahuan*, Punahou High School Yearbook, 1931.

7. MacDonald, *Honolulu Star-Bulletin*, May 8, 1941.

8. Elizabeth MacDonald, *Honolulu Star-Bulletin*, June 4, 1941.

9. Alexander MacDonald, *My Footloose Newspaper Life* (Bangkok: Post Publishing, 1990), 64.

10. Elizabeth McIntosh, interview by the author, October 15, 2011.

11. MacDonald, *My Footloose Newspaper Life*, 68.

CHAPTER 2. WAR

1. Elizabeth McIntosh, interview by the author, October 15, 2010.
2. Gwenfread Allen, *Hawaii's War Years, 1941–1945* (Honolulu: Pacific Monograph, 1999), 32.
3. Elizabeth P. McIntosh Personal Papers, private collection (hereafter cited as McIntosh Papers).
4. Tom Moon, *This Grim and Savage Game: OSS and the Beginning of U.S. Covert Operations in World War II* (Cambridge, MA: Da Capo Press, 2000), 21; Allen, *Hawaii's War Years,* 27.
5. McIntosh Papers; Elizabeth McIntosh, interview by the author, September 19, 2013.
6. Elizabeth McIntosh, interview by the author, June 4, 2012.
7. Nancy Caldwell Sorel, *The Women Who Wrote the War* (New York: Arcade, 1999), 152.
8. Ibid., 154.
9. Ibid., 156.
10. The *kempei tai* functioned as secret police for the IJA and specialized in thought control.
11. Christopher Bayly and Tim Harper, *Forgotten Armies: The Fall of British Asia, 1941–1945* (Cambridge, MA: Belknap Press of Harvard University Press, 2005).
12. Paul Frillman and Graham Peck, *China, The Remembered Life* (New York: Houghton Mifflin, 1968), 147.
13. Ibid., 108.
14. Richard Dunlop, *Behind Japanese Lines, with the OSS in Burma* (Chicago: Rand McNally, 1979), 56–61.
15. Cook and Cook, *Japan at War,* 71.
16. Donald Keene, *So Lovely a Country Will Never Perish: Wartime Diaries of Japanese Writers* (New York: Columbia University Press, 2010), 12.
17. Cook and Cook, *Japan at War,* 237.
18. Allen, *Hawaii's War Years,* 158–59.
19. MacDonald, *My Footloose Newspaper Life,* 73.
20. McIntosh interview, June 4, 2012.
21. Sorel, *Women Who Wrote the War,* 148.
22. See Burl Burlingame, *Advance Force Pearl Harbor* (Honolulu: University of Hawaii Press, 1992).
23. Ibid., 154.
24. Unpublished article, 1942, in McIntosh Papers.

25. Allen, *Hawaii's War Years*, 136; McIntosh interview, September 19, 2013.
26. Allen, *Hawaii's War Years*, 136.

CHAPTER 3. RECRUITMENT

1. McIntosh Papers.
2. Ibid.
3. Emily Yellin, *Our Mother's War: American Women at Home and at the Front during World War II* (New York: Free Press: 2004), 292.
4. Elizabeth McIntosh, interview by the author, October 9, 2010.
5. Elizabeth MacDonald, Homefront Forecast, April 27, 1943.
6. Samuel Hideo Yamashita, *Daily Life in Wartime Japan, 1940–1945* (Lawrence: University of Press of Kansas, 2015), 14–15.
7. Cook and Cook, *Japan at War*, 172.
8. Elizabeth MacDonald, Homefront Forecast, June 1, 1943.
9. McIntosh interview, June 4, 2012.
10. Elizabeth P. MacDonald, *Undercover Girl* (New York: Macmillan, 1947), 3–4.
11. McIntosh interview, June 4, 2012.
12. *The Oahuan*, Punahou High School Yearbook, 1931.
13. MacDonald, *Undercover Girl*, 1.
14. Paul E. Hurlbut, letter from Employment Division of the Civil Service Commission, Box 245, E 225, RG 226, NARA II.
15. Edmond Taylor, *Awakening from History* (Boston: Gambit, 1969), 342.
16. MacDonald, *Undercover Girl*, 5.
17. Ibid., 6. The area from Twenty-Third to Twenty-Fifth Streets NW, between Constitution Avenue and E Street, was filled with temporary buildings such as M and Q, the latter occupied by COI, then OSS, and later the CIA, until it was replaced by the Kennedy Center.
18. Ibid.
19. Philip Warner, *Secret Forces of World War II* (Chelsea, MI: Scarborough House, 1991), 163. Within SOE, the subbranch of SO2 was, before autumn 1941, charged with black propaganda on the European continent. In August 1941 SO2 was separated from SOE to become the Political Warfare Executive (PWE) and took cover under the Political Intelligence Department (PID), which gathered information about the political state of the enemy government. This amounted to a secret agency within a secret agency. The very existence of PWE, as well as its activities, was deemed scandalous by many Britons when it was made public.
20. MacDonald, *Undercover Girl*, 9.

21. Frillman and Peck, *China*, 208.

22. McIntosh, *Sisterhood of Spies*, 295. The anti-Chiang old China hands contingent of OSS came under repeated suspicion for communist sympathies. Most were missionaries or children of missionaries and had connections with the numerous Christian colleges in China. They professed no particular love for communist atheism but were repulsed by what appeared to them a corrupt and callous disregard for the welfare of the Chinese people on the part of the Kuomintang and were especially offended by the extent to which greed had led to high-level Chinese government collaboration with the Japanese. See R. Harris Smith, *OSS: The Secret History of America's First Intelligence Agency* (Berkeley: University of California Press, 1972), 245.

23. Dillon Ripley Papers, Record Unit 7008, Box 9, Smithsonian Institution Archives, Washington, DC.

24. Dixie R. Bartholomew-Feis, *The OSS and Ho Chi Minh: Unexpected Allies in the War against Japan* (Lawrence: University Press of Kansas, 2006), 98.

25. Charles Fenn, *At the Dragon's Gate* (Annapolis, MD: Naval Institute Press, 2004), 6–7. Before the end of the war, Fenn was sent into Indochina on an MO mission to launch rumor campaigns against the Japanese near Hanoi. He came to have a jaundiced eye toward OSS, believing that although it was founded to serve the war effort, it inevitably became a magnet for those who felt their talents would be wasted by being drafted into the ranks. In OSS, he wrote, "those who had not yet been drafted could be classified as 'specialists,' after which they could choose their own military branch; after training emerge as commissioned officers, receiving pay 'commensurate with their previous status as highly paid lawyers or salesmen.'" This led, in his view, to "cluttering up the organization not merely with misfits, but with destructive misfits, because high rank gave men special powers to exercise their incompetence."

26. OSS Personnel Files, Box 0121, E 224, RG 226, NARA II.

27. OSS Personnel Files, Box 42, E 224, RG 226, NARA II.

28. Mandler, *Return from the Natives*, 61.

29. MacDonald, *Undercover Girl*, 9.

CHAPTER 4. LEARNING TO LIE

1. MacDonald, *Undercover Girl*, 8.

2. See Vicki Constantine Croke, *The Lady and the Panda: The True Adventures of the First American Explorer to Bring Back China's Most Exotic Animal*

(New York: Random House, 2005), for the story of Su-Lin, the first Giant Panda in captivity to have been brought to the United States by Ruth Harkness, dress designer, socialite, and Tibetan explorer. Mrs. Harkness became ill in Shanghai, and Jane stepped in to care for Su-Lin while they were en route to Java.

3. Kermit Roosevelt, *War Report of the OSS (Office of Strategic Services)* (New York: Walker, 1976), 75. See also Richard Dunlop, *Donovan, America's Master Spy* (Chicago: Rand McNally, 1982), 381; and John Whiteclay Chambers, *OSS Training in the National Parks and Service Abroad in World War II* (Washington, DC: U.S. Department of the Interior, National Park Service, 2008).

4. Jeff Silverman, "Spies in the Clubhouse," *OSS Society Journal*, Fall 2011, 34.

5. Chambers, *OSS Training in the National Parks*, 59–61. See also Aaron Bank, *From OSS to Green Berets: The Birth of Special Forces* (Novato, CA: Presidio, 1986), 4.

6. Elizabeth McIntosh, interview by the author, June 12, 2012.

7. Jane Foster, *An Unamerican Lady* (London: Sidgwick and Jackson, 1980), 108.

8. "Advanced Course for Morale Operations," Box 12, fldr. 131, E 161, RG 226, NARA II.

9. "Far Eastern Orientation Course," Box 12, fldr. 146, E 161, RG 226, NARA II.

10. Ibid.

11. MacDonald, *Undercover Girl*, 14.

12. Troy Sacquety, *The OSS in Burma: Jungle War against the Japanese* (Lawrence: University of Kansas Press, 2013), 19.

13. MacDonald, *Undercover Girl*, 16; McIntosh interview, September 19, 2013.

14. Sacquety, *OSS in Burma*, 113.

15. Lawrence C. Soley, *Radio Warfare: OSS and CIA Subversive Propaganda* (New York: Praeger, 1989), 161.

16. Cook and Cook, *Japan at War*, 172.

17. Elizabeth McIntosh, interview by the author, June 5, 2012.

18. James C. McNaughton, *Nissei Linguists: Japanese Americans in the Military Intelligence Service during World War II* (Washington, DC: U.S. Department of the Army, 2006), 63.

19. Soley, *Radio Warfare*, 172, 184.

20. Rene Defourneaux, *The Winking Fox: Twenty-Two Years in Military Intelligence* (Indianapolis: Indiana Creative Arts, 1997), 106.
21. Soley, *Radio Warfare*, 184.
22. OSS Records, Box 169, fldr. 2264, E 139, RG 226, NARA II.
23. Robert J. McMahon, *Colonialism and Cold War: The United States and the Struggle for Indonesian Independence, 1945–1949* (Ithaca, NY: Cornell University Press, 1981), 92. See also John Keegan, *The Second World War* (New York: Viking, 1990), 263.
24. "Joint U.S. Intelligence Committee Report," JCS Box 151, fldr CCS350.05, RG 226, NARA II.
25. MacDonald, *Undercover Girl*, 39.
26. Ibid., 44.
27. Dunlop, *Donovan*, 382.
28. U.S. Office of Strategic Services, *Assessment of Men: Selection of Personnel for the Office of Strategic Services* (New York: Rinehart, 1948), 54.
29. Ibid., 6.
30. MacDonald, *Undercover Girl*, 45.
31. Ibid., 45–47.
32. U.S. OSS, *Assessment of Men*, 346.
33. OSS Personnel Files, 1941–1945, Box 245, E 224, RG 226, NARA II.
34. Foster, *Unamerican Lady*, 111.
35. McIntosh Papers.
36. MacDonald, *Undercover Girl*, 54.

CHAPTER 5. IN THEATER

1. *YANK's Magic Carpet* (Calcutta, India: Staff of the China-Burma-India Edition of *YANK*), 8.
2. Foster, *Unamerican Lady*, 113.
3. McIntosh Papers.
4. MacDonald, *Undercover Girl*, 62.
5. Elizabeth McIntosh, interview by the author, November 5, 2012.
6. Julia and Paul Child Papers, 1925–1993, MC 644, Box 4, fldr. 49, Arthur and Elizabeth Schlesinger Library on the History of Women in America, Radcliffe Institute for Advanced Study, Harvard University, Cambridge, MA (hereafter cited as Child Papers).
7. Ibid.

8. Fenn, *At the Dragon's Gate*, 12–13.
9. MacDonald, *Undercover Girl*, 73.
10. OSS Personnel Files, 0475, E 224, RG 226, NARA II.
11. Elizabeth McIntosh, interview by the author, June 1, 2013.
12. Along with Joy Homer, Frame managed to infiltrate Chinese delegations and expose Japanese agents, as well as those sent by Chiang Kai-shek's head of secret police to spy on the British. See MacDonald, *Undercover Girl*, 108.
13. Child Papers, Box 4, fldr. 49.
14. MacDonald, *Undercover Girl*, 250.
15. OSS Personnel files, Box 67, E 224, NARA II; McIntosh, *Sisterhood of Spies*, 250–51. The ferment stirring among young Indian men at the time was palpable. Paul Child compared it to the "boiling of lava under the mountain." See Child Papers, Box 4, fldr. 49.
16. Maureen L. P. Patterson, "Pre-independence Back-Channel Reporting on India, 1944–46" (remarks prepared for conference on American Reporting on India and Pakistan, 1947–1997, Southern Asian Institute, Columbia University, New York, April 4–5, 1997). Patterson submitted her reports to the India Section of the British Empire Division of OSS R&A, headed by Dr. W. Norman Brown, well-known Sanskrit scholar. Brown's R&A section was known as a hotbed of Nationalist sympathies.
17. Frank McLynn, *The Burma Campaign: Disaster into Triumph, 1942–45* (New Haven, CT: Yale University Press, 2011), 95.
18. Child Papers, Box 4, fldr. 49.
19. McLynn, *Burma Campaign*, 338. For the opulence of Mountbatten's headquarters, see also Philip Ziegler, *Mountbatten: The Official Biography* (London: Collins, 1985), 279.
20. See E. Bruce Reynolds, *Thailand's Secret War: The Free Thai, OSS, and SOE during World War II* (Cambridge: Cambridge University Press, 2005).
21. Michael L. Lewis, *Inventing Global Ecology: Tracking the Biodiversity Ideal in India, 1947–1997* (Athens: Ohio University Press, 2003), 41–42.
22. Child Papers, Box 4, fldr. 49.
23. Ibid.
24. Reynolds, *Thailand's Secret War*, 245. Cordell Hull in the U.S. State Department kept the situation heated by declaring that Britain's postwar plans included establishing a "Southeast Asia Federation of Burma, Malaya, Thailand, and Indonesia" in addition to colonizing Thailand.
25. Child Papers, Box 4, fldr. 49.

26. Foster, *Unamerican Lady*, 114.
27. Child Papers, Box 4, fldr. 49.
28. "Washington and Field Station Files," Box 120, fldr. 1642, E 139, RG 226, NARA II.
29. JCS Geographic Files, CCS 185, Box 133, E 190, RG 226, NARA II.

CHAPTER 6. OPERATION BLACK MAIL

1. Thaddeus Holt, *The Deceivers: Allied Military Deception in the Second World War* (New York: Skyhorse, 2007), 297.
2. JCS Geographic Files, CCS 488, 185, Box 133, E 190, RG 226, NARA II.
3. MacDonald, *Undercover Girl*, 78.
4. Ibid., 80.
5. Edmond Taylor, *The Strategy of Terror: Europe's Inner Front* (Boston: Houghton Mifflin, 1940), 205.
6. OSS Records, Box 183, fldr. 691, E 108, RG 226, NARA II.
7. McIntosh, *Sisterhood of Spies*, 260.
8. Bonner F. Fellers, *Psychology of the Japanese Soldier* (Washington, DC: Bibliogov, 2012), 34. Fellers cites a study showing that 25 percent of Japanese university students opposed the militarists and war with the United States. Fellers' papers are housed at the Hoover Institution in Stanford, California.
9. Elizabeth McIntosh, interview by the author, September 6, 2014.
10. McIntosh, *Sisterhood of Spies*, 262.
11. OSS Records, Box 106, E 144, RG 226, NARA II.
12. Elizabeth McIntosh, interview by the author, June 6, 2013.
13. OSS Records, Box 106, E 144, RG 226, NARA II.
14. Ibid.
15. Child Papers, Box 4, fldr. 49.
16. Ibid.
17. MacDonald, *My Footloose Newspaper Life*, 84.
18. OSS Records, Box 169, E 139, RG 226, NARA II.
19. Elizabeth McIntosh, interview by the author, November 11, 2013.

CHAPTER 7. RUMORS AND THREATS

1. Vyacheslav von Plehve was Tsar Nicholas's minister of the interior in 1904. He suggested a "Small Victorious War" with Japan would halt the tide of revolution and expand the Russian empire in the Far East.

2. OSS Records, Box 106, E 144, RG 226, NARA II.

3. Samuel Eliot Morison, *The Liberation of the Philippines, Luzon, Mindanao, the Visayas, 1944–1945*, vol. 13 of *History of the United States Naval Operations in World War II* (Edison, NJ: Castle Books, 2001), 162–63.

4. Keene, *So Lovely a Country*, 48.

5. OSS Records, JCS, Box 133, E 190, RG 226, fldr. 385, NARA II.

6. Lafcadio Hearn, *Kokoro: Hints and Echoes of Japanese Inner Life* (Tokyo: Tuttle Publishing, 2011), 26.

7. OSS Records, Box 106, E 144, RG 226, NARA II.

8. See Ruth Benedict, *The Chrysanthemum and the Sword: Patterns of Japanese Culture* (Cambridge, MA: Harvard University Press, 2005).

9. OSS Records, Box 106, E 144, RG 226, NARA II.

10. OSS Records, Box 60, E 99, RG 226, NARA II.

11. Bartholomew-Feis, *OSS and Ho Chi Minh*, 98.

12. Jennet Conant, *A Covert Affair: Julia Child and Paul Child in the OSS* (New York: Simon & Schuster, 2011), 87.

13. Child Papers, Box 4, fldr. 49.

14. The coast watcher organization performed a vital service to southwestern Pacific operations. It was code-named Ferdinand, after the bull in the children's story who did not fight but just smelled the flowers. See Eric Feldt, *The Coast Watchers: How a Few Daring Men Trapped on Japanese Islands Warned the Allies of Enemy Attacks* (New York: Bantam Books, 1979).

15. "MO Channels," Box 106, E 144, RG 226, NARA II.

16. "Detachment 505," Box 106, E 144, RG 226, NARA II.

17. Smith, *OSS*, 21.

18. OSS Personnel Files, 1941–1945, Box 42, E 224, RG 226, NARA II.

19. MO Production, Detachment 505, Box 106, E 144, RG 226, NARA II.

20. Intelligence Material, Detachment 505, Box 106, E 144, RG 226, NARA II.

CHAPTER 8. LAYING DOWN THE SWORD

1. McIntosh Papers. See also Child Papers, Box 4, fldr. 49.

2. All IJA and IJN personnel carried a copy of the *Sinjinkun* (field service regulations) written by Hideki Tojo: "Meet the expectations of your family and home community by making effort upon effort, always mindful of the honor of your name. If alive, do not suffer the disgrace of becoming a prisoner; in death, do not leave behind a name soiled by misdeeds."

3. John W. Dower, *War Without Mercy: Race and Power in the Pacific War* (New York: Pantheon Books, 1986), 11.

4. Benedict, *Chrysanthemum and the Sword*, xi. This was eventually borne out when the emperor, for whom Japanese citizens were willing to die, told his people in a quavering voice that they must "bear the unbearable" and surrender to peace. They did so.

5. Elizabeth McIntosh, interview by the author, May 10, 2012; Benedict, *Chrysanthemum and the Sword*, 41.

6. Alexander H. Leighton, *Human Relations in a Changing World: Observations on the Use of the Social Sciences* (New York: E. P. Dutton, 1949), 49.

7. OSS Records, JCS, Box 133, fldr. 385, E 190, RG 226, NARA II.

8. OSS Records, Box 106, E 144, RG 226, NARA II.

9. Feldt, *Coast Watchers*, 33.

10. Richard J. Aldrich, *Intelligence and the War against Japan: Britain, America, and the Politics of Secret Service* (Cambridge: Cambridge University Press, 2000), 163.

11. Okamoto was one of only 40 defectors and 1,085 deserters in the Pacific and CBI theaters in 1944, but desertion was becoming common enough that soldiers were composing haiku on the subject. See Yamashita, *Daily Life in Wartime Japan*, 170.

12. MacDonald, *Undercover Girl*, 93.

13. OSS Records, Box 106, E 144, RG 226, NARA II.

14. MacDonald, *Undercover Girl*, 94. For more on Gold Dust, see Sacquety, *OSS in Burma*.

15. Cook and Cook, *Japan at War*, 130.

16. MacDonald, *Undercover Girl*, 96.

17. William R. Peers and Dean Brelis, *Behind the Burma Road: The Story of America's Most Successful Guerrilla Force* (Boston: Little, Brown, 1963), 181.

18. MacDonald, *Undercover Girl*, 97.

19. Child Papers, Box 4, fldr. 49.

20. Ibid.

21. Ibid.

CHAPTER 9. A WOMAN IN CHARGE

1. Oliver Caldwell, *A Secret War: Americans in China, 1944–1945* (Carbondale: Southern Illinois University Press, 1972), 123–24.

2. Ibid.

3. Ibid.
4. Elizabeth McIntosh, interview by the author, October 4, 2011.
5. OSS Records, Box 0101, E 224, RG 226, NARA II.
6. Caldwell, *Secret War*, 124.
7. MacDonald, *Undercover Girl*, 123–24.
8. Ibid., 107.
9. OSS Records, Box 106, E 144, RG 226, NARA II.
10. MacDonald, *Undercover Girl*, 47.
11. Ibid.
12. Ibid, 105.
13. Sacquety, *OSS in Burma*, 55–56.
14. OSS Records, Box 106, E 166, RG 226, NARA II.
15. Peers and Brelis, *Behind the Burma Road*, 214.
16. Sacquety, *OSS in Burma*, 22, 54.
17. OSS Records, Box 60, E 99, RG 226, NARA II.
18. Ibid.
19. Elizabeth McIntosh, interview by the author, February 2, 2012.
20. McLynn, *Burma Campaign*, 378.
21. Ibid., 373.
22. Elizabeth McIntosh, interview by the author, November 10, 2012; Cook and Cook, *Japan at War*, 127.
23. Keene, *So Lovely a Country*.
24. McIntosh Papers; Elizabeth McIntosh, interview by the author, November 11, 2012.
25. McIntosh Papers; McIntosh interview, November 11, 2012.
26. McIntosh Papers.
27. Calcutta Production Unit, Box 60, E 99, RG 226, NARA II.
28. MacDonald, *Undercover Girl*, 112.

CHAPTER 10. ON TO CALCUTTA

1. MacDonald, *Undercover Girl*, 117.
2. Calcutta Production Unit, Box 106, E 144, RG 226, NARA II.
3. MacDonald, *My Footloose Newspaper Life*, 83.
4. MacDonald, *Undercover Girl*, 122.
5. Calcutta Production Unit, Box 6, E 144, NARA II.
6. Ibid.
7. Detachment 202, 8 February, 1945, Box 60, E 99, RG 226, NARA II.

8. "Materials for Bittersweet," January 9, 1945, Box 106, E 144, RG 226, NARA II.

9. Ibid., January 18, 1945.

10. MacDonald to Bateson, January 29, 1945, Box 106, E 144, RG 226, NARA II.

11. "Unit Various," MO Production Detachment 101, January 29, 1945, Box 106, E 144, RG 226, NARA II.

12. MacDonald to Severyns, January 15, 1945, Box 106, fldr. 1102, E 144, RG 226, NARA II.

13. Projects, Box 106, fldr 1102, E 144, RG 226, NARA II.

14. Peers and Brelis, *Behind the Burma Road.*

15. "Rumors for Annamites," February 15, 1945, Box 106, E 144, RG 226, NARA II.

16. Elizabeth McIntosh, interview by the author, December 31, 2014.

17. Alexander MacDonald, Box 106, E 144, RG 226, NARA II.

18. Ibid.

19. McLynn, *Burma Campaign*, 12–13.

20. MacDonald, *My Footloose Newspaper Life*, 90.

21. "Ramree Town," OSS Arakan Field Unit, p. 3, Box 106, E 144, RG 226, NARA II.

22. Ibid.

23. Peers and Brelis, *Behind the Burma Road*, 23.

24. "Ramree Town," 5–6.

25. McLynn, *Burma Campaign*, 419, 427.

26. Registry No. MHC 312, Box 106, E 144, RG 226, NARA II.

27. MacDonald, *Undercover Girl*, 130–31.

28. Ibid.

29. Ibid.

30. Ibid., 131–32.

31. Conant, *Covert Affair*, 98–102; Elizabeth McIntosh, interview by the author, October 10, 2012.

32. Elizabeth McIntosh, interview by the author, October 2, 2012.

33. MacDonald to Severyns, Box 106, E 144, RG 226, NARA II.

34. MacDonald, *My Footloose Newspaper Life*, 87–88.

35. Ibid.

36. "JN 27 Radio Scripts," May 1, 1945, May 22, 1945, Box 133, E 144, RG 226, NARA II.

37. Reynolds, *Thailand's Secret War*, 265.

38. Foster, *Unamerican Lady*, 120–21. Trincomalee was the British naval headquarters in the Pacific theater and the staging ground for British and American air operations against the Japanese in Burma and Malaya. It also served as an interrogation center for Japanese POWs.

39. MacDonald to Foster, February 15, 1945, Box 106, E 144, RG 226, NARA II.

40. OSS Personnel files 1944–1945, Box 245, E 224, RG 226, NARA II.

41. MacDonald, *Undercover Girl*, 146; Elizabeth McIntosh, interview by the author, March 4, 2014.

42. MacDonald, *Undercover Girl*, 147.

CHAPTER 11. CHINA

1. Otha C. Spencer, *Flying the Hump: Memories of an Air War* (College Station: Texas A&M University Press, 1992), xi; Felix Smith, *China Pilot: Flying for Chiang and Chennault* (Washington, DC: Brassey's Inc., 1995), 11; Theodore Harold White and Annalee Jacoby, *Thunder out of China* (New York: Da Capo Press, 1980), 154.

2. MacDonald, *Undercover Girl*, 147–49; Elizabeth McIntosh, interview by the author, June 18, 2012; McIntosh Papers.

3. MacDonald, *Undercover Girl*, 147–49; McIntosh interview, June 18, 2012; McIntosh Papers.

4. MacDonald, *Undercover Girl*, 150.

5. Ibid., 149.

6. Child Papers, Box 4, Fldr. 50.

7. OSS Personnel Files, Box 245, E 224, RG 226, NARA II.

8. MacDonald, *Undercover Girl*, 155.

9. Child Papers, Box 4, fldr. 50

10. MacDonald, *Undercover Girl*, 155.

11. Ibid., 170; OSS Records, JCS Box 29, fldr. 385, RG 226, NARA II.

12. MacDonald, *Undercover Girl*, 170.

13. Child Papers, Box 4, fldr. 50.

14. Fenn, *At the Dragon's Gate*, 7.

15. "Final Report of OSS Activities in China," August 1, 1945, p. 2, E 264, RG 226, NARA II.

16. Kermit Roosevelt, *War Report of the OSS II: The Overseas Target* (New York: Walker, 1976), 435–36.

17. Elizabeth McIntosh, interview by the author, October 4, 2013.

18. "Policy on Publicity Regarding Japanese Prisoners of War," JCS, Box 285, E 133, RG 226, NARA II.

19. Ding Cong, *Half a Century's Friendship* (Doylestown, PA: James A. Michener Art Museum, 1966), 4–5. Published in conjunction with the exhibition titled *William A. Smith, A Retrospective*, shown at the James A. Michener Art Museum.

20. Smith, *China Pilot*, 39.

21. Daniel Ford, *Flying Tigers: Claire Chennault and the American Volunteer Group* (Washington, DC: Smithsonian Institution Press, 1991), 157. For Chennault's background and his recruitment of pilots for the AVG in defense of prewar China, see Charles R. Bond and Terry H. Anderson, *A Flying Tiger's Diary* (College Station: Texas A&M University Press, 1984); and Frillman and Peck, *China*. There are many versions of the story behind the name "Flying Tiger."

22. Frillman and Peck, *China*, 85, 148.

23. Foster, *Unamerican Lady*, 134–35.

24. Child Papers, Box 4, fldr. 50. See also Frillman and Peck, *China*, 196.

CHAPTER 12. THE LAST SUMMER

1. OSS South East Asia, Box 245, E 224, RG 226, NARA II; OSS Promotion Board, Box 245, E 224, RG 226, NARA II.

2. Foster, *Unamerican Lady*, 131–32.

3. MO Production Unit, Detachment 505, Box 106, E 144, RG 226, NARA II.

4. Ibid.

5. Foster, *Unamerican Lady*, 126. The British were old hands when it came to bartering with "operational whiskey." The Royal Navy allowed alcohol on ship; the Americans did not. When the *King George* was in need of equipment for radar repair, she signaled a nearby destroyer, offering a bottle of whiskey in exchange for the spare parts. Someone replied by loudspeaker: "Man, for a bottle of whiskey you can have this whole goddamned ship!" See Nicholas Evan Sarantakes, *The Allies against the Rising Sun: The United States, the British Nations, and the Defeat of Imperial Japan* (Lawrence: University Press of Kansas, 2009), 296.

6. Japanese Underground Newspaper, Project 113, Box 106, E 144, RG 226, NARA II.

7. Ibid.

8. *Takami Jun Nikki*, vol. 4, p. 39, quoted in Keene, *So Lovely a Country*.

9. McLynn, *Burma Campaign*, 445.

10. Schools and Training Branch, June 1945, RG 226, NARA II.

11. Donovan to Heppner, May 10, 1946, Box 106, E 144, RG 226, NARA II.

12. See McNaughton, *Nisei Linguists*. The U.S. government not only interned its own citizens but removed 6,610 Germans, Japanese, and Italians from thirteen Latin American countries and imprisoned them in the United States—an often overlooked aspect of this period of history. See Jan Barboe Russell, *The Train to Crystal City: FDR's Secret Prisoner Exchange Program and America's Only Family Internment Camp during World War II* (New York: Scribner, 2015).

13. MacDonald, *Undercover Girl*, 162.

14. "Pointed Sabotage Campaigns," Box 106, E 144, RG 226, NARA II; Elizabeth McIntosh, interview by the author, October 5, 2012.

15. "OSS Operations in China," 4; McIntosh Papers.

16. "Radio Wars," interview with John Creddy, Gordon Auchincloss, and Elizabeth McIntosh, American RadioWorks, http://americanradioworks.public radio.org/features/wwii/b1.html.

17. Ibid.

18. Soley, *Radio Warfare*, 178–82.

19. McIntosh Papers.

20. MacDonald, *My Footloose Newspaper Life*, 94.

21. Dillon Ripley, "Incident in Siam," Dillon Ripley Papers, RU 7008, Box 7. See also Reynolds, *Thailand's Secret War*, 334–36.

22. "GI Samaritan Wants China Tot to Be Saved," *New York Daily News*, June 1, 1949.

23. "War Dogs Guarded, Yank Jazz Lullabyed GI's Chinese Waif," *New York Daily News*, June 1949.

24. Ibid.

25. "The GI and the Kid Parted (Briefly) at the Orphanage," *New York Daily News*, June 10, 1949.

26. JCS, Box 285, E 133, RG 226, NARA II.

27. Smith, *OSS*, 223.

28. Elizabeth McIntosh, interview by the author, January 27, 2010.

CHAPTER 13. A GREAT CATASTROPHE

1. McIntosh interview, June 4, 2012.
2. MacDonald, *Undercover Girl*, 203–4.
3. Ibid., 204.
4. In later years the appearance of commemorative statues of comfort women in Seoul and various Korean communities in the United States generated much controversy. An estimated 100,000–200,000 Korean and other Asian women were forced to serve as sex slaves for the IJA. Japanese estimates are as low as 20,000, and the Japanese insist that many were "voluntary." See "Japanese Nationalist Protest of 'Comfort Women' Sculpture Fails," *Los Angeles Times*, July 12, 2013.
5. MacDonald, *Undercover Girl*, 209.
6. Ibid., 212.
7. McIntosh Papers; Child Papers, Box 4, fldr. 50.
8. MacDonald, *Undercover Girl*, 219.
9. OSS Records, JCS, Box 29, fldr. 385, E 134, RG 226, NARA II.
10. Ibid.
11. Ibid.; Elizabeth McIntosh, interview by the author, December 31, 2013.
12. JCS, box 29, fldr. 385, E 134, RG 226, NARA II.
13. OSS Operations Final Report, p. 10, McIntosh Papers.
14. Child Papers, box 4, fldr. 50.
15. Ibid.; Bob Bergin, "Kunming, China: Setting for Daring Wartime Operations," *OSS Society Journal*, Summer/Fall 2010, 39.
16. MacDonald, *Undercover Girl*, 222.

CHAPTER 14. MERCY MISSIONS

1. MacDonald, *My Footloose Newspaper Life*, 95–96.
2. MacDonald, *Undercover Girl*, 227.
3. Child Papers, Box 4, fldr. 51.
4. Bill Streifer, "The OSS in Korea: Operation Eagle," *American Intelligence Journal* 30, no. 1 (2012): 33.
5. William A. Smith, "In Weihsin Prison Camp," *OSS Society Journal*, Fall 2011, 28.
6. Bill Streifer, "Operation Cardinal: So You Must Be a Spy," *American Intelligence Journal* 29 (2011): 75.

7. "Special Report on POW Teams," September 3, 1945, Box 4, E 130, RG 226, NARA II.

8. Streifer, "Operation Cardinal," 76.

9. "Special Report on POW Teams," September 3, 1945, Box 4, E 130, RG 226, NARA II.

10. Streifer, "OSS in Korea," 33.

11. Child Papers, Box 4, fldr. 51.

12. Elizabeth P. McIntosh, *In Memorium* (Doylestown, PA: James A. Michener Art Museum, 1966), 6. Published in conjunction with the exhibition titled *William A. Smith, A Retrospective*, shown at the James A. Michener Art Museum.

13. "Special Report on POW Teams," September 3, 1945, Box 4, E 130, RG 226, NARA II.

14. Smith, "In Weihsin Prison Camp," 29.

15. Ibid.

16. Ibid.

17. AGAS comprised thirty-five men in August 1945 and carried out escape, evasion, and intelligence missions and eventually rescue of Allied POWs in China. During its period of operations, AGAS assisted in the rescue of more than eight hundred pilots and airmen from enemy-occupied territory in Asia.

18. OSS Personnel Files, Box 589, E 224, RG 226, NARA II.

19. Child Papers, Box 4, fldr. 5.

CHAPTER 15. OPERATION ICEBERG

1. Foster, *Unamerican Lady*, 160.

2. Quoted in Michael Warner's "The Creation of a Central Intelligence Group," *Studies in Intelligence*, Fall 1995, 111.

3. Ibid.

4. OSS Personnel Files, 1941–1945, Box 589, E 224, RG 226, NARA II.

5. "*ICEBERG*, BASIC PLAN," Box 25, E 110, RG 226, NARA II.

6. "Basic Plan for Batavia," Box 25, E 110, RG 226, NARA II.

7. "Interview with Captain Perks," Box 25, E 110, RG 226, NARA II.

8. "Most Recent Plan for Entry into the N.E.I.," Box 25, E 110, RG 226, NARA II.

9. Sorel, *Women Who Wrote the War*, 160.

10. Elizabeth McIntosh, interview by the author, August 20, 2014.

11. MacDonald, *Undercover Girl*, 240–41.

12. Child Papers, Box 4, fldr. 52.

13. Ibid.

14. Eulogy draft for Al Cox, McIntosh Papers.

15. Foster, *Unamerican Lady*, 149–50.

16. Ibid., 152.

17. "Current Political Situation in Batavia," Box 1, fldr. 8, E 110, RG 226, NARA II.

18. "Humpy," September 20, 1945, Box 25, E 110, RG 226, NARA II.

19. Foster, *Unamerican Lady*, 154.

20. OSS Records, Box 2, E 224, RG 226, NARA II.

21. Ripley, "Incident in Siam."

22. Ibid.

23. Ibid.

24. For the saga of the USS *Houston* and her captured crewmen, see James D. Hornfischer, *Ship of Ghosts* (New York: Bantam Books, 2006).

25. Ibid.

26. Alexander MacDonald, *Bangkok Editor* (New York: Macmillan, 1949), 2.

CHAPTER 16. GOING HOME

1. Child Papers, Box 4, fldr. 51.

2. Child Papers, Box 3, fldr. 35.

3. OSS Personnel Files, Box 245, fldr. 0121, E 224, RG 226, NARA II.

4. Child Papers, Box 3, fldr. 35.

5. Child Papers, Box 4, fldr. 51.

6. OSS Personnel Files, Box 42, E 224, RG 226, NARA II.

7. OSS Personnel Files, Box 513, E 224, RG 226, NARA II.

8. Child Papers, Box 4, fldr. 51.

9. Ibid.

10. "Termination of Employment of OSS Personnel," November 11, 1945, Box 245, E 224, RG 226, NARA II.

11. Foster, *Unamerican Lady*, 158.

12. Ibid., 160.

13. MacDonald, *My Footloose Newspaper Life*, 103.

CHAPTER 17. HOME

1. MacDonald, *Undercover Girl*, 298.

2. McIntosh Papers.

3. McIntosh interview, November 11, 2012.

4. Foster, *Unamerican Lady*, 162.

5. Institute of Pacific Relations, San Francisco Bay Region Division Records, Box 23, Hoover Institution Archives, Stanford, CA.

6. Ibid.

7. Clayton D. Laurie, *The Propaganda Warriors: America's Crusade against Nazi Germany* (Lawrence: University Press of Kansas, 1996), 123. For the OSS-OWI power struggle over control of VOA, see Alan L. Heil Jr., *Voice of America: A History* (New York: Columbia University Press, 2003), 42.

8. Elizabeth McIntosh, interview by the author, October 15, 2012.

9. Foster, *Unamerican Lady*, 166–67.

10. Elizabeth McIntosh, interview by the author, January 18, 2014.

11. Conant, *Covert Affair*, 279.

12. William M. Leary, *Perilous Missions: Civil Air Transport and CIA Covert Operations in Asia* (Tuscaloosa: University of Alabama Press, 1984), 81–82.

13. David C. Wolf, "To Secure a Convenience: Britain Recognizes China, 1950," *Journal of Contemporary History* 18, no. 2 (April 1983): 299–326.

14. Ibid.

15. Dunlop, *Donovan*, 496–98.

16. Elizabeth McIntosh, interview by the author, February 15, 2014.

17. Ibid.

18. Bob Bergin, "OSS Undercover Girl," *World War II History*, July 2007, 79.

19. Laren Kessler, *Clever Girl: Elizabeth Bentley, the Spy Who Ushered in the McCarthy Era* (New York: HarperCollins, 2003), 131.

EPILOGUE

1. *Inky* was the story of a midwestern farm boy whose father becomes a POW during the Korean War. The boy becomes the man of the house and, in addition to running the farm, raises a puppy to be a seeing-eye dog. The boy's father returns home depressed and blinded by his wounds. Inky becomes an important member of the family. The book went through several print runs in the 1950s, and many copies were eventually donated to the Fisher House for recovering veterans.

2. Elizabeth McIntosh, interview by the author, January 17, 2014.

3. Child Papers, Box 4, fldr 46; Conant, *Covert Affair*, 1–12, 22.

4. Child Papers, Box 2, fldr. 25.

5. Ibid.

6. Foster, *Unamerican Lady*, 218.

7. Child Papers, Box 2, fldr. 25.

8. Conant, *Covert Affair*, 316.

9. Eulogy draft, Al Cox, McIntosh Papers.

10. "Chinese Waif out of Orphanage," *New York Daily News*, June 20, 1949, 3.

11. Dower, *Embracing Defeat*, 59.

12. Ibid., 179.

13. Ibid., 169.

14. McIntosh, *Sisterhood of Spies*, xvii.

BIBLIOGRAPHY

INTERVIEWS

Arthur Reinhardt

Susan Tennenbaum

Elizabeth P. McIntosh

PERSONAL PAPERS AND ARCHIVES

Dillon Ripley Papers, Smithsonian Institution Archives, Washington, DC.

Elizabeth P. McIntosh Personal Papers, private collection.

Franklin D. Roosevelt Collection, Hyde Park, NY.

Institute of Pacific Relations, San Francisco Bay Region Division Records, Hoover Institution Archives, Stanford, CA.

OSS Records, Record Group 226, National Archives and Records Administration, College Park, MD.

Paul and Julia Child Papers, Arthur and Elizabeth Schlesinger Library on the History of Women in America, Radcliffe Institute for Advanced Study, Harvard University, Cambridge, MA.

Vassiliev's Notebooks, KGB files, Library of Congress, Washington, DC.

Venona decrypted transcripts, Library of Congress, Washington DC.

NEWSPAPERS

Honolulu Star-Bulletin

Homefront Forecast (NEA Service)

New York Daily News

JOURNAL AND MAGAZINE ARTICLES

Bergin, Bob. "Kunming, China: Setting for Daring Wartime Operations." *OSS Society Journal,* Summer/Fall 2010.

———. "OSS Undercover Girl." *World War II History,* July 2007

Silverman, Jeff. "Spies in the Clubhouse." *OSS Society Journal,* Fall 2011.

Smith, William A. "In Weihsin Prison Camp." *OSS Society Journal,* Fall 2011.

Streifer, Bill. "Operation Cardinal: So You Must Be a Spy." *American Intelligence Journal* 29 (2011).

———. "The OSS in Korea: Operation Eagle." *American Intelligence Journal* 30, no. 1 (2012).

Warner, Michael. "The Creation of a Central Intelligence Group." *Studies in Intelligence,* Fall 1995.

Wolf, David C. "To Secure a Convenience: Britain Recognizes China, 1950." *Journal of Contemporary History* 18, no. 2 (April 1983): 299–326.

BOOKS

Aldrich, Richard J. *Intelligence and the War against Japan: Britain, America and the Politics of Secret Service.* Cambridge: Cambridge University Press, 2000.

Allen, Gwenfread E. *Hawaii's War Years, 1941–1945.* Honolulu: Pacific Monograph, 1999.

Allen, Louis. *Burma: The Longest War 1941–45.* New York: St. Martin's Press, 1984.

Bank, Aaron. *From OSS to Green Berets: The Birth of Special Forces.* Novato, CA: Presidio, 1986.

Bartholomew-Feis, Dixie R. *The OSS and Ho Chi Minh: Unexpected Allies in the War against Japan.* Lawrence: University Press of Kansas, 2006.

Bayly, Christopher, and Tim Harper. *Forgotten Armies: The Fall of British Asia 1941–1945.* Cambridge, MA: Belknap Press of Harvard University Press, 2005.

Benedict, Ruth. *The Chrysanthemum and the Sword: Patterns of Japanese Culture.* Cambridge, MA: Harvard University Press, 2005.

Bond, Charles R., and Terry H. Anderson. *A Flying Tiger's Diary.* College Station: Texas A&M University Press, 1984.

Bose, Sugata. *A Hundred Horizons: The Indian Ocean in the Age of Global Empire.* Cambridge, MA: Harvard University Press, 2006.

Burlingame, Burl. *Advance Force Pearl Harbor.* Honolulu: University of Hawaii Press, 1992.

Caldwell, Oliver J. *A Secret War: Americans in China, 1944–1945*. Carbondale: Southern Illinois University Press, 1972.

Carroll, Peter N. *The Odyssey of the Abraham Lincoln Brigade: Americans in the Spanish Civil War*. Stanford, CA: Stanford University Press, 1994.

Chalou, George C., ed. *The Secrets War: The Office of Strategic Services in World War II*. Washington, DC: National Archives and Records Administration, 1992.

Chambers, John Whiteclay. *OSS Training in the National Parks and Service Abroad in World War II*. Washington, DC: U.S. Department of the Interior, National Park Service, 2008.

Conant, Jennet. *A Covert Affair: Julia Child and Paul Child in the OSS*. New York: Simon & Schuster, 2011.

Cong, Ding. *Half a Century's Friendship*. Doylestown, PA: James A. Michener Art Museum, 1966. Published in conjunction with the exhibition titled *William A. Smith, A Retrospective*, shown at the James A. Michener Art Museum.

Cook, Haruko Taya, and Theodore F. Cook. *Japan at War: An Oral History*. New York: New Press, 1992.

Croke, Vicki Constantine. *The Lady and the Panda: The True Adventures of the First American Explorer to Bring Back China's Most Exotic Animal*. New York: Random House, 2005.

Defourneaux, Rene. *The Winking Fox: Twenty-Two Years in Military Intelligence*. Indianapolis: Indiana Creative Arts, 1997.

Donaldson, Scott. *Achibald MacLesh: An American Life*. New York: Houghton Mifflin, 1992.

Dower, John W. *Embracing Defeat: Japan in the Wake of World War II*. New York: W. W. Norton, 1999.

———. *Japan in War and Peace: Selected Essays*. New York: New Press, 1993.

———. *War without Mercy: Race and Power in the Pacific War*. New York: Pantheon Books, 1986.

Dunlop, Richard. *Behind Japanese Lines, with the OSS in Burma*. Chicago: Rand McNally, 1979.

———. *Donovan, America's Master Spy*. Chicago: Rand McNally, 1982.

Feldt, Eric A. *The Coast Watchers: How a Few Daring Men Trapped on Japanese Islands Warned the Allies of Enemy Attacks*. New York: Bantam Books, 1979.

Feller, Carolyn M., and Constance J. Moore. *Highlights in the History of the Army Nurse Corps*. Rev. and expanded ed. Washington, DC: U.S. Army Center of Military History, 1996.

Fellers, Bonner F. *Psychology of the Japanese Soldier*. Parts 1 and 2. Washington, DC: Bibliogov, 2012.

Fenn, Charles. *At the Dragon's Gate*. Annapolis, MD: Naval Institute Press, 2004.

Fitch, Noel Riley. *Appetite for Life: The Biography of Julia Child*. New York: Doubleday, 1997.

Ford, Corey. *Donovan of OSS*. Boston: Little, Brown, 1970.

Ford, Daniel. *Flying Tigers: Claire Chennault and the American Volunteer Group*. Washington, DC: Smithsonian Institution Press, 1991.

Foster, Jane. *An Unamerican Lady*. London: Sidgwick and Jackson, 1980.

Frillman, Paul, and Graham Peck. *China: The Remembered Life*. New York: Houghton Mifflin, 1968.

Furnival, J. S. *Colonial Policy and Practice*. New York: New York University Press, 1956.

Gilmore, Allison B. *You Can't Fight Tanks with Bayonets: Psychological Warfare against the Japanese Army in the Southwest Pacific*. Lincoln: University of Nebraska Press, 1998.

Grose, Peter. *Gentleman Spy: The Life of Allen Dulles*. Boston: Houghton Mifflin, 1994.

Haynes, John Earl, Harvey Klehr, Alexander Vassiliev, Philip Redko, and Steven Shabad. *Spies: The Rise and Fall of the KGB in America*. New Haven, CT: Yale University Press, 2009.

Hearn, Lafcadio. *Glimpses of Unfamiliar Japan*. Boston: Houghton, Mifflin, 1895; Internet Archive, 2009. https://archive.org/details/glimpsesunfamil 09heargoog.

———. *Kokoro: Hints and Echoes of Japanese Inner Life*. Tokyo: Tuttle Publishing, 2011.

Heil, Alan L., Jr. *Voice of America: A History*. New York: Columbia University Press, 2003.

Hersh, Burton. *The Old Boys: The American Elite and the Origins of the CIA*. New York: Scribner's, 1992.

Higham, Charles. *Trading with the Enemy: An Exposé of the Nazi-American Money Plot, 1933–1949*. New York: Doubleday, 1982.

Holt, Thaddeus. *The Deceivers: Allied Military Deception in the Second World War*. New York: Skyhorse, 2007.

Hoover, Calvin B. *Memoirs of Capitalism, Communism, and Nazism*. Durham, NC: Duke University Press, 1965.

Hornfischer, James D. *Ship of Ghosts*. New York: Bantam Books, 2006.

Iriye, Akira. *Pearl Harbor and the Coming of the Pacific War: A Brief History with Documents and Essays*. Boston: Bedford/St. Martin's, 1999.

Joaquin, Nick. *Culture and History: Occasional Notes on the Process of Philippine Becoming*. Manila, Philippines: Solar Pub., 1988.

Kahin, George McTurnan. *Nationalism and Revolution in Indonesia*. Ithaca, NY: Cornell University Press, 1952.

Keegan, John. *The Second World War*. New York: Viking, 1990.

Keene, Donald. *So Lovely a Country Will Never Perish: Wartime Diaries of Japanese Writers*. New York: Columbia University Press, 2010.

Kessler, Lauren. *Clever Girl: Elizabeth Bentley, The Spy Who Ushered in the McCarthy Era*. New York: HarperCollins, 2003.

Koke, Louis L. *Our Hotel in Bali: How Two Young Americans Made a Dream Come True—A Story of the 1930s*. New York: January Books, 1987.

Kotani, Ken, and Chiharu Kotani. *Japanese Intelligence in World War II*. Oxford: Osprey, 2009.

Kush, Linda. *The Rice Paddy Navy: Espionage and Sabotage behind Japanese Lines in China during World War II*. Oxford: Osprey, 2012.

Latimer, Jon. *Deception in War*. London: John Murray, 2003.

Laurie, Clayton D. *The Propaganda Warriors: America's Crusade against Nazi Germany*. Lawrence: University Press of Kansas, 1996.

Leary, William M. *Perilous Missions: Civil Air Transport and CIA Covert Operations in Asia*. Tuscaloosa: University of Alabama Press, 1984.

Leighton, Alexander H. *Human Relations in a Changing World: Observations on the Use of the Social Sciences*. New York: E. P. Dutton, 1949.

Lewis, Michael L. *Inventing Global Ecology: Tracking the Biodiversity Ideal in India, 1947–1997*. Athens: Ohio University Press, 2003.

Linebarger, Paul Myron Anthony. *Psychological Warfare*. Washington, DC: Infantry Journal Press, 1948.

MacDonald, Alexander. *Bangkok Editor*. New York: Macmillan, 1949.

———. *My Footloose Newspaper Life*. Bangkok: Post Publishing, 1990.

MacDonald, Elizabeth P. *Undercover Girl*. New York: Macmillan, 1947.

Mandler, Peter. *Return from the Natives: How Margaret Mead Won the Second World War and Lost the Cold War*. New Haven, CT: Yale University Press, 2013.

McIntosh, Elizabeth P. *In Memorium*. Doylestown, PA: James A. Michener Art Museum, 1966. Published in conjunction with the exhibition titled *William A. Smith, A Retrospective*, shown at the James A. Michener Art Museum.

————. *Sisterhood of Spies: The Women of the OSS*. Annapolis, MD: Naval Institute Press, 1998.

McLynn, Frank. *The Burma Campaign: Disaster into Triumph, 1942–45*. New Haven, CT: Yale University Press, 2011.

McMahon, Robert J. *Colonialism and Cold War: The United States and the Struggle for Indonesian Independence, 1945–49*. Ithaca, NY: Cornell University Press, 1981.

McNaughton, James C. *Nisei Linguists: Japanese Americans in the Military Intelligence Service during World War II*. Washington, DC: U.S. Department of the Army, 2006.

Meier, Andrew. *The Lost Spy: An American in Stalin's Secret Service*. New York: W. W. Norton, 2008.

Mills, Francis B., Robert Mills, and John W. Brunner. *OSS Special Operations in China*. New Jersey: Phillips Publications, 2002.

Moon, Tom. *This Grim and Savage Game: OSS and the Beginning of U.S. Covert Operations in World War II*. Cambridge, MA: Da Capo Press, 2000.

Morison, Samuel Eliot. *The Liberation of the Philippines, Luzon, Mindanao, the Visayas: 1944–1945*. Vol. 13 of *History of the United States Naval Operations in World War II*. Edison, NJ: Castle Books, 2001.

Morros, Boris, and Charles Samuels. *My Ten Years as a Counterspy*. New York: Dell, 1959.

O'Donnell, Patrick. *Operatives, Spies, and Saboteurs*. New York: Citadel Press, 2004.

Peers, William R., and Dean Brelis. *Behind the Burma Road, the Story of America's Most Successful Guerrilla Force*. Boston: Little, Brown, 1963.

Price, David H. *Anthropological Intelligence: The Deployment and Neglect of American Anthropology in the Second World War*. Durham, NC: Duke University Press, 2008.

Reynolds, E. Bruce. *Thailand's Secret War: The Free Thai, OSS, and SOE during World War II*. Cambridge: Cambridge University Press, 2005.

Rogers, James Grafton. *Wartime Washington: The Secret OSS Journal of James Grafton Rogers, 1942–1943*. Edited by Thomas F. Troy. Frederick, MD: University Publications of America, 1987.

Roosevelt, Kermit. *War Report of the OSS (Office of Strategic Services)*. New York: Walker, 1976.

————. *War Report of the OSS II: The Overseas Target*. New York: Walker, 1976.

Rose, Alexander. *Washington's Spies: The Story of America's First Spy Ring*. New York: Bantam Books, 2006.

Rose, Cornelia Bruere. *National Policy for Radio Broadcasts*. New York: Ayer, 1971.

Rosenberg, Rosalind. *Beyond Separate Spheres: Intellectual Roots of Modern Feminism*. New Haven, CT: Yale University Press, 1982.

Russell, Jan Barboe. *The Train to Crystal City: FDR's Secret Prisoner Exchange Program and America's Only Family Internment Camp during World War II*. New York: Scribner, 2015.

Sacquety, Troy J. *The OSS in Burma: Jungle War against the Japanese*. Lawrence: University Press of Kansas, 2013.

Said, Edward W. *Orientalism*. New York: Vintage Books, 1978.

Sarantakes, Nicholas Evan. *The Allies against the Rising Sun: The United States, the British Nations, and the Defeat of Imperial Japan*. Lawrence: University Press of Kansas, 2009.

Smith, Bradley F. *The Shadow Warriors: O.S.S. and the Origins of the C.I.A*. New York: Basic Books, 1983.

Smith, Felix. *China Pilot: Flying for Chiang and Chennault*. Washington, DC: Brassey's Inc., 1995.

Smith, R. Harris. *OSS: The Secret History of America's First Central Intelligence Agency*. Berkeley: University of California Press, 1972.

Soley, Lawrence C. *Radio Warfare: OSS and CIA Subversive Propaganda*. New York: Praeger, 1989.

Sorel, Nancy Caldwell. *The Women Who Wrote the War*. New York: Arcade, 1999.

Spencer, Otha C. *Flying the Hump: Memories of an Air War*. College Station: Texas A&M University Press, 1992.

Tamayama, Kazuo, and John Nunneley. *Tales by Japanese Soldiers of the Burma Campaign 1942–1945*. London: Cassell, 2000.

Taylor, Edmond. *Awakening from History*. Boston: Gambit, 1969.

———. *The Strategy of Terror: Europe's Inner Front*. Boston: Houghton Mifflin, 1940.

Taylor, Jean Gelman. *The Social World of Batavia: Europeans and Eurasians in Dutch Asia*. Madison: University of Wisconsin Press, 1983.

Taylor, Philip M. *Munitions of the Mind: A History of Propaganda from the Ancient World to the Present Era*. 3rd ed. Manchester, UK: Manchester University Press, 2003.

Tierney, Dominic. *FDR and the Spanish Civil War: Neutrality and Commitment in the Struggle That Divided America*. Durham, NC: Duke University Press, 2007.

Troy, Thomas F. *Donovan and the CIA: A History of the Establishment of the Central Intelligence Agency*. Frederick, MD: Aletheia Books, 1981.

U.S. Office of Strategic Services. *Assessment of Men: Selection of Personnel for the Office of Strategic Services*. New York: Rinehart, 1948.

Waller, Douglas C. *Wild Bill Donovan: The Spymaster Who Created the OSS and Modern American Espionage*. New York: Free Press, 2011.

Warner, Philip. *Secret Forces of World War II*. Chelsea, MI: Scarborough House, 1991.

Wedemeyer, Albert C. *Wedemeyer Reports!* New York: Holt, 1958.

Weinstein, Allen, and Alexander Vassiliev. *The Haunted Wood: Soviet Espionage in America—The Stalin Era*. New York: Random House, 1999.

White, Theodore Harold, and Annalee Jacoby. *Thunder out of China*. New York: Da Capo Press. 1980.

Wohlstetter, Roberta. *Pearl Harbor: Warning and Decision*. Stanford, CA: Stanford University Press, 1962.

Yamashita, Samuel Hideo. *Daily Life in Wartime Japan: 1940–1945*. Lawrence: University of Press of Kansas, 2015.

———. *Leaves from an Autumn of Emergence: Selection from the Wartime Diaries of Ordinary Japanese*. Honolulu: University of Hawaii Press, 2005.

YANK's Magic Carpet. Calcutta, India: Staff of the China-Burma-India Edition of *YANK*, 1944.

Yellin, Emily. *Our Mothers' War: American Women at Home and at the Front during World War II*. New York: Free Press, 2004.

Ziegler, Philip. *Mountbatten: The Official Biography*. London: Collins, 1985.

INDEX

EPM indicates Elizabeth P. McIntosh and letter n with page number indicates notes.

OSS intel networks and, 92; OSS MO Ceylon and, 75; as OSS recruit, 44–45; Pacific crossing with Frame, 70; postwar life of, 208; at Queen's Hotel, Kandy, Ceylon, 73; Ramree Island Battle and, 122; sabotage projects and, 148; Selective Service Committee and, 92–93
Battleship Row, Pearl Harbor, 17–18
BBC, white propaganda and, 43
Beals, Victor, 118
Beck, Simone "Simca," 204
Benedict, Ruth, 50, 89–90, 95, 98–99
Bengal famine of 1943, 143
Bentley, Elizabeth, 201
Berlin Airlift, 198
Berno, Harry, 66, 175
Bertholle, Louisette, 204
Bicât, André, 102
Bicât Sausages, 102
Birch, John, xiii, 189
black propaganda: Berno on OWI's mission vs., 66; British SOE and, 42–43; creating, 4, 5–6, 55–56; EPM as trailblazer in, xii; EPM's photo-card for Japanese in China, 126; EPM's visits to Ceylon and, 125; Hiroshima, after atomic bomb on, 162; Ma on Chinese and, 134–35; missionaries to China and, 110; OSS Detachment 404 in Ceylon and, 67; OSS mission and, 3–4; radio, secondary MO unit and, 55; Radio JOAK, 126–27; SOE subbranch SO2 and, 216n19; as strategic weapon, 47–48. See also diaries, Japanese soldiers'; newspapers, fake; rumors; surrender campaigns; white propaganda
black radio: deception and, xii; Foster's scripts, 76, 91–92; Kunming MO and, 148–49; MacDonald and, 85–86, 126–27; surrender campaigns after atomic bomb, 163. See also Voice of America
blood chit, flying the Hump and, 130, 131
Blucher, Marshal (fictitious), 87–88
Bondurant, Joan, 71–72
books, FBI's removal/censorship of, 203, 204
Borneo: Japanese attack, 23. See also Netherlands East Indies
British: Battle of Ramree Island and, 121–22; black propaganda by, 42–43;

in Calcutta, MO operations and, 118–19; on Chennault's airplanes and Communist China, 199; Communist China recognition by, 200; cooperating on MO with OSS, 128; in Delhi, EPM on Japanese surrender rumor and, 98; "Foot in the Door" policy, 200; Operation Bittersweet in Burma's Arakan and, 120; snatch sorties, 127–28; spying targeting OSS in China, 189; tampering with German personal mail during World War I, 79; on U.S. clandestine activities in CBI, 67, 69
British 1st Burma Division, 24
British Chiefs of Staff: on Japanese soldiers, 77–78
British Combined Chiefs (BCC): on psychological warfare, 3
British Combined Services Detailed Interrogation Center (CSDIC), Delhi, 100
British Detachment 136, 144–45, 152
British Gymkhana Club, Delhi, 72, 98
British Intelligence Bureau, Delhi, 100
British Ministry of Information (BMOI), 67
Buchanan, Daniel C., 147
Buckley, Ed, 201
Budget Bureau, on postwar OSS, 174
Buffalo House, Calcutta, 117
Burma: Allies vs. Japanese aircraft in, 113; altered Japanese postal messages and, 79–83; Battle of Ramree Island, 121–22; Foster's black propaganda and, 144; Hull on Britain's postwar plans for, 220n24; Japanese retreat through, xii, 53–54, 100, 113; Japanese soldiers surrendering in, 99; mountain peoples' loyalties, 110–12; Operation Bittersweet in Arakan, 120; OSS on Fenn and, 44; OSS-British conflict in Thailand and, 73; postwar fighting in, 183; surrender campaign in, 122–23
Burma News, 54
Burma Road, 16, 24
Burma-Siam Railway, 184
Burmese: headmen, winning loyalty of, 110–12; MO Delhi on perceptions of, 97–98

Cairo, EPM on route home and, 190, 191
Calaghan, Major General, 169

Special Six-Year-Old Brandy, for Japanese occupation forces, 208

Spitfires, British, 76, 100, 121

Starling, Lucy, 43

State Department: on Britain's postwar Southeast Asia plans, 220n24; EPM's radio information specialist job with, 196; on Foster's Indonesia report, 195, 196; Foster's passport and, 204, 205; OSS passports and, 93; R&A of OSS after World War II and, 174

Stettinius, Edward, 167

Stevenson, Ralph, 199

Stilwell, Joseph "Vinegar Joe," 44, 71–72, 107, 125

Strategic Services Unit, War Department, 174

Strong, George V., 3–4

Stuart, James, 110, 112

suicide, Japanese: group, 123; national, Foster's directive against, 145–46

Sukarno, Achmed, 56, 181, 194, 195

Su-Lin (panda), 218n2

surrender campaigns: Bicât's offset press and, 101–2; Burma after Ramree Island, 122–23; DT-10, 119; Foster's (July 1945), 146; Gold Dust dissemination of, 102; IJA courier and, 103; Hiroshima, after atomic bomb on, 162–64; Japanese retreat through Burma and, xii, 100; Japanese telegraph network and, 120; JB-1, 101–2; MacDonald on disseminating leaflets over Burma, 121; Red Fort research on, 100–101; releasing POW names and photos and, 138; theories on Japanese and, 96–99, 223n4

survival training, 49

Tai Li (Chiang's spymaster), 92, 110

Tai Tai (Alsatian), 141

Tao Hanzhang, 107

tarantulas, in Ceylon, 84

Taylor, Edmond: Battle of Ramree Island and, 122; on Donovan recruiting artists, 40; EPM's visit to Kandy and, 125; on indirect black propaganda, 79; landing in Thailand, 182–83

Telberg, Ina, 94, 118

Tenet, George, 210

Tennenbaum, Susan, 206

tennis, in New Delhi, 69, 70

Terauchi, Hisaichi, 23

Thailand: EPM's request on cartoons sent into, 119; Hull on Britain's postwar plans for, 220n24; at Japanese defensive line perimeter, 113; MacDonald's orders for, 85; OSS-British conflict in, 73; parachuting OSS guerrilla training team into, 151–52; postwar fighting in, 183; Radio JOAK from, 126–27

32 Feroz Shah Road. *See* OSS MO Delhi

This Is No Picnic (OSS handbook), 60, 61

Thomas, Benton, 169

Thompson, Jim, 165, 184, 190

Thunder out of China (White and Jacoby), 129–30, 204

Tibet, Operation Yak and, 108

Tientsin, China, Japanese occupation of, 16

Ting, Xiao, xiii, 134, 139, 159

Tjarda von Starkenborgh Stachower, Alidius W. L., 169

Tojo, Hideki, 88–89, 96, 222n2

Tokyo, EPM's CIA job in, 207

Tony (German shepherd), 153

Toonerville Trolley, Ceylon, 72, 125

train sabotage, 159

tree men at Mindanao, Philippines, 12

Trincomalee Training Camp, Ceylon: British naval headquarters for Pacific theater in, 226n37; OSS Special Operations training base at, 127, 140, 151

Trojan, getting out of CBI and, 186, 190

Truman, Harry S., 174

Tu, General, 177

Tulley, Grace, 108

Turner, B. M., 86

20th Bomber Command, 88

Undercover Girl (McIntosh), xiv

United Nations, Foster's Indonesian report and, 197

Unspeakable, USS, 189

U.S. 10th Air Force, Calcutta as base for, 117

U.S. Army: on Japanese soldiers, 77; on news censorship after Pearl Harbor attack, 26–27

U.S. Army Nurse Corps: black nurses in, 214n5; captured when Japanese attack Manila, 23; *Republic*, travel to Philippines on, 9

ABOUT THE AUTHOR

Ann Todd has been a contributing author and consultant for the National Geographic Society, given presentations in national parks on OSS operations, and worked as a historian for the National Museum of the Marine Corps. She served in the United States Coast Guard and lives in Dripping Springs, Texas, with her three dogs, Rufus, Patsy, and Bear.

The Naval Institute Press is the book-publishing arm of the U.S. Naval Institute, a private, nonprofit, membership society for sea service professionals and others who share an interest in naval and maritime affairs. Established in 1873 at the U.S. Naval Academy in Annapolis, Maryland, where its offices remain today, the Naval Institute has members worldwide.

Members of the Naval Institute support the education programs of the society and receive the influential monthly magazine *Proceedings* or the colorful bimonthly magazine *Naval History* and discounts on fine nautical prints and on ship and aircraft photos. They also have access to the transcripts of the Institute's Oral History Program and get discounted admission to any of the Institute-sponsored seminars offered around the country.

The Naval Institute's book-publishing program, begun in 1898 with basic guides to naval practices, has broadened its scope to include books of more general interest. Now the Naval Institute Press publishes about seventy titles each year, ranging from how-to books on boating and navigation to battle histories, biographies, ship and aircraft guides, and novels. Institute members receive significant discounts on the Press' more than eight hundred books in print.

Full-time students are eligible for special half-price membership rates. Life memberships are also available.

For a free catalog describing Naval Institute Press books currently available, and for further information about joining the U.S. Naval Institute, please write to:

Member Services
U.S. NAVAL INSTITUTE
291 Wood Road
Annapolis, MD 21402-5034
Telephone: (800) 233-8764
Fax: (410) 571-1703
Web address: www.usni.org